DESIGNING VIRTUAL REALITY SYSTEMS

THE STRUCTURED APPROACH

GERARD JOUNGHYUN KIM

CD-ROM
Included

Designing Virtual Reality Systems

Gerard Jounghyun Kim

Designing Virtual Reality Systems

The Structured Approach

With 191 Figures

 Springer

Gerard Jounghyun Kim, BS, MS, PhD
Department of Computer Science and Engineering
Pohang University of Science and Technology (POSTECH)
Korea

British Library Cataloguing in Publication Data
A catalogue record for this book is available from the British Library

Library of Congress Control Number: 2005923778

ISBN-10: 1-85233-958-6   Printed on acid-free paper
ISBN-13: 978-1-85233-958-6

Printed in the United States of America   (SPI/EB)

9 8 7 6 5 4 3 2 1

Springer Science+Business Media
springeronline.com

To
Dad, who has been my inspiration,
Mom, for her unconditional love,
and God for his grace.

Contents

Section I
Basics of Designing Virtual Reality Systems

Chapter 1
Introduction: VR in a Nutshell

What Is VR?

"Virtual Reality (VR)"[1] is a field of study that aims to create a system that provides a synthetic experience for its user(s). The experience is dubbed "synthetic," "illusory," or "virtual" because the sensory stimulation to the user is simulated and generated by the "system." For all practical purposes, the system usually consists of various types of displays[2] for delivering the stimulation, sensors to detect user actions, and a computer that processes the user action and generates the display output. To simulate and generate virtual experiences, developers often build a computer model, also known as "virtual worlds" or "virtual environments (VE)" which are, for instance, spatially organized computational objects (aptly called the virtual objects), presented to the user through various sensory display systems such as the monitor, sound speakers, and force feedback devices.

One important component of a successful VR system is the provision of interaction, to allow the user not just to feel a certain sensation, but also to change and affect the virtual world in some way. Figure 1.1 captures the basic architecture of a VR system and various associated terminologies.

Goals and Applications of VR

Of, what value is a virtual experience? Obviously, it allows people to get the experience of things that would otherwise be very difficult or even impossible to attain in real life, like going to the South Pole or to the Moon. The virtual experience can even be something imaginary and abstract (rather than real-life inspired), such as experiencing an abstract mathematical world or an

---

[1] The term "VR" is also used to describe the technology or medium used to create and convey the synthetic experience, or even sometimes to the experience itself.

[2] In VR literatures, the term "display" not only refers to the usual "visual" display but also to any sensory output device.

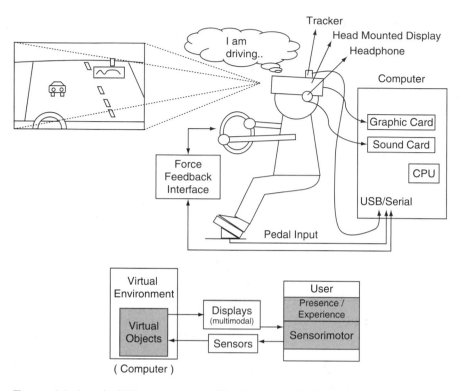

FIGURE 1.1. A typical VR system exemplified by a virtual driving simulation. The user is driving in a virtual world as displayed to him visually through the head-mounted display, aurally through the earphone, and kinesthetically through the handle mechanism. The displays are generated and controlled by the computer program. The computer also accepts user action (e.g., head movement of the user) through sensors and processes it to reflect it to the virtual environment and the display. A more abstract view of the system is shown in the lower block diagram.

imaginary world envisioned by an artist. Thus, it goes without saying that virtual experiences are useful for many purposes including training, education, and entertainment.

One of the sources of confusion regarding the concept of VR is whether or how it is different from the 3D (networked) PC/console games or similarly from the terms like "cyberworld," web-based chatting, etc.. Broadly speaking, 3D games are one type of VR system in the sense that they provide a virtual experience of some sort. However, most 3D games, for commercial reasons, are still keyboard-mouse-based or based on simple interfaces, and 3D game designers are interested in finding a clever scenario that is exciting and engaging so that it will attract and hook more players. Although in developing a successful VR system, one cannot ignore these aspects, the VR scientists are interested more in faithfully reproducing a given experience as much as possible. For instance, a first-person shooting game should be exciting and engaging, whereas a virtual battleground (which might have almost identical content as the first-person shooting game) should be scary and tense (as in a real war). New arcade games that now employ rich 3D graphics, realistic simulations, sound effects, and physical interfaces are more in tune with the general goals of VR.

Two Pillars of VR: Presence and 3D Multimodal Interaction

In this line of thinking, one of the important and distinguishing design goals of VR is the provision of *Presence* for creating a vivid virtual experience (and even for improved task performance in some cases). Presence (or the sense of presence) is defined as the degree to which participants subjectively feel that they are somewhere other than their actual physical location because of the effects of a computer-generated simulation [Bys99]. The effect is often dubbed the "sense of being there" [Hee92]. Humans process external stimuli provided to the visual, auditory, haptic,[3] or proprioceptive,[4] sensory system and transform the stimuli into an internal representation (or mental model), which gives humans the illusion that they are immersed in another space. It would be practically impossible (at least with the current technologies) to delude any VR user into thinking the VEs they experience are real or perfect. Yet with sufficient and clever integration of the sensory stimuli, VR users can still be elicited with a sense of presence and obtain a virtual experience through their ability to conform to the environment, or through the momentary "suspension of disbelief."

Many researchers have identified key elements that promote presence (see Figure 1.2 and Table1.1). Despite a number of different definitions of presence, it is generally accepted that the following aspects are important in promoting it: (1) sensory fidelity and richness, (2) degrees of interactivity, and (3) other psychological cues [Shi03;ISP04]. Sensory fidelity and richness refer to providing a user with an environment that is as realistic as possible, for instance, with a wide field of view (FOV) or immersive display, pictorial realism, multimodal feedback, and first-person viewpoint.

It is quite obvious that display "realism" is important for presence. But considering the possibility of eliciting presence in a "fake" virtual world (something with no counterpart in the real world such as Alice's Wonderland [Car00]), it is natural to search for other contributing factors. In this regard, interactivity and psychological cues can play equally important roles in increasing presence. Interactivity refers to the amount of involvement or

---

[3] The sense of touch and force.
[4] The sense of movements in the joints.

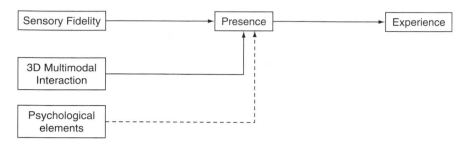

FIGURE 1.2. One of the major contributing factors to creating a vivid virtual experience is presence which is strengthened by various factors.

capability of the user with respect to experiencing the virtual world. Typical examples of interaction would include the capability to navigate throughout the environment, manipulate objects, change their properties, initiate object simulation (e.g., motions, deformations), communicate with other entities, and so on. An appropriate interaction design can increase presence by strengthening the bond or sense of belonging between the user and the virtual world.

Other psychological cues associated with the design of the virtual world, such as predictability and consistency, use of auxiliary/background objects, emotional content, use of plots, and situational awareness have been reported to affect presence in varying ways [ISP04]. On the other hand, distractions from the environment, the cumbersomeness, obtrusiveness or novelty of the devices, and simulation sicknesses can be factors for lowering the level of the experience or presence. However, humans have an amazing capability to adapt to their environment and such negative effects tend to decrease with time of exposure to various such stimuli (physical or psychological). Table 1.1 summarizes the various factors that affect presence in a positive or negative way. A VR system developer, perhaps unlike a 3D game developer, would have to consider the varying effects of these presence factors to create the best virtual experience often with respect to limited computational and hardware resources. Psychological cues are indirect cues in the sense that they alone do not promote presence by themselves, but rather act as means to cancel the negative elements such as distraction (e.g., when focused, one fails to notice the boundaries of the narrow display screen).

The second important element in creating a successful virtual experience is the use of natural and usable interaction (and an appropriately designed interface). From intuition and from the evolutionary viewpoint, an interaction scheme based on the (1) three-dimensional space, (2) involvement of the whole body, and (3) one that takes advantage of the multimodality of

TABLE 1.1.   Possible factors in promoting or demoting the sense of presence.

	Number of sensory outputs (multimodality) and consistency among them
Sensory fidelity	How realistic each sensory output is (modality realism)
	Visual: display size/FOV, image quality, object detail and size, depth cues / stereoscopy, etc.
	Aural: sound quality, spatialization, etc.
	Kinesthetic: existence and realism of force feedback, extent of force feedback (e.g., point contact vs. areal contact), etc.
	Stimulation realism of other modality displays (smell, air flow, tactility, etc.)
	Viewpoint (first person)
	Simulation/behavior fidelity
Interactivity	Existence of interaction (Can user do anything at all?)
	Degrees of interaction (How much can user do?)
	Style of interaction (Is the interaction natural and realistic as in real life?)
Psychological/ content variables (indirect influence)	Characters and storyline / Emotion / Arousal
	Willingness to suspend disbelief
	Previous experience
	Attention and focus
Negative factors to presence	Obtrusiveness of devices
	Heavy HMD, wired and tethered sensors, etc.
	Interference from real world (e.g., noise)

human sensory organs would be the most natural (for instance, versus the current keyboard-mouse-based desktop interface). It has already been mentioned that interaction itself and the style of interaction can affect the user's sense of presence. A badly designed interface can create user discomfort and even simulation sickness and negatively affect the quality of the virtual experience. However, given the limitation in hardware and computational resources, designing the most usable and ergonomic interface is a challenging task that requires many cycles of trial and error. In many cases, the goals of naturalness, usability, and even task efficiency are often in conflict in modeling interaction and designing the interface. A VR system developer must not overlook these human factors issues and pursue a user-centered design approach through careful task analysis, leveraging existing design guidelines for 3D multimodal interfaces, and even one's own experimentation.

We can think of a spectrum of "VR-ness," as a function of the level of presence and interaction style. Figure 1.3 shows that at one end of the spectrum the real world exists, which serves as the basis of an environment with the highest possible presence and usability (actually it is possible that interfaces which cannot exist in the real world may be more usable). At the other end exists an environment such as online text chatting with minimal presence and richness in terms of ways to interact.

Conceptual ◄──────		──────► Spatial	

Spectrum Features	Online (Text) Chatting	DeskTop 3D Game	Typical Virtual Reality	Real World
Interaction	Text	Keyboard / Mouse	3D Motion Voice Force Feedback	Language Gesture Facial expression
	Unimodal / Passive	◄──────	──────►	Multimodal / Active
Display	Text	Graphics	Graphics Video Audio ...	...
	Non immersive ◄──────		──────►	Immersive

FIGURE 1.3. The spectrum of VR-ness.

Building a Virtual Reality System

Developing and maintaining a VR system is a very difficult task. It requires in-depth knowledge in many different disciplines, such as sensing and tracking technologies, stereoscopic displays, multimodal interaction and processing, computer graphics and geometric modeling, dynamics and physical simulation, performance tuning, and so on. The major features and requirements that particularly distinguish VR systems from other software systems are (1) the real-time performance requirement, while maintaining an acceptable level of realism and presence, (2) the problem of modeling the object's appearance and physical properties in addition to, and in relation to, its function and behavior, and (3) consideration of many different styles and modalities of interaction techniques, according to different tasks and input/output devices. The difficulty lies in the complexity of having to simultaneously consider many system goals, some of which are conflicting.

Building a VR system usually requires the following stages of effort in an iterative fashion. In the first stage, the requirements of the virtual experience are analyzed and the overall flow and scene structures are roughly sketched including the time and conditions for interaction. Essential input/output devices or the required amount of computational power should be estimated. Based on the requirements, the major virtual objects are modeled. The geometries are created (most often) using computer-aided design tools; then the developers program their behaviors using graphics/VR library routines. The virtual objects and other computational elements need to be organized to form a scene and the scene is programmed to be rendered and displayed to the user at a reasonably high frame rate (e.g., at 20 Hz to ensure smooth animation of objects). Special VR sensors and display devices are interfaced into the system. The overall system is further refined by analyzing the various required interaction tasks and designing particular interfaces for them. Finally, various presence factors may be added to enhance the virtual experience as much as possible within the bounds of required performance (e.g., 20-Hz frame rate). The overall process may be viewed as a classic spiral software engineering process [Boe88] as depicted in Figure 1.4 [Seo03].

As with any software, VR software should be developed in stages and in an iterative manner. The earliest iterations should focus on the usual aspects, such as requirements analysis, object and feature identification, class hierarchy, gross system behavior, user task modeling, and general software architecture. Once this stage of specification matures, the next stage would involve more VR-related aspects, addressing performance issues and which computational modules identified in the first stage would be refined further. This would most likely include refinement of the user task models into interaction models, and the formation of appropriate computational and geometric Level of Detail (LOD)[5] models. Incremental simulation/execution can be applied to validate and revise important object behaviors, predict the approximate performance, and make further decisions for process distribution (if appropriate tools exist).

---

[5] Level of detail models are geometric models of an object created at varying degrees of complexity for real-time rendering purposes (See Chapter 3).

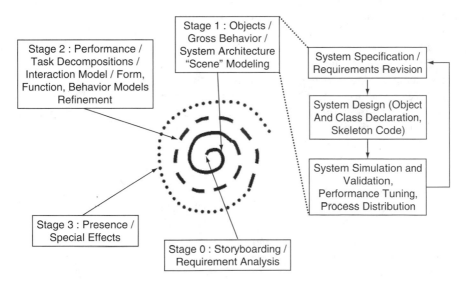

FIGURE 1.4. The Spiral model of VR system development [Seo02]. (Reprinted with permission from ACM © 2004).

Once the performance aspect has been treated to a certain degree, the third stage of iterations can address the issue of improving presence. In other words, the third stage decides whether to further employ nonhardware elements known to promote presence. Although these presence-enhancing elements (e.g., increasing input/output modalities, providing higher degrees of interactivity, increasing simulation fidelity, varying types of interaction, minimizing distraction, employing special effects, etc.) may possess only secondary importance in terms of system functionality (and may be regarded as targets of interest in much later stages of design), I believe that they are sufficiently important to be considered upstream as a defining quality in a VR system is the provision of presence. However, we stress that consideration of these elements is still grounded on at least some preliminary specification of the most critical functionalities and performance requirements of the system.

About This Book

Many technical challenges lie in all facets of VR system development. This book is organized in such a way that it follows the development process depicted in Figure 1.4, and for each stage, describes the problem and possible solutions. It is different from, (and it is hoped, more useful than) other introductory books on virtual reality in that it provides concrete examples and practical solutions (with actual code examples) to the technical challenges in building a VR system instead of just explaining the high-level concepts, following a specific development methodology. The book is primarily written for first-level graduate students. However, advanced undergraduate students or IT professionals can also follow the book without much difficulty.

The first part of the book covers the very basics in building a VR system in a systematic way and explains various technical issues in object modeling and scene organization. The second part of the book dives into the core (one of the pillars) of virtual reality dealing with 3D multimodal interaction, and designing for usable and natural interaction. I start with reviewing various special VR input and output devices. Understanding their nature is critical for the user-centered approach to VR system design. Then, I go over how to conduct an interaction task analysis and design software/hardware interfaces. As modeling and animating human characters are very important, I devote one chapter to it as a special case of object modeling. Simulation of important object behaviors such as physical simulation and collision detection/response are also treated separately. Objects, characters, behaviors, and scene modeling are all deeply related to the issue of providing a high sense of presence to the user. The companion CD includes the actual codes developed in stages from examples that appear in the chapters (for detailed instructions as to how to use them, refer to the readme files on the CD).

Final Notes

Also, note that there are other advanced topics not covered in this book such as the implementation of camera-based interaction, the use of image-based approaches (to modeling and rendering), biological man–machine interfaces, and so on. Among those topics not treated in the book, Augmented Reality (AR) is a particular type of VR system, and in AR, synthetic graphics/images/text are registered and overlaid onto the real scene (or on video imagery) using a special device called the see-through head-mounted display or cameras and image/graphics compositing systems. In this sense, there is another continuum of VR-ness, called the *Mixed Reality* [Mil94], in terms of how much of the displayed scene is real (see Figure 1.5). Multiuser virtual environments can add yet another dimension to the virtual experience. With the advent of the high-speed Internet connection, networked VR application is also growing in importance.

The underlying and enabling technologies of VR can be applied to many other areas, not just creating a virtual experience. For instance, VR can be viewed as an advanced form of Human–Computer Interaction (HCI), a new enriched communication medium, or an intuitive information visualization method. Frederick Brooks of the University of North Carolina, Chapel Hill has long advocated that the role of virtual reality should be that of "Intelligence Amplification (IA)" (as opposed to artificial intelligence) [Rhe91]. He once stated that

...I believe the use of computer systems for intelligence amplification is much more powerful today, and will be at any given point in the future, than the use of computers for artificial intelligence (AI). ... In the AI community, the objective is to replace the human mind by the machine and its program and its database. In the IA community, the objective is to build systems that amplify the human mind by

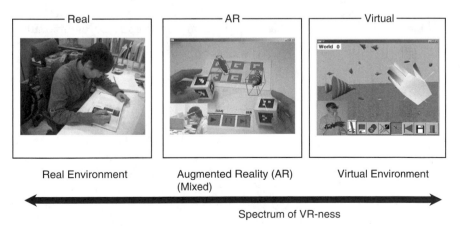

FIGURE 1.5. The Mixed Reality continuum [Mil94].

providing it with computer-based auxiliaries that do the things that the mind has trouble doing. . . .

I note that the type of VR system treated in this book is only representative of larger possibilities. I leave it to the readers to think more about what exactly VR may, should, or can be, or what really constitutes a virtual experience. This book focuses more on the practical methods and technical basis and details of constructing a typical VR system.

Acknowledgments

I first thank the people at Springer-Verlag who saw the value in bringing about this book, especially Catherine Drury and Beverly Ford, the editors. The content of the book reflects much of the research work I have done for the past several years at POSTECH with my hardworking students. In addition, they helped me prepare, edit, and format the manuscript and many of the figures. In particular, I would like to thank (in no particular order) Dr. Jinseok Seo, Dr. Namgyu Kim, Gun A. Lee, Sungkil Lee, Jonghyun Ryu, Sangyoon Lee, Jane Hwang, Kwanghoon Ko, Seokhee Jeon, Dr. Ungyeon Yang, Yongjin Kim, Jaehoon Chung, Jaeyoung Chun, Seonghoon Lim, and Bohyun Cho. I also thank my colleagues and friends who supported me in many ways, ranging from technical input to motivational encouragement. Thanks to Dr. Skip Rizzo, Dongju Lee, Woosuk Kim, Sajin Kang, Clara and Cyndy, Pastor Joseph W. Lee and the lovely people at the East Light Korean Church, Prof. Seungyong Lee, Prof. Youngju Suh, Prof. Sungho Han, Prof. Kyo Kang, my advisor Dr. George Bekey, Dr. Heedong Ko, Prof. Kaye Wohn, and the Trojan and USC Robotics Lab alums, and lastly but not the least, Prof. Chanmo Park, who brought me here to this wonderful institution of POSTECH where everything was made possible. Finally, I thank my family. To my wife, Sooah, "without your care, patience, support, and love, this would not have been possible." And, to my children, Andrew and Ellen "thanks for being there!"

Summary

Virtual reality is a field of study which aims to create a system that provides a synthetic experience for its user(s). A VR system usually consists of various types of displays for delivering the stimulation, sensors to detect user actions, and a computer that processes the user action and generates the display output. VR is characterized by its defining objectives to achieve high user-felt presence in the virtual environment and the use of natural 3D multimodal interfaces. Through presence and natural interaction, VR finds uses in education, training, entertainment, and many other application areas. VR systems are highly complex and require a structured approach to building them, starting with the basic functionalities and refining them with more VR features.

Pondering Points

- What are application possibilities for virtual reality other than education, training, and entertainment?
- How can user-felt presence be beneficial to one's task performance?
- Make a case for and against the role of realism in producing a convincing experience.
- Can there be a VR system that is not mainly computer-based?
- Is the real-life-based way of interaction the most natural and easy to use for humans?
- How can preconception affect users in the virtual environment?
- Is VR just another superfluous novelty or fad, or does it have a unique cost-effective benefit?
- Can one feel "present" when reading books, playing video games, watching movies, or through online chatting? What good can come from employing special modality output devices and natural interaction?

Chapter 2
Requirements Engineering and Storyboarding

Good system engineering practice is vital to the successful development of VR systems, more so than ordinary software systems because VR systems have multifaceted requirements (not just to make correct computations). In fact, a typical development process for VR systems will go through many cycles of revisions, as there is a lack of design guidelines on how to effectively integrate various resource-consuming computations and interactive techniques.

Thus, in building a VR system, we must start with identifying and describing its requirements. Requirements [IEE94] are statements identifying a capability, physical characteristic, or quality factor that bounds a product or process need for which a solution will be pursued. Requirements refer to the desired properties of the system and the constraints under which it operates and is developed. Requirements should be documented and specified as clearly as possible, for ease of revision and later maintenance. Although requirements engineering is a difficult and cumbersome process, it should be done at least for the important core part of the system. These descriptions are best captured and maintained using computational support tools and formalisms, but in actuality, even hand-drawn sketches and documents (such as the storyboards) would be useful [Cim04].

Requirements may be functional or nonfunctional. Functional requirements describe system services or functions. Nonfunctional requirements are constraints on the system or on the development process. There are many ways to go about doing requirements engineering for a VR system. For instance, we start with the functional requirements such as those about the scenes, virtual objects comprising the scene, behaviors, and the style of interaction.

Storyboarding is one way to start off the requirements engineering process. A storyboard is a visual script designed to make it easier for the director and cameraman to "see" the shots before executing them [Cri04]. It saves time and money for the producer and is used for making movies, commercials, and animation. There are structured ways to make storyboards, but for now, informal sketches and annotations suffice for our purpose (See Figure 2.1).

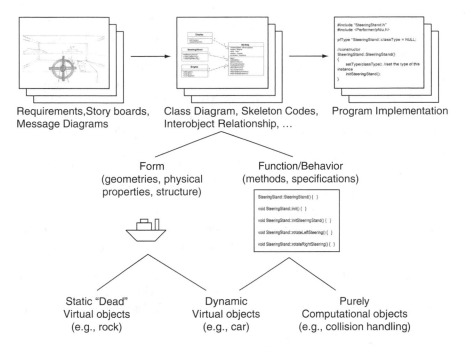

Requirements,Story boards,   Class Diagram, Skeleton Codes,   Program Implementation
Message Diagrams   Interobject Relationship, ...

Form
(geometries, physical
properties, structure)

Function/Behavior
(methods, specifications)

Static "Dead"   Dynamic   Purely
Virtual objects   Virtual objects   Computational objects
(e.g., rock)   (e.g., car)   (e.g., collision handling)

FIGURE 2.1. Modeling and implementing virtual objects in an object-oriented fashion.

The overall scenario, as represented in the simple form of sequences of "cuts" (or static scenes) in the storyboard, can be further refined and include some dynamics. One useful method is to use the Message Sequence Diagrams (MSD) [DeM79], or use cases [Car98]. The MSD depicts typical scenarios of internal and external behaviors of a VR world in terms of sequences of data or control signals exchanged among objects in the system (See Figure 2.4). Using the MSDs, one can test the system for later model validation, but more importantly, it enables the developer to identify important objects in the system. Constructing MSDs also aids in identifying the sequences of the messages among various objects and picturing how they interact with one another. In particular, external devices can be treated as an object for human–computer interaction. Object classes are then constructed by examining the identified objects and grouping them according to the commonality in their attributes.

Objects, better referred to as "virtual objects," are the constituents of a virtual environment through which the user will obtain the virtual experience. Although there is a natural mapping from virtual objects to the "objects" in the object-oriented programming paradigm, virtual objects are rather just a modeling concept at least at this stage. As these virtual objects are later implemented as "objects" in an object-oriented computational platform (which would be a natural thing to do), they are interchangeably referred to as both a modeling concept and a specific computational implementation. Virtual objects, for their physical connotation, indeed lend themselves naturally to the object-oriented system development methodology, and this book chooses to illustrate the implementation details using the object-oriented platform. Note that the object-oriented approach can be used to model the concrete virtual objects and scenes they compose in the VE, and to abstract various functional services required to execute and manage them, for instance, device management, rendering control, object and scene creation/consolidation/importing, event management and communication, process management, and so forth. We use the Open-SceneGraph [Ope04] and the SGI Performer[1] to illustrate many of the concepts explained in this book (actual code samples may be found on the companion CD). OpenSceneGraph is an open-source high-performance 3D graphics toolkit written entirely in standard C++ and OpenGL. SGI Performer is a popular commercial package for developing virtual reality applications.

For a large-scale virtual environment with many sorts of objects, sketching a rough object class diagram can be useful. A class diagram shows the existence of classes and their relationships in the logical and brief view format. The standard class diagram notation such as that of the Unified Modeling Language (UML) [Fow97] can be used. The diagram includes association, aggregation, composition, and inheritance relationships. Relationships provide a path for communication between objects. It is important to begin the overall modeling process with a consistent view of the object-orientation. With a clear picture of a system configuration in terms of constituent objects and information flows between them, the detailed specification behavior, function, and form for each object can begin.

Virtual objects, just like physical objects, can be characterized by three main aspects: the form, function and behavior. *Form* refers to the outer appearance of virtual objects, and their physical properties and structure.[2] We usually associate "appearance" with the visual sense (how it looks), however, a form or appearance must be judged with respect to ways it can stimulate humans through the display devices. Thus, form may include appearances also in terms of audition, haptics (force feedback), and other modalities that humans possess. For simplicity, we concentrate on the visual part for now, but later in the book, we will talk about modeling and simulation of nonvisual appearances. Other physical properties (which may be required for physical simulation) such as mass, material property, velocity, and acceleration may be included as part of form information.

---

[1] Performer is a registered trademark of Silicon Graphics, Inc. A free month-long evaluation version of Performer is available at www.sgi.com.
[2] Structure refers to the spatial/logical relationship among component objects in the case where the given object is a composite one.

Function refers to encoding what virtual objects do (i.e., primitive tasks) to accomplish their behavior (defined below), whether autonomously or in response to some external stimuli or event, and *behavior* refers to how individual virtual objects dynamically change and carry out different functions over a (relatively long) period of time, usually expressed through states, exchange of data/events, and interobject constraints. It is somewhat difficult to clearly draw the line between function and behavior. Functions may be viewed as primitive behaviors that are mostly atomic and taking a relatively short amount of time. Separating them, nevertheless, is useful for modular design of object dynamics. The description of objects, as part of a formal or informal specification of the overall application or system, must address these aspects. Note that there may be objects without form (purely computational objects such as device interfaces) or without function or dynamic behavior (e.g., static nonmoving objects such as virtual rocks).

So, for instance, the form specification/description would start by capturing the initial approximate shape/volume as well as the physical configuration of those objects (e.g., a simple hand-drawn sketch will do). As the description gets more mature and goes through a number of refinement iterations, the objects could decompose into smaller components (e.g., by breaking a car into its components, such as body, wheels, doors, etc.). Values of important attributes (e.g., size, color, mass, object type, etc.) may be added to this description as well. These descriptions are best captured and maintained using computational support tools and formalisms, but in actuality, hand-drawn sketches and documents (such as the storyboards) would still prove useful. More detailed explanations of the modeling and initial implementation process are given in Chapters 3 and 4.

Construction of virtual objects and their world often requires many revisions, and changing one aspect of the world will undoubtedly affect other aspects of it. For instance, different shapes and configurations (positions and orientations in space) can result in different dynamic behaviors. A jet fighter has different aerodynamic characteristics from that of a passenger airplane. Form can also affect functionality. For instance, two different robots differing in size may have different work volumes and capabilities. Such a development cycle is difficult to handle when working in a single level of abstraction and considering these design spaces in isolation.

Object functions and behaviors can equally be described using tools as primitive as plain text to more structured and diagrammatic representations such as procedural scripts, state transition diagrams, data flow diagrams, constraint languages, and the like. The choice of representation should be based on the complexity and nature of the object behavior and also on the type of behavior model supported by the VR development platform (so that the description can be easily mapped to and implemented at a later time). For instance, some game engines support state-based automata to express and implement intelligence into objects. Less fancy VR development platforms only support procedural programming for object behavior implementations. See Chapter 4 for more details. Figure 2.1 illustrates this initial modeling process as demonstrated in this book.

Another equally important functional requirement concerns user interaction. The storyboard and the MSD identify the important junctions and events at which user input is required. The task required to be carried out by the user should be refined to some degree and matched with the capabilities of the hardware devices and computational power of the computing hardware. The method of interaction modeling and interface design is treated in Chapter 5.

A related problem to interaction is the designation of the proper display devices. Different display systems are suited for different tasks and situations. For instance, HMDs are more suited for close-range manipulation tasks, whereas large projection displays are suited for navigation and walk-through application. Whether to employ head-tracking, haptics, 3D sound, and so on is an important interaction-related decision to make. Generally, sensors and displays cannot be changed during their use. They are also generally expensive, and one might not have the luxury of choosing the best possible displays and sensors. A clever design of the contents can overcome some of the limits introduced by low-end displays and sensors. Thus, at an early stage, having a rough idea of the nature of the user tasks and interactions (e.g., style of input and response to input) is helpful in determining the right displays and sensors and in recognizing the limits and bounds introduced by the hardware for providing a suitable level of presence and usability. Also note that there may be interaction objects (those that are purely functional such as device polling, or those also with form such as menus) to consider as well. Putting the user in the center of the system design process is very important as many VR systems fail simply because they are not user friendly.

The important nonfunctional requirements to consider at this stage are requirements for the overall system performance and device constraints. The performance requirement is rather simple. A virtual reality system is a real-time system, and must make computations for simulations, synchronize its output with various input devices, and maintain display updates at a rate at which human users will feel comfortable. For instance, for smooth computer graphic animations, the simulation for updates should be made at about at least $15 \sim 20$ times per second. Other input or display devices may require different timing requirements (for instance, haptic equipments ideally require an update rate of up to 1000 Hz for delivery of smooth force feedback). Note that 1/15th second is an amount relative to the capability of the computational and graphics hardware. Thus, if the functional requirement cannot be accommodated by the nonfunctional constraints such as the performance bounds or the devices, they have to be addressed in some way, either by making a business decision to purchase the appropriate equipment or later by designing to overcome the resulting distraction factors through clever content psychology. The important thing is that this be known in the early design stage.

Finally, a developer needs to understand, once again, that making these requirements and implementing them is an iterative process, starting from a rough picture and being refined stage by stage. To what degree should the requirements and implementation be done? That depends on the discretion of the developer.

Example: Ship Simulator Design

We illustrate this initial modeling process more concretely by illustrating the design of a simple virtual ship simulator. The objective of the example application is to assist trainees to navigate in and out of the pier and anchor without colliding with other vessels or the coast. Figure 2.2 lists the initial requirements for the simulator. Given these high-level goals and informal requirements of the system, we start with sketches of the storyboards as shown in Figure 2.3.

Requirements (Level 1)

- The virtual ship simulator (named *Ship Simulator*) helps users (named *User*) operate a vessel (named *My Ship*) and practice docking without colliding with other vessels (named *Other Ship*) or the coast.
- Initial View
  - The default view (named *Camera*) is the scene as seen from the control bridge where the *User* controls its ship (*MyShip*). The *User* can see the outside environment through the windows in the bridge.
- Interaction
  - The control bridge includes a steering wheel (named *Steering Wheel*) and an engine lever (named *EngineTelegraph*) for the *User* to steer and control the velocity of the *My Ship*.
  - The *User* can look around the interior of the bridge and change its view named *Camera*).
  - The basic mode of control via keyboard (named *Keyboard*) and mouse (named *Mouse*) must be supported. *Ship Simulator* shall accept input from the *Keyboard* to control *My Ship*.
- Models
  - The bridge includes a steering wheel (named *Steering Wheel*) and an engine lever (named *Engine Telegraph*).
  - The scene must also include object models for sky, sea, *other ship*, terrain, and pier.
- Simulation
  - *Ship Simulator* controls several automatically navigated vessels (*Other Ship*).
  - *Othership's* initial positions and moving directions are chosen randomly.
  - *Otherships* change their speed and directions every 10 seconds.

FIGURE 2.2. The initial requirements for the virtual ship simulator.

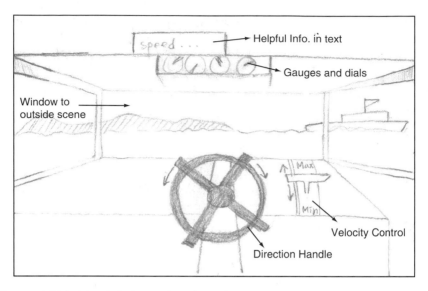

FIGURE 2.3(a). The default starting view of the *ShipSimulator*. The interior of the control bridge is seen with the steering wheel, engine lever, outside view, and gauges. The *User* can look around the control bridge.

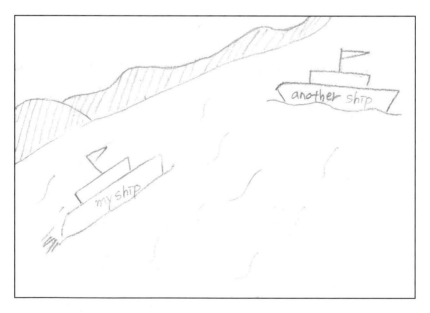

FIGURE 2.3(b). The external view of Figure 2.3a. A number of ships (including *MyShip*) move around the sea. This view can be selected by separate keyboard/ mouse control.

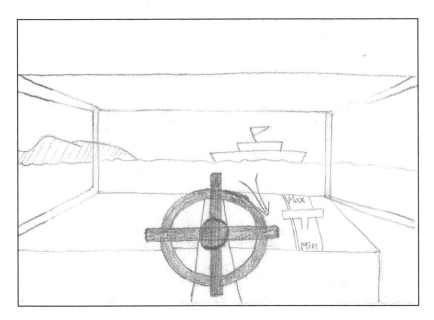

FIGURE 2.3(c). As the *User* steers the ship using the handle (named *SteeringWheel*), the scene through the window is changed accordingly.

FIGURE 2.3(d). The external view of Figure 2.3c.

FIGURE 2.3(e). As the *User* manipulates the engine lever (named *EngineTelegraph*) and controls the velocity of *MyShip*, the scene through the window changes accordingly.

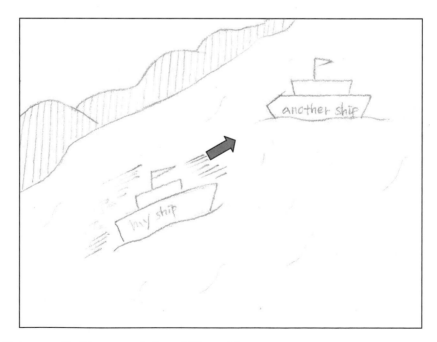

FIGURE 2.3(f). The external view of Figure 2.3e.

As shown in this simple storyboard, the three major objects are identified first: the trainee vessel (called *MyShip*), other automatically controlled vessels (called *OtherShip*), and the central simulation control module (called *ShipSimulator*). *MyShip* is composed of, among other things, *SteeringWheel and EngineTelegraph* (the user interface for vessel control). We also identify an interface object: the *Keyboard* (for various ship and training control functions) and an object representing the camera position, *Camera*.

The specification starts by creating simple scenarios using the MSD as depicted in Figure 2.4. Figure 2.4a is the first simple example of the MSD, a trainee interaction scenario for "looking around" on the control bridge. When the *User* enters a key, it is stored by the interface object *Keyboard*, and the *User* checks what kind of keys were pressed (e.g., "z" for looking to the left), and the *Camera* is updated accordingly. A similar interaction scenario is given in Figures 2.4b and c where the *User* communicates to the *Keyboard* (pressing the up/down/left/right arrow keys) to control the speed and the course of *MyShip*. In Figure 2.4d, the *OtherShip* sets its own initial position and direction in a random fashion and changes its speed and direction periodically every 10 second.

An initial class definition (with major functionalities specified based on the content of the messages exchanged) and the class diagram is designed as depicted in Figure 2.5. Figure 2.5 shows the simplified class diagram created by constructing various MSDs. Notice that the interaction object

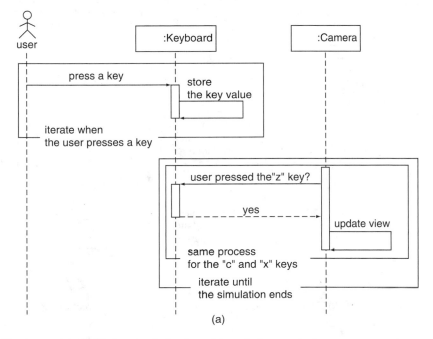

FIGURE 2.4(a). MSD for simple keyboard-based view control.

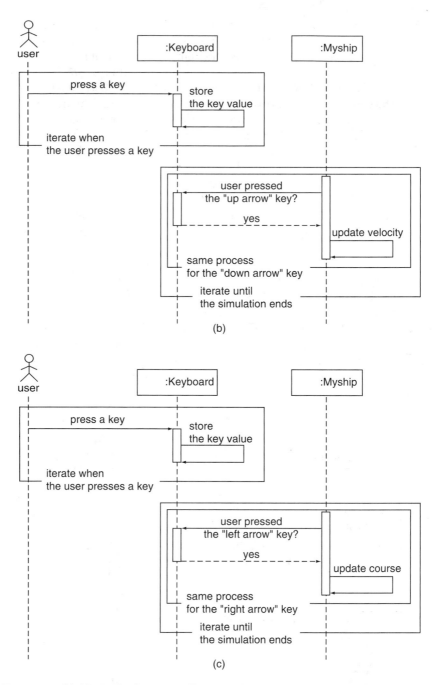

FIGURE 2.4(b),(c). MSD for controlling *MyShip's* velocity and direction using the arrow keys.

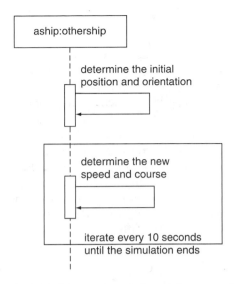

FIGURE 2.4(d). MSD for initializing and updating an instance of an *OtherShip*.

Keyboard and the *ShipSimulator* are purely "functional" without any form. As noted, the relations between classes are clarified at this stage of the modeling. A trainee can operate *MyShip* through *Keyboard*, then *MyShip* changes *Camera*. He or she can also change the orientation of *Camera* through *Keyboard* but the change in *Camera* does not affect *MyShip*. This initial class diagram will be subject to revision during the next phases of development.

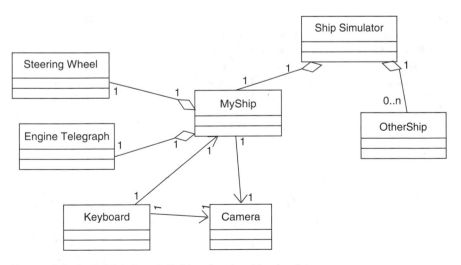

FIGURE 2.5. An initial class definition for the ship simulator.

Summary

VR system design starts with listing the requirements and carefully analyzing them as to whether virtual reality is even needed in the first place. The requirements must be centered around the user's expectation and capabilities. For instance, an experience-oriented requirements will result in a system with emphasis on presence, whereas a task-oriented requirements will place emphasis on efficient interaction. Based on the requirements, the overall scenario can be constructed using storyboards. "Virtual" objects that make up the scene are identified and the basic specifications for their form, function, and behavior should be made. Other aspects of the system such as device constraints, interaction, major special effects, and presence cues are also noted in this early stage of system development. Major interobject relationships are made more explicit by drawing class diagrams and message sequence diagrams.

Pondering Points

- Characterize the form, function, and behavior for a virtual human, virtual rock, virtual airplane, and virtual wind.
- What are possible barriers to making a VR system run in real-time?
- Make a case for, and against, carrying out requirements engineering at all.
- Make a case for, and against, using abstract formalism, support tools, or even documentation for requirements and system specifications.
- Is the object-oriented paradigm most fitting for implementing VR systems?
- Can having too many interaction points in the VR content be detrimental to inducing a good convincing virtual experience?
- In achieving the intended level of virtual experience, how can one make a good decision, for instance, between purchasing a special device for the increased effect, and staying with the less capable one and overcoming its shortcoming using other tricks?

Chapter 3
Object and Scene Modeling

Object Modeling and Initial Implementation

Virtual objects, for their natural physical connotation, indeed find themselves naturally mapped to the objects in the object-oriented system development methodology. Note that the object-oriented approach not only can be used to model the objects and scenes in the VE, but also abstract the various computational services needed for the VE, for instance, device management, rendering control, object importing, event management, process management, and so forth. In this chapter, we look at different ways to implement the form and function/behavior of the virtual objects based on the rough requirements and specification exemplified in the previous chapter.

Geometric (Form) Modeling/Implementation

Most VR applications are usually developed in the sequence of form modeling, followed by function/behavior programming. The most popular method of form modeling is to use Computer-Aided Design (CAD) systems. Then, if necessary, the CAD output must be converted into the appropriate file format or data structure to be used by the VR execution environment (e.g., for rendering and displaying it). The VR development/execution environment is a computational layer built on top of an underlying basic system support (such as for graphics, device interfaces, and system control) that provides abstraction for developers to program (through a set of library routines) and run their programs. Figure 3.1 (left) shows the structure of this computational structure.

Figure 3.1 (right) also shows the structure of a CAD system which is in fact another computer graphic application. It allows users to enter commands through the keyboard and the mouse, and visually construct the appearance/geometry of an object. The geometry and other properties of the object in construction all have internal computational representations

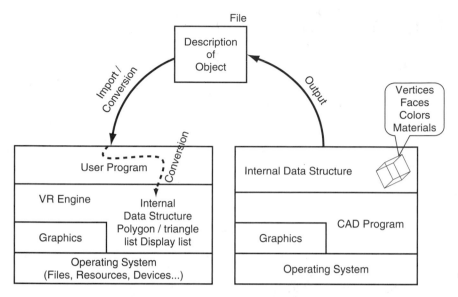

FIGURE 3.1. A VR execution environment and importing a CAD model for a virtual object.

(or data structures). For these objects to be "used" and drawn for your VR system, they need to be put in a certain file format and then be imported into your run-time VR environment. Whatever file formats or internal representations that different modelers and computer graphics systems use, they ultimately must be converted into a list of (flat) polygons/triangles, because that is what today's graphics hardware uses to produce images on the screen. There exist popular CAD systems, and there exist popular VR run-time environments, and they are not necessarily compatible with one another. For instance, a popular geometric modeler 3DSMax[1] produces an output file in a format called the ".obj" files, and certain VR development/execution environments will not be able to import the file format and convert it into the list of polygons to render them on the screen. One of the first things that the VR developer must worry about is this compatibility: whether a given CAD model can be imported into the chosen VR development/execution environment. Certain VR packages advertise that they are able to import various kinds of file formats, but it is always safe to doublecheck for "full" compatibility.

CAD data not only include the geometry information, but also much other useful information such as the hierarchical structure of the object, color, texture, lighting properties, material, and even simple behavior or animation sequences. Certain environments will only be able to import

---

[1] 3DSMax is a registered trademark of the Discreet, Inc.

part of this information. Note that the imported information is merged into yet another internal representation that a given particular VR environment will use. Even though the job of object modeling is often committed to the graphic designers (i.e., expert CAD users), it is beneficial for a VR developer to be familiar with the modeling process and the internal model representations used by the CAD system, because the way objects are modeled and represented internally can later have an impact on the performance of the virtual reality system that uses these object models.

Various Representations for Geometry

In this line of reasoning, we discuss the basis for representing various types of geometry. One of the simplest ways to represent geometry is through mathematics such as algebraic equations. Figure 3.2 shows a few varieties. Representing such mathematical objects can be divided into several flavors: the parametric, explicit, and implicit forms (see Figure 3.3).

Thus, for instance, an internal representation for an "explicit" line would have an identifier for the object and the entity type (i.e., it is a line) and the values for the coefficients of the line equation. Or, a "parametric" curve/ surface can be specified in a similar fashion by providing the control points (by mouse clicks). Certain computations are made easier depending on the type of mathematical representation used. For instance, although the implicit representation can be used conveniently for collision detection (as illustrated in Figure 3.4), the parametric representation is more convenient for figuring out "where" something (such as a point) is on a given surface or a curve.

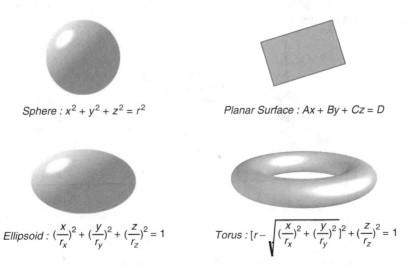

Sphere : $x^2 + y^2 + z^2 = r^2$

Planar Surface : $Ax + By + Cz = D$

Ellipsoid : $(\frac{x}{r_x})^2 + (\frac{y}{r_y})^2 + (\frac{z}{r_z})^2 = 1$

Torus : $[r - \sqrt{(\frac{x}{r_x})^2 + (\frac{y}{r_y})^2}]^2 + (\frac{z}{r_z})^2 = 1$

FIGURE 3.2. Examples of algebraic representations of various geometric entities.

	Explicit Form	Implicit Form	Parametric Form
Sphere	$y = \sqrt{r^2 - x^2 - z^2}$	$x^2 + y^2 + z^2 = r^2$	$x = r\cos\phi\cos\theta, -\pi/2 \le \phi \le \pi/2$ $y = r\cos\phi\sin\theta, -\pi \le \theta \le \pi$ $z = r\sin\phi$
Ellipsoid	$y = r_y\sqrt{1 - (\frac{z}{r_z})^2 - (\frac{x}{r_x})^2}$	$(\frac{x}{r_x})^2 + (\frac{y}{r_y})^2 + (\frac{z}{r_z})^2 = 1$	$x = r_x\cos\phi\cos\theta, -\pi/2 \le \phi \le \pi/2$ $y = r_y\cos\phi\sin\theta, -\pi \le \theta \le \pi$ $z = r_z\sin\phi$
Torus	$y = r_y\sqrt{r^2 - 1 - (\frac{z}{r_z})^2 + r\sqrt{(\frac{z}{r_z})^2 - (\frac{x}{r_x})^2}}$	$[r - \sqrt{(\frac{x}{r_x})^2 + (\frac{y}{r_y})^2}]^2 + (\frac{z}{r_z})^2 = 1$	$x = r_x(r + \cos\phi)\cos\theta, -\pi \le \phi \le \pi$ $y = r_y(r + \cos\phi)\sin\theta, -\pi \le \theta \le \pi$ $z = r_z\sin\phi$

FIGURE 3.3. Variations in mathematical representations: parametric, implicit, and explicit forms.

Although these mathematical equations can be useful, it would be quite difficult to model a certain object entirely mathematically (e.g., what is the mathematical representation for a chair?). To construct more complex-looking objects (such as a chair), one good way might be to use the mathematical representation for the primitives, but put the primitives together "manually." One such approach is Constructive Solid Geometry (CSG) (see Figure 3.5). In CSG-based CAD systems, an intuitive set of operators such as

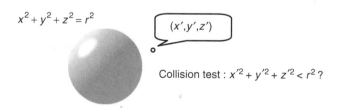

$x^2 + y^2 + z^2 = r^2$

(x', y', z')

Collision test : $x'^2 + y'^2 + z'^2 < r^2$?

$x = r\cos\phi\cos\theta, -\pi/2 \le \phi \le \pi/2$
$y = r\cos\phi\sin\theta, -\pi \le \phi \le \pi$
$z = r\sin\phi$

Values of ϕ and θ indicate where point(x, y, z) is on the surface of the sphere.

FIGURE 3.4. Different mathematical representations used for collision detection and point localization.

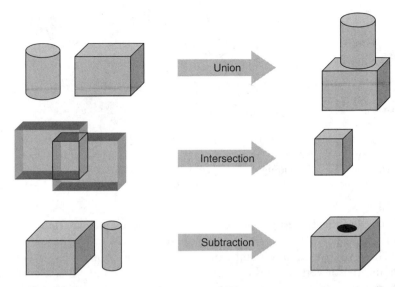

FIGURE 3.5. The modeling concept of Constructive Solid Geometry (CSG).

union, intersection, and difference can be applied to compose and create complex-looking objects. The mathematics behind this (for computing the resultant shape) is very complicated and beyond the scope of this book. Another approach is to use constraints. Constraints are helpful, for instance, in positioning one object in relation to another in a precise way. For instance, a constraint that says, "face X needs to align with edge Y and edge Z" can be input prior to making the manual placement, and this way, the degrees of freedom (needed to place the face along the edge Y and Z) can be limited in order to guide the placement in the most convenient way. After the primitives are put together, the overall geometric configuration can be captured simply by recording the relative position and orientation (e.g., 4 × 4 transformation matrices; see later part of this chapter) between the constituent primitives. A virtual object composed of several constituent primitives (or subobjects) can be represented hierarchically using a tree data structure. In this hierarchy, the coordinate system of children objects (constituents of the parent object) is defined relative to that of the parent object. When a motion (or certain transformation) is applied to the parent, all of its children are affected by it as well.

Another simple way to model objects is through manually constructing an object using even more primitive entities such as polygons, triangles, edges, and vertices. Note that (flat) polygonal representation is what is required by the graphics hardware for rendering. Because a polygon is made up of vertices and edges, a polygonal-based modeler would allow users to place vertices and connect them to form edges and faces, in the virtual 3D space, to construct a polygonal object model (see Figure 3.6). Such a model

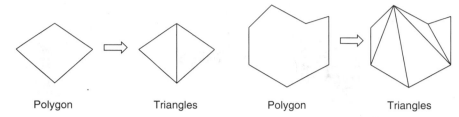

Polygon   Triangles   Polygon   Triangles

FIGURE 3.6. Polygons constructed by placing vertices in 3D space and specifying their connectivity. Note that their surfaces may not be flat. Thus, they are decomposed into triangles by subdividing the polygons by a triangularization process. Any polygon can be split into a number of triangles.

is also called the **B-Rep (Boundary Representation)** or wire-frame because the exact surface is not really mathematically defined (only the boundaries are). However, we cannot assume that the polygons constructed by specifying a number of vertices and their connectivity will be flat. This is because a polygon with more than four vertices is not guaranteed to lie on a flat plane (however, triangles are). Thus, polygons are often ultimately further decomposed into triangles by a separate process (i.e., triangularization[2]).

These can be simply displayed with the content being "hollow" (surfaces not filled in). Naturally, it will be difficult to model complex shapes (especially those with fancy curves and surfaces) by means of this method. Even smooth curves or surfaces can be approximated with polygon models given a sufficient amount of vertices, edges, and faces (see Figure 3.7). However, this is problematic, because it would be too tedious for the user to input the positions of these vertices and their connectivity information. Perhaps the best approach is offer the CAD user an intuitive and natural interface to indirectly create basic primitives in a parametric way and compose them using a method such as the CSG and constraint-based methods. Then, automatic polygonalization and triangularization algorithms can be called to produce the polygon/triangle list data structure (and the file format to be exported).

One shortcoming of using the automatic polygonalization (or triangularization) method is the lack of flexibility in controlling the number of polygons they produce for a given model. The performance of a graphics subsystem is quite dependent on the number of polygons of the objects to be drawn. Some CAD systems do offer advanced polygonalization (or triangularization) routines in which the output can be specified with the number of target polygon counts, and even specification of different parts for different degrees of polygonalization (or triangularization). Also note that a polygon list can be easily converted into a triangle list (because any polygon can be split into a number of triangles).

---

[2] Triangulation is also often called tessellation.

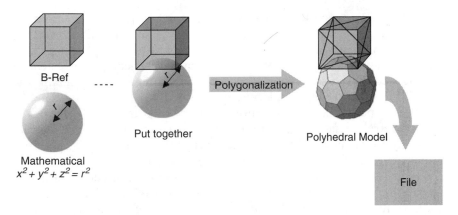

FIGURE 3.7. Modeling an object using a CAD system with various representations, and converting them into a polygonal data/file.

The final method of modeling is the procedural modeling method. As its name implies, one can create and specify the geometry of the model, relative locations and orientations of subobjects, their color, and other properties in a procedural manner, that is, by writing a program that consists of commands that accomplish the job (see Figure 3.8). Library routines from

Making a sphere

```
pfGeoSet   *sphereGset;
pfGeode    *geode;

//make unit sphere at (0,0,0)
//using 100 triangular faces
sphereGset= pfdNewSphere(100, arena);
geode->addGSet(sphereGset);

//parent node in scene graph
scene Graph Root->addChild(geode);

//set radius of sphere
sceneGraphRoot->setScale(20);

//set sphere origin position
sceneGraphRoot->setTrans(10,20,30);
```

Making a cube

```
pfGeoSet   *cubeGset;
pfGeode    *geode;

//make unit cube at (0,0,0)
cubeGset= pfdNewcube(arena);
geode->addGSet(cubeGset);

//parent node in scene graph
sceneGraphRoot->addChild(geode);

//set xyz length of cube
sceneGraphRoot->setScale(20,20,30);

//set cube position
sceneGraphRoot->setTrans(10,20,30);
```

FIGURE 3.8. Procedural routines for creating and placing primitive objects such as a sphere and a cube using the Performer programming library.[3]

---

[3] Performer is a registered trademark of Silicon Graphics, Inc.

computer graphics or VR engines usually include a small set of routines for creating simple primitives (in a parametric way) such as cubes, spheres, cones, ellipses, and the like. Again, it would be quite difficult to represent a complex shape using this method. However, it is sometimes convenient to use these code-generated parametric primitives to prescribe changes to the model (e.g., shape change, replacing textures or colors) during run-time.

Remember that there can be information relevant to "form" other than just geometry. Nongeometric form information can include the usual object hierarchy, color, material, and physical properties such as mass, position, velocity, acceleration, force, angular velocity, angular acceleration, torque, and so on. Developers can define additional properties as needed. The object modeler (e.g., CAD system) may allow encoding of such information in addition to the geometry. If not, the user must document it separately manually or using other tools.

An external data importer of a given VR development/execution should interpret the form information created by the object modeling and merge it into its own object model. As mentioned before, even though many types of information may be specified using a given modeling tool, when imported into the VR development/execution platform, some of the information can be lost (see Figure 3.9). For instance, using a modeling tool like

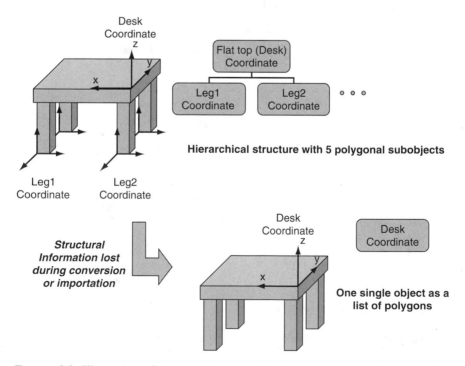

FIGURE 3.9. Illustration of the possible loss of information during the model file import process.

3DSMax, one can create not only nice-looking geometries for an object, but also its structure, simple behavior, and animation sequences. However, when importing the ".obj" file into a certain VR platform, not all information may survive in the conversion process. One of the most critical pieces of "form" information is the object hierarchy (i.e., subobjects and their relationships). In 3DSMax, the object may have consisted of subobjects in a hierarchical manner, with each subobject having an independent status with a separate polygon list. However, a given VR platform, in reading and importing the ".obj" file may reconstruct the object as one monolithic polygon list for the whole object. Thus, for instance, one will not know where the right leg of a human model is (or which polygons correspond to those for the leg) because the resultant model is just a big polygon list. A more desired conversion process would be one that can preserve or reconstruct the data as a hierarchical tree of polygon lists, the same as the input.

Performance-Conscious Form Modeling

Most approaches to dealing with the real-time performance requirements of VR systems have focused on reducing the number of objects/polygons that need to be processed by the graphics hardware. Image-based rendering is an extreme example of this approach, which essentially eliminates any use of 3D polygons. Instead it uses and requires computations on images. The images can be for individual objects or for a good part of the whole environment. Creative use of textures or image-based modeling is a good performance optimization technique that not only provides reasonable realism, but also relieves users of the burden of tedious modeling efforts (see Chapter 5). However, its full-blown usage for VR is yet an open question due to some unresolved issues, such as the low interactivity, visibility problems, storage requirements, and the intensive image processing required for correct view generation.

Another approach to reducing the graphics overhead is to figure out, at a given frame to be drawn, the part of the virtual world visible from the given viewpoint and only render that. These techniques usually rely on a particular model structure (e.g., indoor building) or designation of occluding and their occludee objects or polygons. However, these approaches require assumptions that may not be applicable to the construction of general VR worlds.

One of the most popular ways to tune a VR system performancewise is to use the levels of detail (LOD). An object may be associated with, not one, but multiple geometric models of varying details, known as the LODs, and the system can dynamically switch among them to maintain an acceptable frame rate depending on system load and the importance of the object. The conventional approach to preparing for (geometric) LODs for virtual objects is through a process called *polygon budgeting* [Hof97]. With polygon budgeting, important (regarding their potential rendering cost) virtual objects in the scene are identified and assigned the appropriate number of polygons, depending on the scene complexity and the limitations of the target graphic hardware. The budget is used by the model builders as a guide as they create the geometric models using the geometric modelers and CAD systems. In practice, models are usually created with utmost detail, then, simplified in reverse (using mesh simplification algorithms[4]) down to several levels of detail as needed.

One of the standing problems with simplification algorithms is the preservation of geometric features (e.g., topology, curvature, vertex position, etc.). There is an inherent trade-off between degrees of simplification and preservation of the original appearance, features, and shape. Moreover, these algorithms (as implemented in the geometric modelers) are applied to the overall model, and do not usually allow the user to "selectively" simplify or preserve certain segments or features that may be visually significant. Ideally, with the polygon budget, the geometries must be created and refined from a rough model to a detailed one as part of a hierarchical and incremental development process. Such a process promotes a performance-conscious design by forcing the developer to focus on the more critical features in form, function, and/or behavior in a top-down manner. Intermediate models obtained from the hierarchical modeling approach can naturally be used for LODs.

Scene Construction

Once the object's forms and behaviors (see next sections for behavior modeling) are roughly modeled, they need to be "put in place" in the 3D space to compose a scene (at least an initial one). Note that the scene can be changed in time as objects may move, are newly introduced, or destroyed. In order to place an object in a scene, there has to be a fixed standard reference coordinate system. Any graphics or VR platform assumes the existence of such a coordinate system, usually called the "World" coordinate system. The locations and orientations of all the virtual objects need to be set (or converted to) with respect to this assumed World coordinate system, because the graphics hardware, for instance, assumes that all object coordinates are with respect to that of the World, and projects them to the screen.

Object Placement by Series of Action

In order to specify a position and orientation of an object, the object itself must possess a coordinate system on its own, called the object or local coordinate system. The local coordinate system is (most usually) attached

---

[4] Most popular geometric modelers include a mesh simplification functionality. A good survey of simplification algorithms is given in [Lub99].

somewhere on the object itself and in a "convenient" orientation at modeling time by the user. In a sense, this local coordinate system represents the object (thus, it makes sense that the local coordinate system be placed in a "strategic" position on the object). For instance, a virtual desk object might have a local coordinate system placed in the corner of its flat top (so the origin of the object coordinate system would be here) with its x-axis aligned to the length, y-axis aligned to the depth, and z-axis pointing perpendicular to the flat top (see Figure 3.10). However, it does not matter where and how the location and orientation of the object coordinate are placed.

The position and orientation of the object "in the world" are defined by where and how the "object's coordinate system" is placed in relation to the "world coordinate system." This analogy can be extended to an object-to-object relationship. That is, the position and orientation of one object with respect to another object can be defined by where and how one object's coordinate system is placed in relation to the other object's coordinate system. In such a case, two coordinate systems form a parent (reference)–child relationship. Cascaded parent–child relationships among objects (or equivalently their coordinate systems) can be formed, with the ultimate parent being the "World" coordinate system (we come back to this issue later).

Given an object coordinate system and its reference or parent (e.g., World) coordinate system, the object's location can be specified by stating how to place the object coordinate system origin at the desired location with respect to the reference coordinate system. Initially, the object (or equivalently its local coordinate system) is assumed to be at, and aligned with, its parent coordinate system. Thus, as shown in Figure 3.10, the location of object O by default would be at coordinate (0, 0, 0), then respecified to be at coordinate (−10, 30, 20) by simply adding the displacement of (−10, 30, 20), or equivalently moving O by −10 in the x-direction, 30 in the y-direction, and 20 in the z-direction of the World coordinate system.

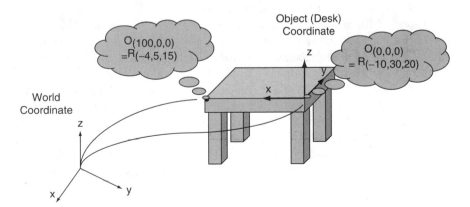

FIGURE 3.10. The World coordinate system and the object/local coordinate system for the desk.

Note that although this new position is $(-10, 30, 20)$ with respect to the parent coordinate system, it is also at $(0, 0, 0)$ with respect to the local object coordinate system. To avoid confusion, we attach a superscript (such as R for the "Reference," or O, "Object") to the coordinates to indicate their reference coordinate system. Thus, after the movement, coordinates $^O(0, 0, 0)$ and $^R(-10, 30, 20)$ refer to the same point, the (new) location of the object. If the object needs to be moved again, for instance by $(10, 10, 10)$, then the displacement is simply added to the current location, producing $^R(0, 40, 30)$.

By the same logic, the object would always be located at the origin of its own local coordinate system, $^O(0, 0, 0)$. What about the location of a "local" point (or vertex) $^O(px, py, pz)$ on this object? Assuming that the object does not change its shape during the movement or placement operation (i.e., rigid motion without deformation), its local coordinates will remain the same. However, coordinates of the local point with respect to the parent World coordinate system will change by the amount of the movement. That is, $^O(px, py, pz)$ and $^R(px - 10, py + 30, pz + 20)$ refer to a same point in space.

The operation is represented as

$$^R X_{\text{New}} = \text{Trans}(^R X_{\text{Old}}, \text{displacement})$$

$$= {}^R X_{\text{Old}} + \begin{pmatrix} dx \\ dy \\ dz \end{pmatrix}$$

$$X_{\text{New}} = X_{\text{Old}} + \begin{pmatrix} dx \\ dy \\ dz \end{pmatrix}$$

Note that the expression operates with respect to one coordinate system. Thus, it is safe to drop the superscript R. VR programming libraries include variations of the movement operator shown above. For instance, a hypothetical call such as *Move (object1, 10, 20, 30)* will carry out the operation above, adding the displacement to the current location of object1 with respect to its parent coordinate system. Another hypothetical call such as *Absolute_move (object1, 10, 20, 30)* would place object1 at location $(10, 20, 30)$ with respect to the origin of the parent coordinate system of object1.

In addition to the position, the orientation of an object also needs to be specified. One method of doing this is by describing by how much to rotate its own (local) coordinate system around the axis of the parent (or reference) coordinate system. For instance, we might rotate[5] the object (or equivalently

---

[5] All rotations are according to the right-hand rule (i.e., the right thumb directed toward the positive direction of the axis, and the direction of the remaining fingers denoting counterclockwise direction of rotation.

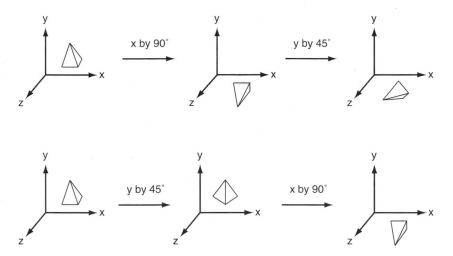

FIGURE 3.11. The order of applying rotation matters.

its local coordinate system) through the x-axis of the parent reference coordinate system (which is not moving) by some value α, then rotate through the y-axis by β, and finally rotate through the z-axis by γ. If we applied the rotation by each axis in a different order, the object would be oriented differently, as depicted in Figure 3.11. This stems from the fact that mathematically applying rotation transformation is not commutative, that is, the order of the application matters.

Thus, to conveniently specify the orienting operation without confusion, one often uses the convention called the Fixed axis angles. Fixed axis angles are a set of three angles, α, β, and γ. When these three values are given as an orientation specification between two coordinate systems, one reference and the other rotated, it is understood that the object is rotated by α in the x-axis of the reference coordinate system, then by β in the y-axis, and then by γ in the z-axis, "in that order." Similarly to the translation, the rotation process can be modeled as applying a mathematical operator (see below).

$$^R X_{New} = \text{FixedAxis\_}Rot(^R X_{Old}, {}^R\text{axis\_set}, \alpha, \beta, \gamma)$$

where ^{R}axis_set denotes the three axes of the (reference) coordinate system R (sometimes, the axis order might be explicitly specified).

Similarly to object moving, when initially specifying the orientation of an object, it is assumed to be aligned with its reference coordinate system. Thus, as shown in Figure 3.12, the pose of object O1 by default would be aligned to the axis of the reference coordinate system. The actions of three rotations are applied to newly orient the object. The Fixed axis rotation operation can be mathematically represented as applying three linear transformation matrices in series, to any point of the object expressed in its own local coordinate system.

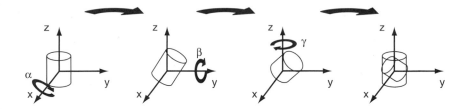

Rotating by Fixed axis convention, α=30, β=40, γ=60

FIGURE 3.12. Orientation specification with Fixed axis angles.

$$^R X_{\text{New}} = \text{FixedAxis\_Rot}(^R X_{\text{Old}}, \ ^R \text{axis\_set}, \ \alpha, \ \beta, \ \gamma)$$

$$= Rot(^R z, \ \gamma)^* Rot(^R y, \ \beta)^* Rot(^R x, \ \alpha)^{*R} X_{\text{Old}}$$

$$= {}^R Rot^{\text{Fixed axis}} * {}^R X_{\text{Old}}(\text{in a single matrix format})$$

$$X_{\text{New}} = Rot^{\text{Fixed axis}} * X_{\text{Old}}$$

where *Rot (i, w)* is a linear function representing an operation to rotate around the axis *i* by *w* degrees. Note that the expression operates with respect to one coordinate system (in this case the *R*). Thus, it is safe to drop the superscript *R*. *Rot(z, γ)*, *Rot(y, β)*, *Rot(x, α)* are given by the following simple formulas (in matrix forms).

$$Rot(^R z, \ \gamma) = \begin{bmatrix} \cos \gamma & -\sin \gamma & 0 \\ \sin \gamma & \cos \gamma & 0 \\ 0 & 0 & 1 \end{bmatrix}$$

$$Rot(^R y, \ \beta) = \begin{bmatrix} \cos \beta & 0 & \sin \beta \\ 0 & 1 & 0 \\ -\sin \beta & 0 & \cos \beta \end{bmatrix}$$

$$Rot(^R x, \ \alpha) = \begin{bmatrix} 1 & 0 & 0 \\ 0 & \cos \alpha & -\sin \alpha \\ 0 & \sin \alpha & \cos \alpha \end{bmatrix}$$

Fixed axis angle convention is needed when all three orthogonal axes are involved in sequence in specifying the relative orientation between two coordinate systems. However, rotation around an individual axis (whether the axis is one of the reference coordinate axes or an arbitrary vector) can be specified with the axis vector and the amount of rotation (e.g., degrees) as one mathematical operator. Expressing the rotation axis as a vector $\vec{k} = {}^R (kx, \ ky, \ kz)$ in the reference coordinate and the amount of rotation θ, the rotation is represented by a mathematical operator:

$$^R X_{\text{New}} = {}^R Rot\_by\_single\_axis({}^R\vec{k},\ \theta)^{*R} X_{\text{Old}},$$

$$X_{\text{New}} = Rot\_by\_single\_axis(\vec{k},\ \theta)^{*} X_{\text{Old}},$$

Without confusion, the superscript R can be dropped. The formula for *Rot_by_single_axis* is given by (in matrix form) [Cra86]

$$Rot\_by\_single\_axis\ (\vec{k},\ \theta) = \begin{bmatrix} kxkxv\theta + c\theta & kxkyv\theta - kzs\theta & kxkzv\theta + kys\theta \\ kxkyv\theta + kzs\theta & kykyv\theta + c\theta & kykzv\theta - kxs\theta \\ kxkzv\theta - kys\theta & kykzv\theta + kxs\theta & kzkzv\theta + c\theta \end{bmatrix}$$

where $c\theta = \cos\ \theta$, $s\theta = \sin\ \theta$, and $v\theta = 1 - \cos\ \theta$. Note that to replace the rotated object in its original position, the inverse of the rotation operator is applied:

$$(^R Rot^{\text{Fixed axis}})^{-1} = Rot(^R x,\ -\alpha)^{*} Rot(^R y,\ -\beta)^{*} Rot(^R z,\ -\gamma)$$

or,

$$(Rot\_by\_single\_axis(k,\ \theta))^{-1} = Rot\_by\_single\_axis(k,\ -\theta)$$

There is another rotation operator called the Euler rotation operator. In the Euler rotation, the rotation is applied with respect to the "rotating" local coordinate system of the object. For instance, one can rotate around the local z axis (which is initially coincident with the z axis of the reference coordinate system) by γ, then around the local y axis (which by now would have rotated from its original pose and be different from the fixed reference y axis) by β, then finally around the local x axis by α. The operation can be represented as below (note that to be clear the axis order is explicitly specified as a subscript). It so happens that the Euler rotation operation is equivalent to the Fixed axis rotation when the axis rotation order is reversed as shown in the formula below (derivation is not shown).

$$^R X_{\text{New}} = Rot^{Euler}{}_{ZYX}(^R X_{\text{Old}},\ ^R axis\_set, \alpha, \beta, \gamma)$$

$$= Rot^{Fixed\ axis}{}_{XYZ}(^R X_{\text{Old}},\ ^R axis\_set, \alpha, \beta, \gamma)$$

Similarly to the translation case, **VR** programming libraries contain variations of the rotation operators shown above. A hypothetical operator such as *Fixed_Axis_Rotate (object1, α, β, γ)* would rotate *object1* with respect to its parent coordinate system by the convention (with axis order of xyz) by α, β, and γ (and similarly for *EulerZYX_Rotate (object1, α, β, γ)*). Another hypothetical operator such as *Rotate_axis (object1, k, d)* would rotate *object1* through vector $\vec{k}$ by angle d.

To summarize, one way to specify the location and orientation of an object with respect to another reference coordinate system is to express them in a series of operators (and associated parameter values) applied to the object with respect to the reference. Note that the order of application is important. Motion usually involves both translation and rotation, and in

Object Moving

```
pfGeoSet    *cubeGset;
pfGeode     *geode;
pfDCS       *objectDCS;
```

```
//make unit cube at (0,0,0)
cubeGset = pfdNewcube (arena);
geode->addGSet (cubeGset);
```

```
//attach cube to parent node in scene graph
objectDCS->addChild (geode);
```

```
//moving cube position x to 10, y to 20, z to 30
objectDCS->setTrans(10,20,30);
```

Object Rotating

```
pfGeoSet    *cubeGset;
pfGeode     *geode;
pfDCS       *objectDCS;
```

```
//make unit cube at (0,0,0)
cubeGset= pfdNewcube (arena);
geode->addGSet (cubeGset);
```

```
//attach cube to parent//node in scene graph
objectDCS->addChild(geode);
```

```
//Rotate cube//Euler angle = (90,0,45)
objectDCS->setRot (90,0,45);
```

FIGURE 3.13. The SGI Performer library calls (and required parameters) for positioning (or equivalently moving) and orienting (or equivalently rotating) an object.

applying rotations and translations, the resultant position or orientation will be different depending on whether the rotation is applied first or the translation is applied first (we come back to this issue again). Figure 3.13 shows example library calls available in SGI Performer and the required parameters for rotating or translating an object.

Dealing with Multiple Frames of Reference

So far, even though we talked a little bit about different types of coordinate systems (such as reference and local), we have really operated within one coordinate system, moving or rotating an element (e.g., vector, point, etc.) expressed in one coordinate system to a new location in the same coordinate system. Although it is most convenient, during motion simulation (which is the specification of position or orientation in time) or rendering (part of which is projecting objects to a display screen), that all involved objects be expressed in one frame of reference, virtual objects, in general, are not expressed in just one (for instance, the World) coordinate system.

In fact, all the coordinates of the primitives (e.g., polygons, faces, edges, vertices, etc.) that make up an object are (initially) expressed with respect to the object coordinate system. For instance, a coordinate of a vertex (1, 1, 1) that belongs to object1 will be with respect to object1's coordinate system, whereas another vertex (1, 1, 1) that belongs to object2 will be with respect to object2's coordinate system. Thus, although they both have the representation (in fact, a confusing one) of (1, 1, 1), they refer to different positions in the (whole) space. As already mentioned, thus, when specifying a coordinate,

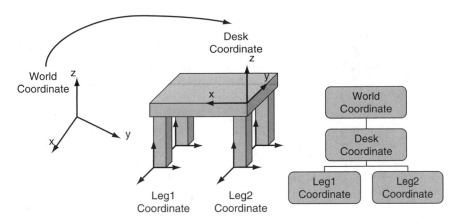

FIGURE 3.14. Hierarchy (or chain) of relations among objects (and their coordinate system).

to avoid confusion, one must express the coordinate system to which it belongs (or the reference coordinate system).

Similarly, a position and orientation of an object with its own local coordinate system may be specified with respect to another object coordinate system (we have learned how to do this in the previous section). A typical case is when an object contains subobjects (as in a desk having four legs as distinct subobjects; see Figure 3.14). The subobject locations and orientations are conveniently specified with respect to the parent object (the parent object becomes the reference instead of the World). For instance, it is more natural to specify the leg of the desk as being located at the corner of the flat top, that is, in reference to the flat top object, rather than in reference to some other unrelated entity. Thus, a cascade (or hierarchy) of interobject (or intercoordinate) relations can be formed with the World coordinate system being the final, root, and absolute reference coordinate system among objects in a scene as shown in Figure 3.14. In essence, this hierarchy expresses the whole scene, the constituent objects, and their location and orientations. Thus, what we need is a mechanism to express locations and orientations of all objects expressed with respect to different coordinate systems ultimately into a single unified one (e.g., the World) so that one can easily carry out certain computations for display or simulation.

Re-Expressing Coordinates

We have seen that rotation operators can be expressed in a matrix format, and rotation matrices have a nice property that a product of rotation matrices results in another (one) rotation matrix (i.e., a series of rotations around respective axes is equivalent to one rotation). In fact, a rotation matrix between two 3D coordinate systems is defined as a matrix composed of three (unit) column vectors, each representing the axis of one coordinate system with respect to the other coordinate system. This rotation matrix is equivalent to the matrix that is formed by multiplying the series of rotations (in order) to make one coordinate system coincide with the other (as we have explained so far). By the theories of linear algebra, a rotation matrix carries out a change of basis. That is, multiplying a rotation matrix by a coordinate expressed in one coordinate system changes the coordinate to be expressed in another coordinate system (see Figure 3.15).

Recall, for instance, Rot^{Euler}, rotates an object originally at $^RX_{Old}$ into a new location, $^RX_{New}$. Thus, there are two interpretations for what the rotation matrix can do, as illustrated in Figure 3.15. One is re-expressing the coordinates of an entity and the other is to rotate the entity in the same coordinate system (e.g., Euler rotation). To express the capability of the coordinate re-expression (or change of basis), we put a super- and subscript in the rotation matrix, in the left top, the target coordinate system, and in the

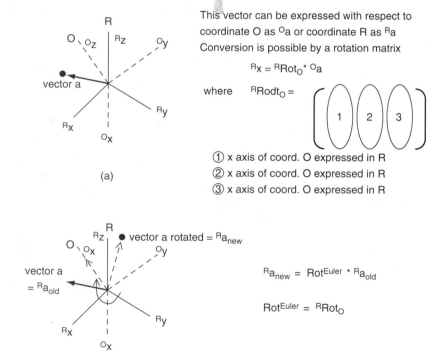

FIGURE 3.15. Two interpretations of the rotation matrix: (a) an entity is re-expressed in another coordinate system that is rotated from the reference. The conversion is made possible by multiplying a rotation matrix defined between the two frames; (b) the same rotation matrix can be interpreted to rotate an entity within one coordinate system.

lower right, the source coordinate system. The same interpretation is possible for translation as well. Figure 3.16 illustrates that a displacement between two translated coordinate frames can be used to express the position of an entity with respect to the two coordinate frames, or equivalently two different positions within one coordinate system.

To reiterate, by the theory of linear algebra, we can express a rotation matrix, $^1Rot_2$, using the basis of coordinate systems 1 and 2. $^1Rot_2$, as a matrix will contain in its columns the basis of coordinate system 2 expressed in the basis of coordinate system 1. For instance,

$$^1Rot_2(^1x, 90) \text{ in matrix form} = \begin{bmatrix} 1 & 0 & 0 \\ 0 & 0 & -1 \\ 0 & 1 & 0 \end{bmatrix}$$

We can see that the columns of this matrix express the axis of coordinate system 2 in terms of its reference basis: $(1, 0, 0)$, $(0, 1, 0)$, and $(0, 0, 1)$. What about the reverse operation, $^2Rot_1(^2x, \theta = -90)$? The reverse operation can be found by constructing this matrix with its columns as the basis of coordinate system 1 expressed in 2 (we can figure out what θ will amount to; that is, rotating 2 with respect to 1 through the x-axis by 90 degrees is

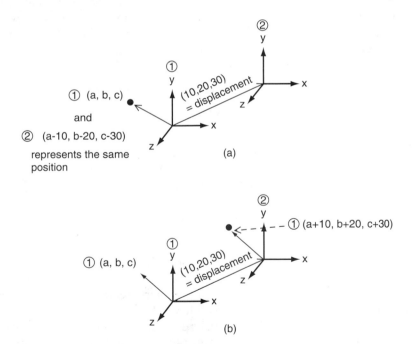

(a)

(b)

FIGURE 3.16. Two interpretations of the displacement between two coordinate systems; (a) an entity is re-expressed in another coordinate system that is translated from the reference; (b) the same displacement can be used to translate the entity within one coordinate system.

equivalent to rotating 1 with respect to 2 through the x-axis by -90 degrees). It turns out, by the theories of linear algebra, because the columns of rotation matrices are orthonormal, their inverses are just their transposes; that is,

$$^2Rot_1(^2x,\theta = -90) = {}^2Rot_1 = {}^1Rot_2^{-1} = {}^1Rot_2^T$$

Although the rotation matrix allows us to convert coordinates between two coordinate systems with different orientations, it does not account for translation. Because movements (or specification of an object location) usually involves both translation and rotation, it is convenient to combine the vector addition/subtraction (for translation) and matrix multiplication (for rotation) into one compact matrix representation (which is a 4×4 matrix as we show). In order to accomplish this, the homogeneous coordinate system is used to represent entities in the 3D space (e.g., position, vector) upon which the 4×4 matrix is applied. With homogeneous coordinates we add a 1 as a fourth component to represent vectors in 3D space, and the 4×4 matrix includes a fourth row $(0, 0, 0, 1)$ to handle this additional component. Representing a 3D entity with such a fourth component does have a mathematical meaning, but this is not treated in this book. For now, we accept the convention for the simple purpose of convenience. Thus, the 4×4 matrix (or better termed as 4×4 transformation matrix) includes the rotation matrix as its first submatrix and the amount of translation in its fourth column as shown in the following.

$$^2T_1 = \begin{bmatrix} & {}^2_1Rot & & dx \\ & & & dy \\ & & & dz \\ 0 & 0 & 0 & 1 \end{bmatrix}$$

and

$$^2x = {}^2T_1 * {}^1x$$

where

$$^1x = \begin{pmatrix} a \\ b \\ c \\ 1 \end{pmatrix}$$

Note that the 4×4 transformation matrix represented this way applies rotation, then the translation. The result would be different if translation were applied first. This is easily seen in its decomposition into components as also seen below. Here, T^{Trans} is a 4×4 transformation matrix that applies only translation (with its R submatrix equal to the identity matrix I), and likewise, T^{Rot} is a 4×4 transformation matrix that applies only rotation (with its d component 0).

$$^2T_1 = T^{Trans} T^{Rot} \neq T^{Rot} T^{Trans}$$

where

$$
T^{Trans} = \begin{bmatrix} & & & dx \\ & I & & dy \\ & & & dz \\ 0 & 0 & 0 & 1 \end{bmatrix} \quad \text{and} \quad T^{Rot} = \begin{bmatrix} & & & 0 \\ & ^2_1Rot & & 0 \\ & & & 0 \\ 0 & 0 & 0 & 1 \end{bmatrix}
$$

The 4 × 4 transformation matrices are conveniently used to convert various entities represented in different coordinate systems into another. In fact, whenever objects are to be rendered to the screen by the hardware, all objects must be ultimately converted into the World coordinate system (once everything is converted into the World coordinates, then they are projected to the screen coordinates). Thus, directly encoding the 4 × 4 transformation matrix (i.e., 12 elements) between two coordinate systems is another way of expressing relative object placement, instead of using Fixed axis or Euler angles, or thinking of it as movements from the default coordinate systems.[6] On the other hand, when carrying out simulation or motion calculation, it is convenient to express or interpret the process with the action-oriented approach (such as Euler rotation and translation operators).

Because the 4 × 4 transformation matrix conveniently captures both the rotation and translation between two given coordinate systems, the entire scene can be structured in a chain of 4 × 4 transformation matrices (as shown in Figure 3.17) that specify the physical relationship among them. A changing scene can be implemented by changing the values of the 4 × 4 matrices so that the objects move and rotate in space with respect to time (see Figure 3.18). Most VR programming and development environments use a hierarchical data structure called the scene graph[7] that organizes the scene by a tree, where the coordinate systems of the children objects (constituents of the parent object) are defined relative to that of their parent object. When a motion is applied to the parent node, all of its children are affected by it as well.

Function/Behavior Modeling

Low-level simulation programming constructs or libraries are most often used to add behavior. Such software packages allow relatively simple

---

[6] The 12 elements include 9 elements in the rotation matrix and 3 elements in the translation vector. Relative rotation can be expressed with fewer elements using another mathematical construct called the quaternions.

[7] The scene graph includes the hierarchical structure of the scene/objects plus other additional information such as lighting, cameras, object specific properties, behavior, and so on.

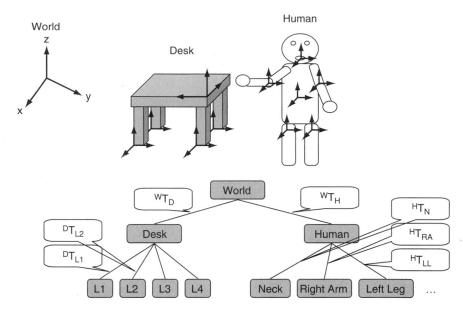

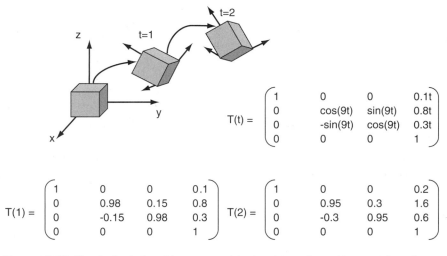

FIGURE 3.17. Hierarchy (or chain) of relations among objects (and their coordinate system) using the 4 × 4 transformation matrices.

$$T(t) = \begin{pmatrix} 1 & 0 & 0 & 0.1t \\ 0 & \cos(9t) & \sin(9t) & 0.8t \\ 0 & -\sin(9t) & \cos(9t) & 0.3t \\ 0 & 0 & 0 & 1 \end{pmatrix}$$

$$T(1) = \begin{pmatrix} 1 & 0 & 0 & 0.1 \\ 0 & 0.98 & 0.15 & 0.8 \\ 0 & -0.15 & 0.98 & 0.3 \\ 0 & 0 & 0 & 1 \end{pmatrix} \quad T(2) = \begin{pmatrix} 1 & 0 & 0 & 0.2 \\ 0 & 0.95 & 0.3 & 1.6 \\ 0 & -0.3 & 0.95 & 0.6 \\ 0 & 0 & 0 & 1 \end{pmatrix}$$

FIGURE 3.18. Physical relationship expressed in 4 × 4 transformation matrices changing in time to express object movements.

encoding of the functional/behavioral aspect of the virtual environment, by hiding and abstracting out low-level details and providing easy-to-use APIs for the programmers. These programming libraries also usually support object-oriented programming, communication with popular VR devices, and capabilities to import various model file formats. Direct programming is the most straightforward method of encoding virtual object behavior (or even scenewide behaviors), however, there are other possibilities.

Many game development platforms offer scriptlike languages, simpler than programming languages, to specify behaviors. With simple scripts, it is sometimes difficult to express complex interobject constraints and relations. Sometimes it is also convenient to encode object behaviors in terms of constraints among the virtual objects (e.g., if one object moves, the others follow). Expressing object function or behavior using Data Flow Diagrams (DFD) or state-based representations can be useful in overcoming this problem. A DFD specifies a single process or a function in terms of how it can be decomposed into a number of subprocesses or objects and their input/output relationships. For instance, the DFD is useful for specifying device interface behaviors, how the raw sensor data are transformed into a usable form by the number of intermediate filtering and conversion processes. The state-based representations can express time- or event-based coordinated behaviors among virtual objects very well. Many Artificial Intelligence (AI) behaviors are modeled using state-based representations such as finite-state machines.

However, in reality, direct programming remains the most prevalent form of function/behavior implementation. This is partly because high-level authoring tools and constructs tend to abstract too many details, and performance tuning and addressing presence can be difficult with these tools, and inappropriate for something other than small-scale, proof of concept prototyping. Many developers still prefer to merely use the API in a creative manner, or even use very low-level graphic system packages (e.g., OpenGL, DirectX[8]) in order to apply various optimization tricks. As such, these different styles of representational constructs (i.e., scripts, constraints, reusable components, state-based representations) are widely used as a way of specifying or documenting behavior prior to diving into programming as a way of planning and documentation. In the next section, we take a closer look at using the constructs to specify the important part of a system during development and implementation as discussed in the next chapter.

Example: Ship Simulator Revisited (Level 1 Form and Function/Behavior)

Figures 3.19 and 3.20 show initial scene graphs and geometric models for the Ship Simulator example introduced in Chapter 2. The whole world is composed of, for now, simply *MyShip* and *OtherShips*. *MyShip* is in turn composed of the *EngineTelegraph* (lever) and the *SteeringWheel*. Note that some objects are omitted for simpler illustration purpose (such as the deck

---

[8] DirectX is a registered trademark of Microsoft Corp.

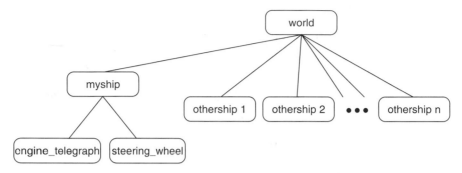

FIGURE 3.19. An initial scene graph for the Ship Simulator example.

FIGURE 3.20. Initial geometrical models for *MyShip* and *OtherShip*.

and windows of *MyShip* and other simple environment objects such as the sky and terrain).

Figures 3.21 through 3.23 illustrate the specifications of the behaviors of three main objects: *MyShip*, *OtherShip*, and *Camera*. Upon start of the whole system (Ship Simulator), *MyShip* automatically enters an initializing state and then transits into four concurrent states waiting for *User's* keyboard input. With the key input, appropriate actions are taken (script-based specification for this part is given on the companion CD). The specification for *OtherShip* is similar. Upon initialization, it automatically starts to make new targets and navigate toward them. A new target is regenerated at a fixed period of time.

Summary

Once important objects and interaction requirements are identified through activities such as storyboarding, they are roughly modeled in terms of their form, function, and behavior. These objects are to be refined iteratively and hierarchically as the development progresses into more details with respect to the given computational resources. Objects are put in place to form a scene in a hierarchical structure of the object coordinate system using operators and 4 × 4 transformation matrices.

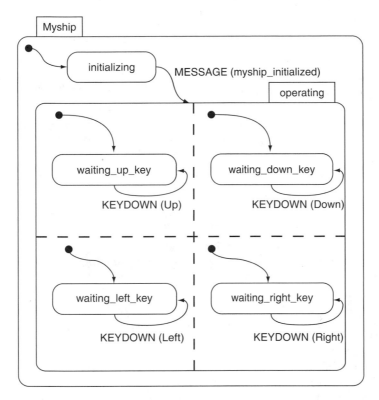

FIGURE 3.21. The statechart for controlling *MyShip*. A more detailed script-based description of the actions taken at each state is given on the companion CD.

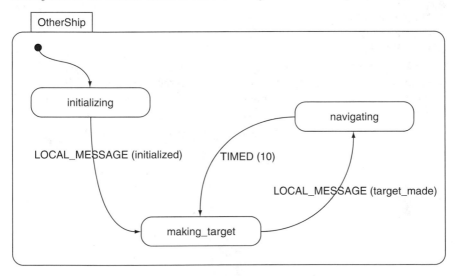

FIGURE 3.22. The statechart for the behavior of *OtherShip*. A more detailed script-based description of the actions taken at each state is given on the companion CD.

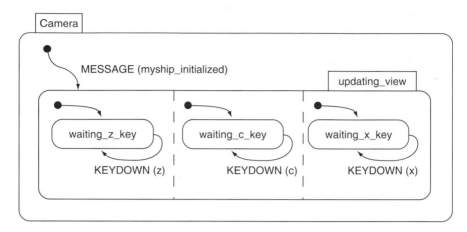

FIGURE 3.23. The interactive behavior of the *Camera* as controlled by the *User* (looking around). A more detailed script-based description of the actions taken at each state is given on the companion CD.

Pondering Points

- Is it possible to express *Rot_by_single_axis* (k, θ) (rotation around an arbitrary vector) in the Euler convention?
- Is it possible to factor out the axis order and amounts of rotation around each principal (fixed) axis from, Rot_by_single_axis (k, θ)?
- Is it better to carry out a simulation of a steering wheel with respect to the World coordinate system or with respect to the Car (Object) coordinate system?
- Suppose that you are designing the behavior of an adversary entity in a first-person shooting game. Express its (semi-intelligent) behavior using a script, data flow diagram, and a state-based representation. Which is the most convenient? Do the same for expressing a "running as waving" behavior for a humanlike character. Which do you think is the best representation to use in terms of expressivity and later maintenance?

Chapter 4
Putting It All Together

After a rough specification (Chapters 2 and 3), an initial implementation can start on a chosen development platform. There are many ways to implement a VR system. In this book, as we have emphasized the advantages of the object-oriented approach, we illustrate the implementation detail using an object-oriented programming language (C++) with a commercial graphics/simulation/VR library called the OpenSceneGraph (on the Microsoft Windows platform; [Ope04]; actual code can be found on the companion CD). A good introductory document (and the package itself) to the OpenSceneGraph can be obtained from a Web site at http://openscenegraph.sourceforge.net for free. The OpenSceneGraph is a portable, high-level graphics toolkit for the development of high-performance graphics applications such as flight simulators, games, virtual reality, or scientific visualization. It is built on top of the OpenGL graphics library and provides many utilities for rapid development of high-performance graphics and VR applications. For instance, its abstraction supports built-in functionalities such as efficient scene data structure management, graphics rendering control, display and window configuration, level of detail nodes, user interface, special effects, intersection checking, lighting, texture, animation, and even multiprocessing. OpenSceneGraph also supports many model and image file formats (for reading and writing).

We also continue to further refine and modify the specifications made in Chapters 2 and 3 following the spiral model advocated in Chapter 1. The central part of a VR application is the "scene graph" data structure. In the previous chapter, we explained how objects form a chain of physical relations to form a scene hierarchy. We also mentioned that this hierarchy would be extended into a data structure called the scene graph that represents not only the hierarchical spatial relations but also much other information about the scene and objects in the scene. Most VR packages including the OpenSceneGraph use a scene graph such as a data structure in one way or another.

A scene graph starts with the topmost root node that encompasses the whole virtual world. The world is then broken down into a hierarchy of nodes representing either spatial groupings of objects, settings of the position of objects, animations of objects, or definitions of logical relationships between objects. The leaves of the graph represent the physical objects themselves, the drawable geometry, and their material properties. The focus of the scene graph is usually the representation of the 3D worlds, and its efficient rendering.

The scene graphs provide an excellent framework for maximizing graphics performance. They provide a way of culling (excluding and not drawing) the objects that will not be seen on the screen, and state sorting of properties such as textures and materials, so that all similar objects are drawn together. Without culling the CPU, buses and the GPU (graphics processing unit) would become swamped with too much data. The hierarchical structure of the scene graph makes this culling process very efficient. In fact, the scene data organized with the scene graph is "traversed" by the system (at each simulation round) and processed (see Figure 4.1). For instance, the scene graph can be traversed by the "CULL" traverser that determines what will get rendered among the data present in the scene graph (for instance, some data might be chosen not to be drawn as they are far from the user viewpoint). The "DRAW" traverser will carry out the rendering process as it traverses the scene graph (it converts all the local coordinates into the world along the traversal using the process explained in Chapter 3 and projects it to the display). The order of the traversal is determined by the hierarchy of the scene graph, in top-down or depth-first fashion starting from the root node (or user specified node) [SGI02].

A typical VR application (such as an OpenSceneGraph application) goes through the following initialization process and execution loop.

Initialization

1. Initialize OpenSceneGraph.
2. Configure the graphics pipeline, display channel, and window association.[1]

---

[1] Read the OpenSceneGraph introductory manual to get more familiar with the concepts of graphics pipeline and channels.

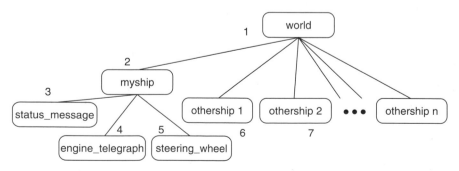

FIGURE 4.1. Scene graph traversal order (depth first).

3. Create (or load) the scene graph.
4. Set the camera and its view frustum.

The Loop

5. Read any external input.
6. Compute simulation and update the objects and scene graph.
7. Update the camera position/orientation.
8. Redraw the scene.
9. Go back to 5.

A channel is equivalent to a camera moving throughout the scene. A camera must have a position, orientation, and a view frustum or view volume. A view volume is a part of the 3D space that will be visible (thus drawn) to the user. It is defined by the "near" and "far" clipping planes and the horizontal and vertical field of view (as shown in Figure 4.2). Note that the camera is just another object that can be dynamically moved and its parameters changed during the course of the application run. The location and orientation of the camera is specified in the same way as the other virtual objects (using the 4 × 4 transformation matrix). In fact, specifying the camera position and orientation using the 4 × 4 transformation matrix can be done by specifying the location vector and two other vectors, the up vector (up direction of the camera) and the direction vector. The third vector orthogonal to the up and direction vectors is obtained by their cross

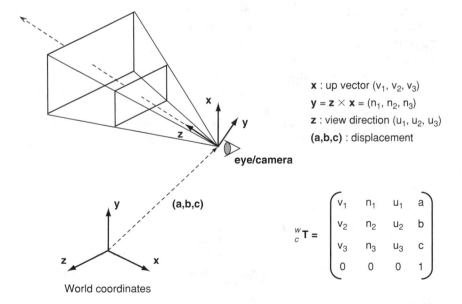

$\mathbf{x}$: up vector (v_1, v_2, v_3)
$\mathbf{y} = \mathbf{z} \times \mathbf{x} = (n_1, n_2, n_3)$
$\mathbf{z}$: view direction (u_1, u_2, u_3)
(a,b,c) : displacement

$$ {}_c^w T = \begin{pmatrix} v_1 & n_1 & u_1 & a \\ v_2 & n_2 & u_2 & b \\ v_3 & n_3 & u_3 & c \\ 0 & 0 & 0 & 1 \end{pmatrix} $$

FIGURE 4.2. The view frustum and camera parameters.

product. These three vectors constitute the rotation matrix between the World frame and the camera frame.

As one can see, after the initialization, there is one monolithic loop process that, in sequence, checks the external input, runs object simulation, updates the scene and the camera according to any input and time progression, and repeatedly redraws the output. In particular, the simulation part of the program corresponds to the object's behavior model, in most cases, coded in plain programming languages in a procedural manner.

Although we assume a single monolithic thread for the overall computation model for simulating and rendering the virtual environment, other types of computational models are certainly possible. The simulation loop can be split up into individual threads or processes that communicate with each other for synchronization purposes, for instance, sensor thread, application/ simulation thread, and rendering thread. The rendering thread can even be split up into two or more separate threads in the case that two (or more) graphics hardware are necessary for multichannel outputs (e.g., for stereo or for multisided display systems). In such a case, care must be taken to synchronize all the graphics hardware. In particular, for active stereo systems where it is important that at one moment all the graphics hardware output images for the left eye and vice versa, the hardware "GenLock" signal is used to synchronize the output scan time of all the graphics hardware. In systems that do not employ active stereo, software frame-level synchronization is often sufficient (i.e., one- or two-frame misalignment is negligible to the human eye if the display is in mono or if using passive stereo).[2]

In another aspect, the rendering process can be even further separated into interleaved threads of the cull (that determines what gets drawn) and draw (the actual rendering) processes. Figure 4.3 shows the interleaving of the application, cull, and draw threads. In OpenSceneGraph, for instance, the scene graph supports multiple graphics contexts for both OpenGL Display Lists and texture objects, and the cull and draw traversals have been designed to cache rendering data locally and use the scene graph almost entirely as a read-only operation. This allows multiple cull–draw pairs to run on multiple CPUs that are bound to multiple graphics subsystems.

Example Design and Implementation (Continued): Level 2 Ship Simulator

We start to modify the Level 1 specifications/requirements to include more details (Figure 4.4). For instance, the following additional hypothetical requirements may be added. We refine the storyboard as shown in Figure 4.5.

---

[2] For active and passive stereo, refer to Chapter 6.

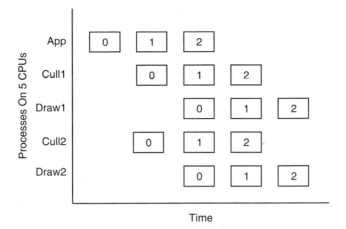

FIGURE 4.3. The multiprocess computational model for a VR program. The numbers in the box indicate the image frame number for which each process is computing.

With the newly refined requirements, we further refine the overall scene and details of form, function, and behavior for each constituent object. Figures 4.6 and 4.7 show the updated MSDs. *MyShip* is now composed of additional subobjects, gauges, and radar. The environment objects, sky and sea surface, are also added (see Figure 4.8). Note that *ShipSimulator*, the functional entity that manages the overall simulation, is an object without any form and thus does not appear in the scene graph.

Requirements (Level 2, added)

- More realistic ship movement
  - E.g. rolling and pitching
  - Rotating radar
- Collision detection
- Status information
  - Gauge display
  - Indication of successful docking

Requirements (Level 3, added)

- Simple weather effects (e.g. fog)
- Wave effects

FIGURE 4.4. Additional Level 2 and 3 requirements for the Ship Simulator example.

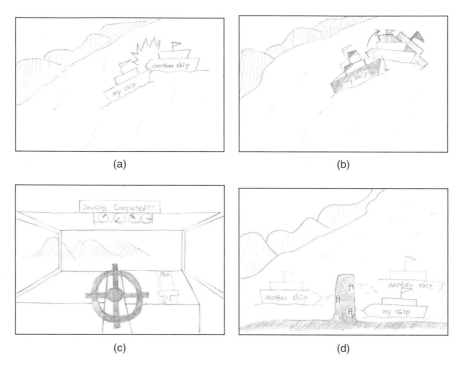

FIGURE 4.5. New storyboards for the Ship Simulator example: (a) a collision between *MyShip* and *OtherShip*; (b) the *User* is informed of the collision and appropriate response (*OtherShip* moving backward for 5 seconds and changing its course; (c) gauges and a message indicating a successful docking; (d) external view of a successful docking.

Polygon Budgeting

For objects with form, we plan for their suitable levels of geometric complexity through the polygon budgeting process [Hof97]. In polygon budgeting, the suitable number of polygons is decided by considering the processing and rendering capacity of the target execution environment (i.e., your computer and graphics board). Table 4.1 assumes that a target platform can process about 100,000 polygons per frame (~5 million polygons per second at 50 frames[3] per second). We initially determine the estimates of the object polygon counts. The number of LODs and their distribution are initially determined by the properties of the application, but they are also subject to change, upon iterative performance and presence tuning during later stages.

---

[3] A sufficiently high frame rate is targeted considering the possibility for stereoscopic rendering that requires twice the normal frame rate.

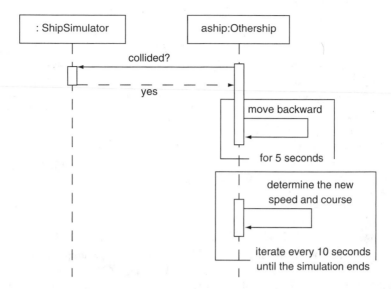

FIGURE 4.6. Updated message diagram between *ShipSimulator* and *OtherShip* for collision handling.

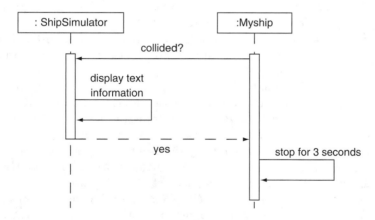

FIGURE 4.7. Updated message diagram between *ShipSimulator* and *MyShip* for collision handling.

Modeling of Function/Behavior

Objects (Ones Without Geometry): ShipSimulator

Figure 4.9 contains a data flow diagram for the *ShipSimulator,* (a formless object that subsumes various control functions for the simulator), and shows how they are coupled to each other. *ShipSimulator* is composed of three processes: *SetInitialPosition* that decides the initial position of *OtherShip,*

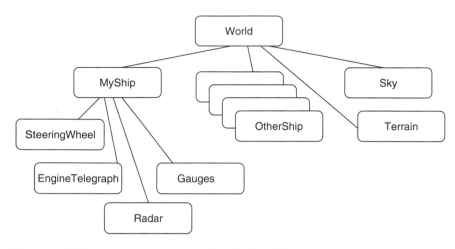

FIGURE 4.8. The updated scene graph for the Ship Simulator example.

CheckCollision that checks collisions with other objects, and *SetMyShipPosition* that accepts a newly joined *MyShip* for training (there may be several users being trained at the same time). All the leaf processes (circular blocks in the DFD) will correspond to an actual block of code in the VR program. Such a computational module may require a "controller" (the rectangular box in Figure 4.9) that is responsible for initiating and coordinating the process executions (when it has one or more leaf processes), and bringing about state transitions.

The internals of the controller may be specified using a state-based representation similar to a statechart [Har90], as shown in Figure 4.10. In this example, the process *SetInitialPosition* generates the event *InitComplete* that triggers a state transition for *ShipSimulator*. This controller changes its state from *Idle* to *DoingSimulation* by the event *start*[†] and the state *DoingSimulation* has two concurrent states that manage *OtherShips* and *MyShips* simultaneously. Because all the instances of *OtherShip* are generated automatically at the beginning, the state *OtherShipControl* changes its substate to the state *CheckingCollision* after the instances of *OtherShip* are created and initialized successfully. The state *MyShipControl* notifies the initial positions/

TABLE 4.1. A Polygon budget table

Object		Number	Polygons per objects	Total polygons
MyShip	LOD1	1	2500	5,000
	LOD2	10	2000	20,000
	LOD3	8	3000	24,000
OtherShip		3	6000	18,000
Env. (Sky,…)		1	10,000	10,000
Total				87,000

Env. (Sky, Terrain,…)

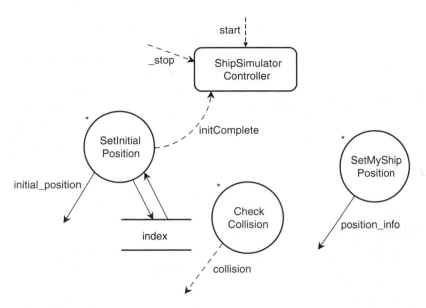

FIGURE 4.9. The data flow diagram of ShipSimulator [Seo02]. (Reprinted with permission from MIT Press © 2004.)

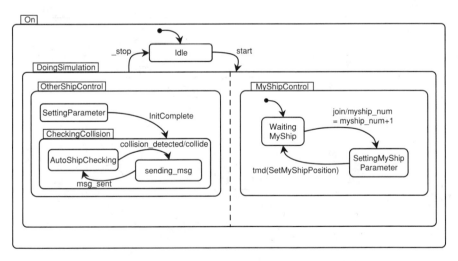

FIGURE 4.10. The state-based representation of the controller "ShipSimulator" [Seo02]. (Reprinted with permission from MIT Press © 2004.)

orientations of instances of the joining *MyShips* and returns to the state *WaitingMyShip*, to wait for another *MyShip* to join for training. Making specifications such as this prior to actual coding makes it easy to mentally visualize and simulate the whole object behavior and promotes a more efficient and structured development process.

Modeling Interactive Behavior: *My Ship*

Although the behavior and function of *MyShip* is simple, it is the only object that has dynamic behavior controlled by user interactions. The state-based specification in Figure 4.11 depicts how a *User* controls the velocity and orientation of a vessel using various keys. *MyShip* communicates with the *Keyboard* object for input events and also transmits events to the *ShipSimulator* to indicate collision or success of docking. Two concurrent states are added, representing the newly satisfied requirements of producing the rolling and pitching motion of the ship.

Modeling of Objects with Form (and their LODs): OtherShip

In this subsection, we demonstrate the process of concurrent consideration and modeling of form and behavior and LOD generation. In the case of *OtherShip*, we start with a very simple form model of a ship (for no particular reason; we could very well start with a rough function/behavior model

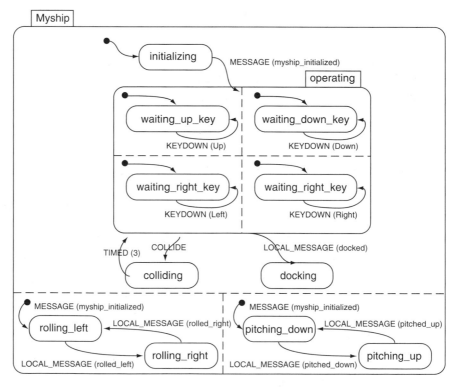

FIGURE 4.11. State-based representation of *MyShip's* behavior.

instead). This simplest form model (G1) is composed of a set of boxes and has 106 polygons, roughly within the estimate of the initial polygon budget (see Table 4.1). The *OtherShips* simply serve as moving environment objects so that the trainees can train to maneuver on the sea. At this point, we can refine the original behavior model (B1) from Chapter 3 to handle collision and produce pitching and rolling motion and rotating radar (not shown in the statechart). The resulting statechart is shown in Figure 4.12. Note that in order to include the new behavior of rotating radar, the form model G1 must be refined into G2, one with the radar. Thus, the next geometric model G2 is produced by adding the "radar" geometry along with other parts for a more realistic appearance (see Figure 4.13).

As one can see, the incremental and hierarchical nature of the modeling process naturally leads to the generation of LOD models both for geometry and behavior. Figure 4.14 depicts the overall refinement process of *Other-Ship* and the arrows represent the sequence of refinement. Note that the flow and number of refinements (or the number of LODs) may vary according to

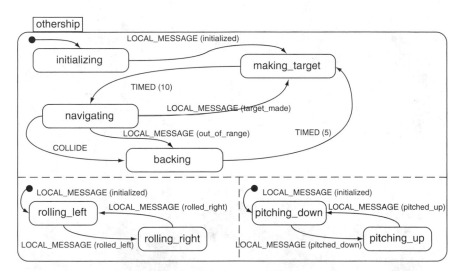

FIGURE 4.12. The updated behavior model of the *OtherShip*.

FIGURE 4.13. Geometric LODs for *OtherShips*. Note that the rotating behavior can be realized with the corresponding subobject [Seo02]. (Reprinted with permission from MIT Press © 2004.)

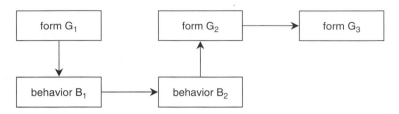

FIGURE 4.14. Refinement process of the object *OtherShip*. Geometries or behaviors with different levels of detail are constructed along the refinement process (the higher the number, the more refined the models are). (Reprinted with permission from MIT Press © 2004.)

the intent of the developer, and as long as the "compatibility" condition (that there exists geometric entities corresponding to entities in the behaviour model) is kept, any geometric and any behavior model can be combined. Figure 4.15 shows a snapshot of the resulting "Level 2"

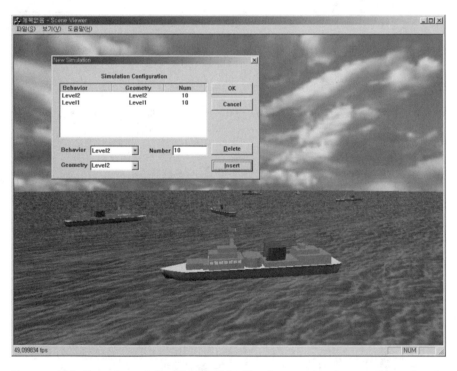

FIGURE 4.15. Snapshot of the Virtual Ship Simulator and excerpts of actual code based on the specification. The ships can be at different levels of detail both in terms of geometry and behavior. The user should experiment with several configurations to try to produce the best effect while maintaining an acceptable frame rate. (Reprinted with permission from MIT Press © 2004.)

```
. . . . (omission) . . . .

//initialize ShipSimulator
void ShipSimulator::initShipSimulator()
{
    . . . . (omission) . . . .

    MyShip::init();
    OtherShip::init();
    SteeringStand::init();
    EngineTelegraph::init();
    VoyageInfoDisplay::init();

    . . . . (omission) . . . .

    createScene();

    . . . . (omission) . . . .
}

. . . . (omission) . . . .

//frame controlled loop
void ShipSimulator::run()
{
    while(myShip->checkESCKey()==false)
    {
        pfSync();

        //update view point
        chan->setViewMat(myShip->getViewMatrix());

        //collision control
        controlCollision();

        pfFrame();
    }
    pfExit();
}

. . . . (omission) . . . .
```

```
. . . . (omission) . . . .

//control collision
void ShipSimulator::controlCollision()
{
    for(int i=0;i<OTHER_SHIP_NUM+1;i++)
    {
        pfVec3* rec=ships[i]->getBoundaryRec();
        for(int j=0;j<OTHER_SHIP_NUM+1;j++)
        {
            if(i!= j)
            {
                if(ships[j]->detectCollision(rec))
                {
                    ships[j]->setCollisionMode();
                    ships[i]->setCollisionMode();
                }
            }
        }
    }
}
```

sample code : ShipSimulator.cpp

FIGURE 4.16. Excerpts of actual code based on the specification. The complete specification and code are contained on the companion CD.

implementation. The actual code can be found on the companion CD (also see Figure 4.16).

Summary

Based on the specifications, we can start with the initial implementation. Starting with their initial rough specifications, the form, function, and behaviors of the virtual objects are incrementally and hierarchically refined into more detail and coded, guided by the polygon budget. Intermediate-level models can be used as level of detail objects.

Pondering Points

- Suppose you used a state-based representation to specify the behavior of one of your virtual objects. How can this behavior be implemented using a common programming language such as C++?
- How would interobject events actually be implemented or handled? For instance, consider a situation where the virtual signal light changes its color to green, and the other virtual car waiting in the road must catch this event and move accordingly.

Chapter 5

Performance Estimation and System Tuning

The Presence and Performance Trade-off

Most people in the VR community seem to agree with the definition of presence as the feeling of being in the VR world and on the importance of provision of presence as a defining quality of VR. Several researchers have studied the elusive notion of presence. Many factors affect presence and some are related to system performance. For instance, it is likely that system load will be increased by providing more sensory channels, increasing visual and simulation fidelity, increasing degrees of interactivity, and so on. System delay and occasional disruption in continuity are reported to have a very negative effect on presence, even more than lowered pictorial realism [Wel96]. Research in this area is still at the preliminary stage, therefore the design guideline for VEs with high presence awaits future research efforts. For the time being, we have to resort to old-fashioned trial and error process for system tuning (for producing the highest presence with the available resources). Even though the trial and error process is perhaps the most primitive and time-consuming process, there currently is not a scientific methodology to do this in a different way. However, by sticking to the structured development strategy overall, the trial-and-error process can be minimized. As the system is tuned, the system can be further refined, while we make trade-offs between expected benefits and required computational cost.

Tuning with the LOD Models

We can, for instance, start the tuning process with trying out different LOD mixes and distribution. Depending on the computational capability of the given processor and graphics board the right LOD mix (e.g., 15 Autoships at G_3/B_3, 50 at G_2/B_2, and 30 at G_1/B_1) can be tuned to produce the best

TABLE 5.1. Simulating 50, 75, and 100 *OtherShips* with Different LODs[a]

	Ave. Frame Rate		
LOD	50	75	100
$L_1(G_1, B_1)$	41	41	40
$L_2(G_2, B_1)$	43	37	30
$L_3(G_2, B_2)$	33	26	22
$L_4(G_3, B_1)$	34	28	25
$L_5(G_4, B_3)$	27	23	18

[a]An LOD is defined by the geometric LOD denoted G_n and the behavioral LOD denoted B_n, where the higher the value of n, the more detailed and more computationally heavy the virtual object is. Adapted from [Seo02]. (Reprinted with permission from ACM © 2004.)

effect, with an acceptable frame rate.[1] Because there will be many *Other-Ships*, we might assume it could dominate the load on the processor and the graphics board. Assuming that the application required about 50 to 100 *AutoShips*, we check the performance by simulating the amount of *Auto-Ships* at five different LODs, as shown in Table 5.1 (Figure 4.15 shows the VR environment).

Table 5.1 shows performance test results in terms of the average frame rates for each chosen LOD. Although results[2] show the expected trivial fact that more complex models produce lower frame rates, we observe that the variances in the frame rates are not linear. For instance, if we were to select a 2-LOD-mix for the case of 50 ships, we might choose L2 and L3, because they have higher details at a similar cost versus L1 and L4, respectively.

Presence/Special Effects: Third Stage of Spiral Process

In Chapter 2, we explained the spiral process, one of the modeling philosophies emphasized in this book. The spiral process has three stages and the basic iterations of 'Requirement Analysis—Design—Validation' occur continuously at each stage. Presence and special effects are considered toward the end of the spiral with close monitoring of the remaining resources after all the basic functionalities are built and reasonably tested. Table 5.1 already shows that even with more than 100 *AutoShips* at high model detail, we would be able to obtain up to $30 \sim 40\,\text{fps}$ performance (with < 50 fps, adding stereoscopy might be sacrificed depending on a careful choice of the LOD mix). Thus, we can attempt to realize the 'Level 3' requirements given in the previous chapter, adding the weather and wave effects.

---

[1] Likewise, the LOD can be simply selected and dynamically switched based on other criteria such as distance from the user, screen projected size, and so on.

[2] The simulation was performed on a desktop PC with an Intel Pentium 4, 1.4-Ghz CPU, 512-M bytes (RDRAM) main memory, and an Nvidia Geforce2 MX graphics card, using MS Windows 2000, WorldToolKit, and MS Visual C++.

Taking Advantage of the Graphics Hardware Features: Fog Effect

It turns out that to implement a simple weather effect such as fog is very simple because of the built-in capabilities of today's graphics hardware. And because it is hardware-supported, there is not much performance drop. In fact, there are many other special effects features that are hardware-supported, such as shadow, texture mapping, particle simulation, and so on. In particular, we take a closer look at taking advantage of images or textures to enhance visual realism and ease of modeling.

Using Images and Textures for Object/Scene Modeling and Fast Rendering

One of the ways to avoid tedious modeling efforts yet achieve reasonable realism is the use of textures. Textures or images also enhance visual photorealism, and today's graphics hardware provide great support for fast texture mapping. Textures are (usually) a rectangular piece of image sample that can be pasted upon the object surface (which would in effect be a collection of polygons or triangles). There are many ways a texture can be pasted upon the object surface. In the simplest case, a texture is applied to a planar surface. The process is depicted in Figure 5.1.

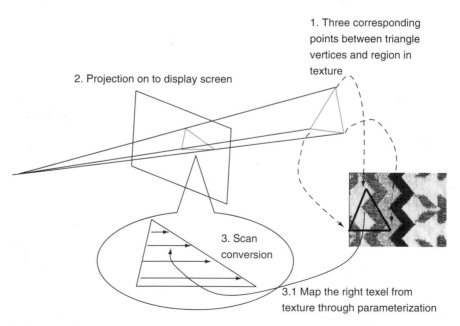

FIGURE 5.1. Pasting a texture on a 3D triangle.

First, the user must specify the corresponding texture pixels (texel) for the three vertices. The three vertices would be projected to the display screen, and during the scan conversion process to render the interior of the projected triangle on the screen, the right color must be brought from the corresponding place in the texture. The final rendered color at that pixel is a function of this texel color and other parameters related to lighting and shading (e.g., viewpoint, triangle/surface normal, shading model, etc.). In order to map the pixels in the screen space to the texture space, each space is parameterized using unified coordinates as shown in Figure 5.2.

There are many other forms of texturing that developers can take advantage of for producing various modeling details, for instance, cylindrical mapping, spherical mapping, environment mapping (for modeling environment reflection on shiny objects), and bump mapping (for modeling protrusions). Most VR, game, or graphics engines provide built-in functionalities for such texture mappings.

In addition to modeling the complex surface properties of objects, textures can be used to represent the object itself. Billboards and moving textures (sprites) are such examples. A billboard is a simple planar primitive with a pasted texture that is continuously rotated to face the viewer (see Figure 5.3). Billboards are often used for (rotationally symmetric) objects that look

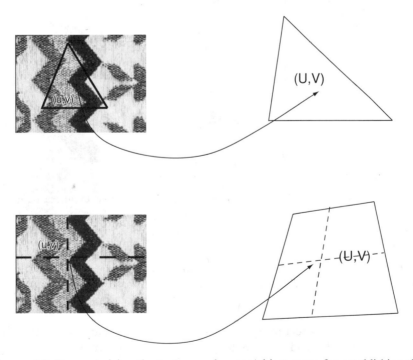

FIGURE 5.2. Parameterizing the texture and screen/object space for establishing the correspondence between (u, v) and (U, V).

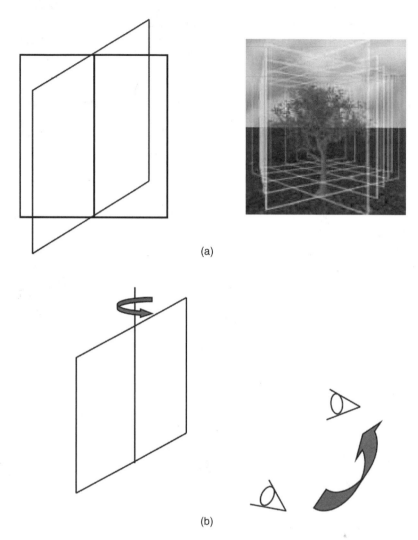

(a)

(b)

FIGURE 5.3. Two cases of billboards: (a) placing multiple planar textures around axis of symmetry; (b) rotating the texture to the changing viewer direction.

similar when viewed in different directions. One variation is to post more than one textured planar primitive in different angles around the axis of symmetry (instead of rotating them to face the viewer). The transparency of the texture is set such that only the relevant object is opaque (e.g., so that objects behind the trees can be seen through).

Sprite or moving texture is another texture-based technique much taken advantage of in the field of computer games for character animation and other special effects. Key postures of a character in a motion sequence are captured as textures and they are replaced in sequence in a short amount of time to

FIGURE 5.4. Six textures switched fast to produce animation effect (Sprite).

produce the animation effect (see Figure 5.4). Sprites can be used not only for character animation but for other special effects such as fire and glow, explosion, water flow effects, clouds, and the like. More advanced image-based methods can generate intermediate images from neighboring images (in the motion or view sequence) for a smoother transition and less distortion.

Finally, textures can be used to model not just objects but a big part (if not all) of the scene, for instance, for background such as the sky or a mountain range. For instance, in the QuickTime VR approach by Chen [Che95], a panoramic image is captured and stored as a cylindrical environment map, and depending on the viewer location and viewing direction, the appropriate part of the environment map is retrieved and rendered to the user (see Figure 5.5).

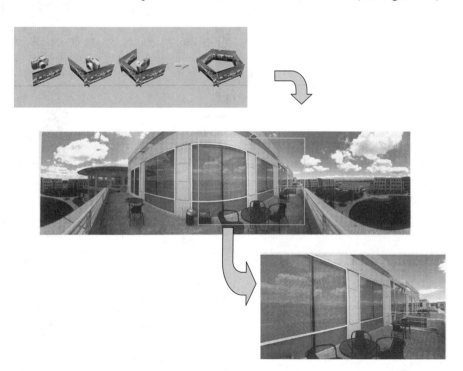

FIGURE 5.5. QuickTime VR. A panoramic environment map is constructed from a number of images and depending on the view direction, a portion from the map is retrieved, warped, and rendered to the user [Che95]. (Reprinted with permission from the ACM © 2004.)

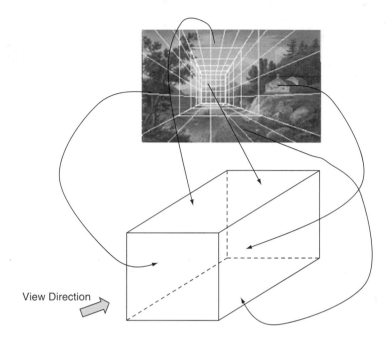

FIGURE 5.6. "Tour into the Picture" by Horry et al. An image is split into different regions around the vanishing point. Each region is mapped into a rectangular box to be used as a environment map [Hor96]. (Reprinted with permission from the ACM © 2004.)

In the approach called "Tour into the Picture" by Horry et al. [Hor97], a static image is split up into regions according to the location of the vanishing point, and each of the pieces is pasted upon the interior of large rectangular box (see Figure 5.6). Object and scene modeling (and even behavior modeling) can be made easier by employing these texture techniques in a creative way.

Adding the Wave Effect

Thus, now we are ready to realize the next remaining special effect to improve the appearance of the sea surface, by using the moving texture technique. Instead of using a big static textured polygon to represent the sea, we can employ a simple logic to rotate through four texture images to mimic the "visual" dynamics of the sea. (See the code on the companion CD for details of this simple special effect trick.) Figure 5.7 shows this newly added behavior of *Sea*. *ShipSimulator* determines the period according to the parameters of the simulation environment, that is, the velocity of the wind and the height of the wave, and generates the event "next_texture."

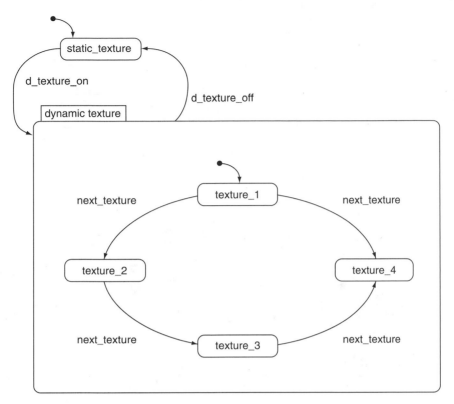

FIGURE 5.7. Moving sea behavior by moving textures.

Summary

Once the basic functionalities are in place, further refinements can be added while considering the overall performance and available computational resources. Such added functionalities may include special effects, physical simulation, and presence-enhancing elements. The environment itself can be made richer by simply adding more objects to the scene subject to resource availability as well.

Pondering Points

- Would you choose to have stereoscopic display, thus effectively reducing the rendering quality by half by having to generate two separate outputs for left and right displays, or to render in monoscopy with higher graphic quality? Explain your answer.
- Would you choose to have many simple environment objects (e.g., rocks) or fewer with higher detail? Explain your answer.

Section II
Making of the Virtual Reality

A VR system is a type of simulation system. The first part of the book went over how to build a simple object-oriented simulation system. Virtual reality systems, more so than other software/hardware systems, are highly complex and heterogeneous. Developers must go through much trial and error for content configuration and performance tuning; thus the system must have high maintainability. For that reason, a structured system building approach was advocated and highlighted in the first part of the book. The second part of the book concentrates on various features that breathe life into a "mere" simulation system and make it a true experiential virtual reality system, namely, 3D multimodal interactions, usable and natural interfaces, physical simulations and avatars, and other presence-promoting effects.

Chapter 6
Output Display

The term '*display*' is usually associated with the 'visual' output. However, in the context of virtual reality, one of whose goals is to mimic the way humans usually interact in the real world, it refers to any modality output, that is, visual, aural, haptic (a term referring to the sense of touch and force feedback), olfactory, thermal, taste, and so on. A VR system, in simulating an experience, may (and should strive to) generate various signals and stimulations in many modalities, and use various display devices to convey them to the human user. Ideally, the display devices should be ergonomically designed, have sufficient fidelity or resolution for the user, and match the perceptual capability of humans. At the same time, the application developers must understand the perceptual capabilities of the human sensory system, and convey the right amount of modality stimulations, integrate and synchronize them, and deliver them to the human user using the right display devices. We start by examining the important parameters of the human visual system, and the various display systems available for VR usage, and how to use them for appropriate visual effects.

The Human Visual System

Let's examine very briefly how the human eye operates to acquire raw visual input. Figure 6.1 shows a simple inside look at the human eye. Light reflected off objects in the world enter the eye, and are refracted first through the cornea (75%), the lens (23%), and the liquids within the eyeball (2%) before reaching the retina in the back of the eyeball. The image is formed upside down on the retina. The retina is a region at which there exist millions of photoreceptor cells. Two types of photoreceptors make up the retina; the rods and the cones. The rods are more sensitive to changes in light intensity (or low-intensity light) and distributed more at the peripheral region. Cones react more to high-intensity light and are concentrated at the center of the retina called the fovea. The image formed at the retina is more focused and has clearer details at the 'foveal' region, whereas the peripheral region is less

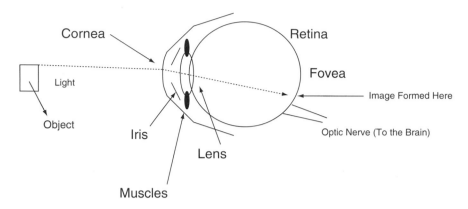

FIGURE 6.1. The anatomy of the human eye.

so, but with greater sensitivity to detecting 'moving' objects. The light intensity/color information from photoreceptor cells of the right and left eyes is relayed to the left and right parts of the brain through the optic nerve.

The amount of light that enters the eyeball is controlled by the iris (the opening of the eye itself is called the pupil) and the associated muscles. The image focus is controlled by the muscles that act on the lens by changing its size and shape. The muscles that control various parts of the eye are collectively called the occulomotor muscles.

There are many parameters, naturally most of them being the attributes of all those that constitute the human eye system, that ultimately determine the quality of the acquired raw visual input. For instance, the density of the photoreceptor cells would be an important factor in determining visual acuity (the minimum size of a recognizable visual pigment). The way the photoreceptors react to light will determine human sensitivity to brightness. Among the many such properties or parameters of our visual system, we make a note of the following.

First is the visual acuity as explained above. Human visual acuity is the minimum lateral length the human eye can perceive. Note that acuity is at its highest resolution in the foveal area (central region of the visual field), and drops at the periphery of the retina. However, in general, humans are known to have about 5-arc min[1] of visual acuity. With this visual acuity, humans would be able to recognize a letter of about 0.4 in (0.8 cm) from a 20-ft distance (this is called 20/20 vision for the left and right eyes; see Figure 6.2).

Human 'visual acuity' should be considered in determining the spatial or angular resolution of the display system with respect to the user's distance from the display. The spatial 'resolution' of the display system refers to the number of pixels that can be displayed in a unit display area, and the angular

---

[1] 1 arc min = 1/60 degrees, and 1 arc sec = 1/60 arc min (confirm).

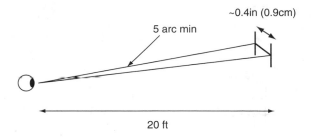

FIGURE 6.2. Visual acuity and 20/20 vision. With about 5-arc min of visual acuity (or 20/20 vision), a letter of 0.4 in can be recognized from a 20-ft distance.

resolution refers to the visual angle the pixel subtends from a particular viewing distance. A display resolution (spatial or angular) is dependent on the value of the pitch, the size of the pixel. Another important visual parameter is the 'Field Of View (FOV)', the angle subtended by the viewing surface from a given observer location. Humans have an FOV of about 120 degrees vertical and 180 degrees horizontal. In fact, because humans can rotate their necks they can obtain virtually 360 degrees spherical FOV. Providing a wide FOV (matching it to that of humans) is a very important factor in promoting the sense of presence. Various display devices, other than monitors, in combination with head-tracking, can be used to provide a wide physical or operational FOV. Given a display system and a user location, one can compute the FOV, and set the resolution of the display system appropriately according to the visual capability of the user (see Figure 6.3).

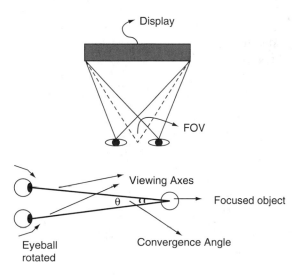

FIGURE 6.3. Field of view and convergence angle.

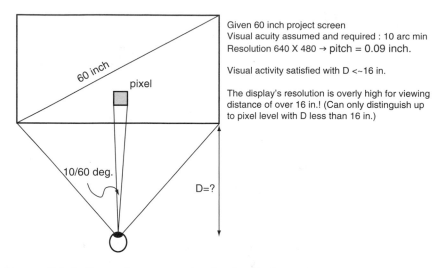

Given 60 inch project screen
Visual acuity assumed and required : 10 arc min
Resolution 640 X 480 → pitch = 0.09 inch.

Visual activity satisfied with D <~16 in.

The display's resolution is overly high for viewing
distance of over 16 in.! (Can only distinguish up
to pixel level with D less than 16 in.)

FIGURE 6.4. Setting various parameters for the display system.

Another important display system parameter is the Critical Flicker Frequency (CCF) and the Refresh Rate (RF). CCF refers to the rate at which the whole display screen is completely rescanned (a display system usually works by continually redrawing each horizontal 'scan' line (or rescanning) at a very high rate) and humans are known to start feeling the display to flicker at a CCF of 50 Hz (see Figures 6.4 and 6.5). The RF (also known as the frame rate) refers to the update of the content to produce smooth animation. Humans usually start to notice that the animation is not smooth when the RF drops below about 10 ∼ 12 Hz. Other display parameters that a developer might be able to control, but not used much in practice are the hue, brightness, and contrast.

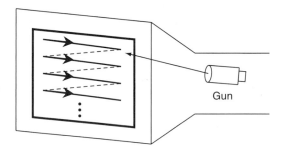

FIGURE 6.5. Scan line and critical flicker frequency in a display monitor.

Human Depth Perception and Stereoscopy

In a macro scale, humans do live attached to a mostly flat ground, making them 2D-oriented creatures. But humans are also 3D-oriented creatures, and operate daily using the depth perception capability in the immediate space around them. Consequently, providing depth information is important in realizing 3D and natural interaction in the virtual environment.

Depth perception is possible in many ways. Physiologically, depth information is extracted from the two slightly different views of the world that are input through the right and left eyes (Figure 6.6). The two images are fused in the brain and the difference (also known as the disparity) between them is processed in the brain to create the sense of depth. This is called depth perception or stereoscopy from binocular disparity (we come back to binocular disparity later). Binocular disparity is a very strong depth perception cue for viewing ranges within 10 ~ 15 m from the eyes.

Another physiological fact used by the brain is the signal that comes from the occulomotor muscles. When looking at objects, humans adjust the size of their eye lens and rotate the eyeballs. Adjusting the size of the eye lens (to focus on an object) is called 'accommodation' and the rotation of the eyeball (to focus also but more for fusing images from two eyes) is called 'convergence' (see Figure 6.7). Note that accommodation and convergence are coupled together; that is, when the eyes converge on a certain object, the accommodation automatically kicks in. The amounts of accommodation and convergence are sensed by the brain to help determine the depth of the object. Although most effective within the range of 5 to 10 m from the user.

There are also many psychological (nonphysiological) cues that help humans sense depth. They include the effect of perspective views (parallel lines coming to a vanishing point on the horizon), object occlusion (feeling that the occluded object is deeper), existence of shadows, motion parallax (far objects seem to move less rapidly), and relative size (far objects look

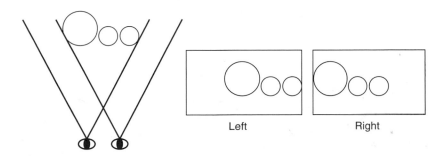

FIGURE 6.6. Slightly different images formed in the left and right eyes.

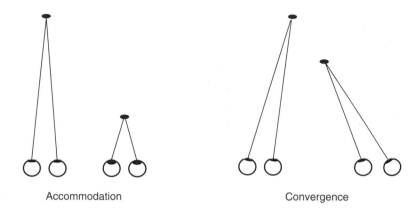

FIGURE 6.7. Accommodation and convergence.

smaller); (see Figure 6.8). Actually, sensing of motion and shadow are both psychological and physiological cues. There are regions in the brain where the visual information is processed, that are responsible for sensing shadow, disparity, and motion. All of these cues are known to be more or less additive (the more cues there are, the richer the depth information is), and can be used effectively to provide the sense of depth in a virtual environment.

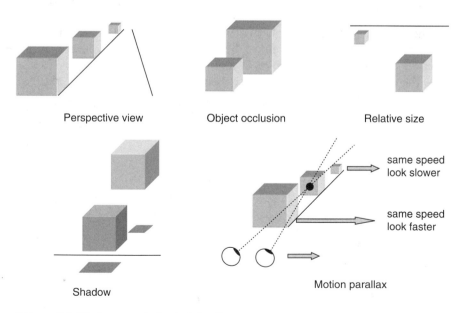

FIGURE 6.8. Various psychological depth cues.

Stereo and Binocular Disparity

To be precise, binocular disparity refers to the difference in retinal images between the two eyes due to the projection of objects at different depths. As shown in Figure 6.9, when one focuses on a point (point A) in space, the depths of the other points (e.g., point B) are felt with respect to the focused point.

The depth of the focused point A becomes the "zero" disparity point, serving as a reference point. Other points in space that are closer or farther in depth will have different retinal projections in the two eyes relative to the zero disparity point. In the figure, the points on the retina at which point B projects are off from the points to which the focused point A projects. This "off" amount is called the disparity. Because there are two eyes, the situation would create two disparity values. The total disparity is the sum of the disparities from the left and right eyes. Note that the disparity value carries a sign with respect to the zero disparity point: for the right eye, + when disparity is off to the clockwise direction and − when off to the counterclockwise direction (and vice versa for the left eye).

Figure 6.10 shows the relationship between the disparity value and the relative depth (distance between the two points in space A and B) [McK92]. The figure shows that the disparity is directly related to the difference in the 'convergence' angles for the two points A and B. In fact, the difference in convergence angles between two points is equivalent to the binocular disparity as measured in terms of the angles. Furthermore, this difference in convergence angles is proportional to the relative depth $(D1 - D2)$. Note that the relative depth has a non linear relationship with D2, the distance to the object. Suppose, in a stereo display system, B represents the display surface; then D2 becomes the viewing distance. That is, the depth felt by the user will be quite different for different viewing distances (e.g. when viewed by a large audience; see Figure 6.11).

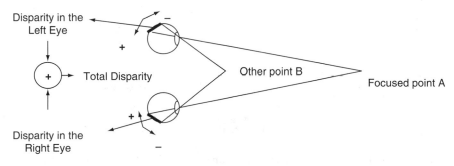

FIGURE 6.9. Binocular disparity.

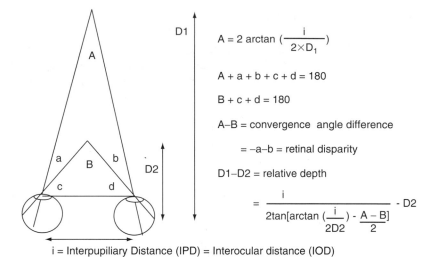

FIGURE 6.10. Disparity, convergence angles, viewing distances, and (relative) depth. (Adapted from [McK92] and reprinted with permission from Presence © 2004.)

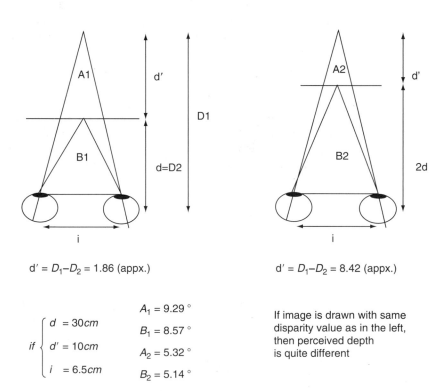

FIGURE 6.11. Two cases: when viewing distance is at d, and when viewing distance is at $2 * d$.

Implementing Stereoscopy Using Screen Parallax

The basic principle in realizing stereo display is to render the "right" image and show it only to the right eye and likewise for the left eye (see Figures 6.12 and 6.13). The trouble is that in most cases, it is not known exactly where the user is looking or where the eyes are converging to (unless we had the hardware to track the eyeballs), thus we assume that the eyes look at infinity as shown in Figure 6.14, and all the disparity values are relative to this

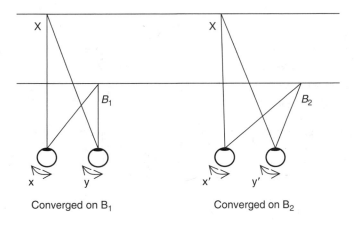

FIGURE 6.12. User actually looking at two different things within same viewing space. Depending on where the user is converged, the disparity values are different for the same point X in the space.

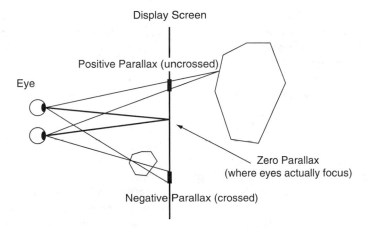

FIGURE 6.13. Screen parallax: positive, negative, and zero.

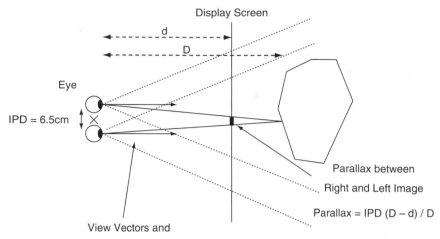

FIGURE 6.14. Defining the view volume for the right and left eyes. The model is based on an assumption that both eyes look straight, or are focused on an object at infinity. The parallax value for a given 3D point is computed with values of the IPD, depth value (z value $= D$), and the distance to the screen d.

infinitely focused point. A set of two images is rendered using two viewing volumes defined as shown in Figure 6.14 (viewing directions of both eyes perpendicular to the screen).

This can create inconsistency in one's depth perception. Even if we knew where the eyes are converged, because the display surface is fixed with respect to the eyes or head, it is practically not possible to resolve this source of error (see Figure 6.15). Ideally, the display should lie perpendicular (and move with the view direction) to the line that connects the focused point to each eyeball in a hypothetical setup shown in Figure 6.15. Another approach is to do a oblique or off-axis projection. Oblique projection can handle cases when the line between center of the screen from the eye is not perpendicular to the screen (see Figuer 6.15)

In natural viewing, the points of convergence and accommodation always coincide; that is, humans automatically converge their eyes for the same distance that they focus. However, an artificial stereoscopic image cannot be viewed without a separation of these two functions. For example, if you are sitting 30 feet from the screen, your eyes will remain focused for 30 feet regardless of where a 3D object is (virtually) projected: on the screen's surface, behind the screen, or in mid-air between the screen and the viewing position.

Thus, regardless of the actual view direction, if we assume that the user is focused on the pixels being drawn on the display surface, 3D points that happen to lie on the image plane (display surface) will serve as the zero

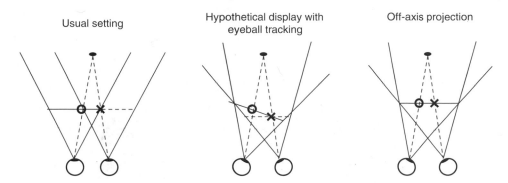

FIGURE 6.15. How disparity must be calculated if the actual point of convergence were known, for instance, by eyeball tracking.

disparity points. The points that are farther from the image plane will project at different points on the image plane and create a '*positive*' screen parallax. Likewise, the points that are closer than the image plane will project at different points on the image plane but in a "crossed" fashion as seen in Figure 6.13, called the '*negative*' parallax. Although the positive or negative parallaxes are differences between points projected with respect to two different focal points (right or left eye), they are directly related to the actual binocular disparity value with respect to the zero disparity point. Note that the screen parallax values are proportional to the depth (distance from the screen where the z coordinate would be zero to the object beyond the screen). For instance, the farther the object is from the screen, the larger the positive parallax value becomes, which means that the screen parallax is directly proportional to the actual binocular disparity.

The only fallout is as the user is looking at different objects; even though the user is forced to focus on the display surface that is physically at a certain fixed distance from the user, the convergence angle changes when looking at the various places in the virtual image. This creates a discord in how convergence and accommodation work together and causes eyestrain, and the greater the separation between accommodation and convergence distances, the greater the chance for eyestrain.

Based on how the current stereoscopic technology works, the overall recommended strategy in producing stereoscopic imagery is to put objects (e.g. the one is interacting with at the moment) near the zero parallax screen if possible, so that there is less conflict between accommodation and convergence. Note that if the screen is relatively small, objects that must have negative parallax can be clipped by the window boundary and the user can falsely get a sense that it has positive (farther into the screen) depth (because of the occlusion by the screen boundary). Such an effect must be avoided by clever manipulation of the content by locating the objects in the middle of the screen and sizing the objects properly (see Figure 6.16).

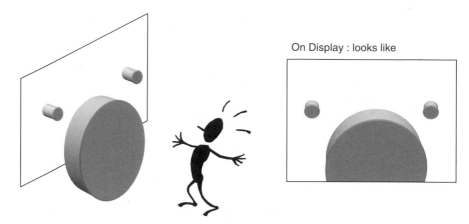

On Display : looks like

FIGURE 6.16. The boundary effect: objects with negative parallax feel like being behind the screen surface with positive parallax; objects should be located in the middle of the screen and sized properly if possible to avoid this effect

Visual Display System (Stereoscopic)

In this section, we review some of the typical visual display systems that are used in virtual reality. Because readers are probably quite familiar with the ordinary monoscopic displays (despite their varieties in sizes and configurations), we focus on the support of stereoscopy.

Autostereoscopy

The first type of stereoscopic display system is the '*autostereoscopic*' ones, meaning that these devices require no extra devices to be worn by the user and provide stereoscopy to the naked eyes (an attractive feature in the usability point of view). Two major approaches of autostereoscopy, similar in the way they work, are the parallax barriers and lenticular sheets. As already mentioned, the secret of creating the effect of three dimensions is to make each eye see different pictures (separated by the appropriately set disparity values for each corresponding pixel).

In a parallax barrier-based system, the display (called the parallax stereogram) is composed of adjacent columns of pixels, each of which forms part of the larger image for the right or the left eye. Parallax barriers are selectively opaque strips of material that can then be used to block alternate columns of these pixels from either the right or the left eye. Each transparent "slit" acts as a window to a vertical slice of the image placed behind it, and the exact width of the slice depends on the position of the eye (see Figure 6.17).

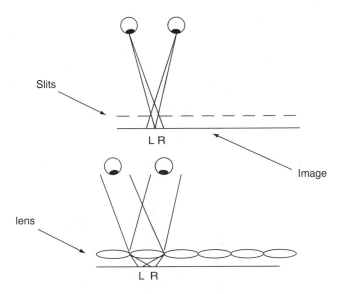

FIGURE 6.17. Parallax barriers and lenticular sheets.

One major problem is that the parallax blocking system relies on the viewer being at precisely the right spot or angle to maintain the effect. If one moves one's head by just few centimeters, the effect easily breaks down. To combat this problem and also make the display work in 2D mode (if needed, for usual everyday 2D-based applications such as word processing), the parallax barriers are implemented using materials that can be made opaque for the 3D effect or back to transparent to give a standard 2D display according to an electric signal.

Traditionally, parallax barriers- (and lenticular sheet-) based systems have been used for static pictures with slit sizes that are predetermined. However, with the latest advances in LCD technology, barriers with variable slit sizes (and even head-tracking) can be built to accommodate different viewing positions, moving pictures, and even disabling the barriers (the 2D viewing mode); (see Figure 6.18).

Lenticular Sheet

Instead of slits in the parallax barriers, lenticular sheets contain a series of cylindrical lenses, put on top of the columns of image strips. The lens focuses on the lenticular image designed so that each eye's line of sight is focused onto different strips. The image placed behind the lenticular sheet is formed in essentially the same way as for the image in the parallax barrier system (see Figure 6.17).

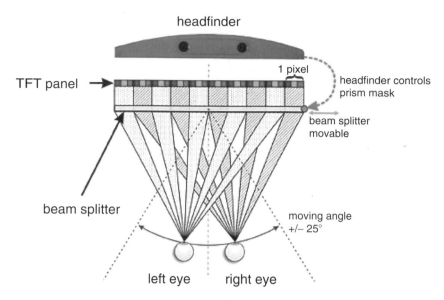

FIGURE 6.18. Autostereoscopic display from SeeReal Technologies, Dresden, Germany. It is based on a principle akin to the (adjustable) parallax barriers with separate head-tracking for larger viewing positions. (Reprinted from [See04] with permission from SeeReal Technologies.)

Nonautostereoscopic Displays

Anaglyphs and Polarized Lights (Passive Stereo)

There are three major types of nonautostereoscopic display systems. They too work on the basic principle of making each eye see a different picture. One of the simplest ways of doing this is to use glasses with two different filtering lenses (say, red and blue), used with a display on which two slightly different images are drawn in the same pair of colors. The filter glass allows one colored picture to be seen by one eye and vice versa (see Figure 6.19). This particular approach is called the '*chromatic*' (using color) anaglyph and there are other anaglyphs based on filtering of other properties of the light.

A similar approach can be done by polarizing the light used to produce the display. The left eye image can be produced with a light with one polarity and the right eye image with another polarity, and viewing the two superimposed images with a polarity filter so that each gets to see the appropriate image. The electric and magnetic vibrations of an electromagnetic wave, such as the light, occur in numerous "planes" or "orientations." A light wave that is vibrating in more than one plane is referred to as unpolarized light. Light emitted by the sun, by a lamp in the classroom, or by a candle flame is an example of an unpolarized light. It is helpful to picture unpolar-

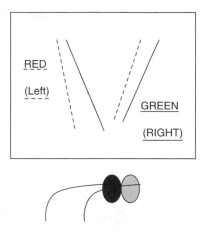

FIGURE 6.19. How chromatic anaglyphs work to create the stereo effect.

ized light as a wave that has an average of half its vibrations in a horizontal plane and half its vibrations in a vertical plane.

It is possible to transform unpolarized light into polarized light. Polarized light waves are light waves in which the vibrations occur in a single plane only. The process of transforming unpolarized light into polarized light is known as polarization. There is a variety of methods of polarizing light. The most common method of polarization involves the use of the Polaroid filter, made of a special material capable of blocking one of the two planes of vibration of an electromagnetic wave (see Figures 6.20 and 6.21) [Hen04].

Three-dimensional movies (or graphic displays) using light polarization are actually two movies being shown at the same time through two projectors. The two movies are filmed from two slightly different camera locations (representing the left and right eyes). Each individual movie is then projected from a slightly different position to the screen through the polarizing filters. The polarizing filter used for the projector on the left may have its polarization axis aligned horizontally and the polarizing filter used for the projector on the

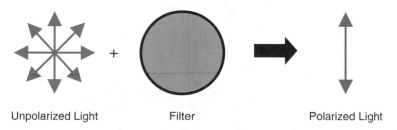

Unpolarized Light   Filter   Polarized Light

FIGURE 6.20. The light polarization process [Hen04].

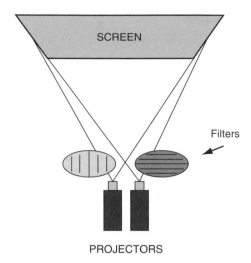

FIGURE 6.21. Using light polarization to produce stereo.

right would have its polarization axis aligned vertically. The audience wears glasses that have a Polaroid filter for each eye. The result of this arrangement of projectors and filters, is that the left eye sees the movie that is projected from the right projector and the right eye sees the movie that is projected from the left projector (see Figure 6.22). This gives the viewer the perception of depth. Note that if only one display system is being used (for instance, rather than two projectors as shown in the figure), the interlacing technique can be used to display the right and left images simultaneously. That is, the even scan lines are used to render the right image and the odd for the left (see Figure 6.23). Note that this would reduce the image resolution in half.

Time Multiplexing (Active Stereo)

The next popular method of creating a nonautostereoscopic system is called the time multiplexed method. The methods so far produced left and right images that are actually rendered simultaneously and filtered for viewing. The

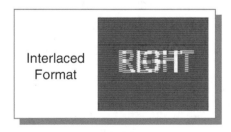

FIGURE 6.22. Taking advantage of interlacing to display the right and left image simultaneously. (Courtesy of Namgyu Kim.)

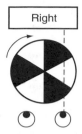

FIGURE 6.23. Time multiplexed stereo using a color wheel.

time multiplexed systems switch very fast between the left and right images, and render only one image at a time. This system is also often called the *active* system as opposed to the polarized glass approach most referred to as the *passive* system. Figure 6.23 shows an example of a time multiplexed system using a color wheel that is appropriately designed and turns, in synchronization with the display, at a rate so that each eye only sees the appropriate image.

A more elegant solution, but based on the same principle, is through the use of shutter glasses. The user wears electronic glasses that operate in synchronization with the display system in that when the left image is shown, the right part of the glass is blocked (so that only the left eye gets the left image) and vice versa. The glasses (or the shutter glasses) are usually made of an LCD so that the "blocking" can be achieved by making the LCD screen/window "black" by a synchronized electric signal (see Figure 6.24).

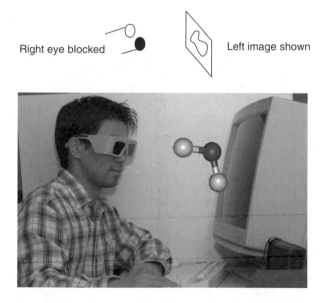

FIGURE 6.24. Time multiplexed stereo display system using shutter glasses.

Because the switching of the image is very fast, the user is not aware that only one image is actually being rendered at a time. In fact, the switching frequency must be set at around 60 Hz for each eye, same as the Critical Flickering Frequency (CFF). Thus the display system must be able to support about 120 Hz of refresh rate to support time multiplexed stereo systems.

Head-Mounted Display

Finally, the third major nonautostereoscopic display system used for VR is the Head-Mounted Display (HMD). HMD usually employs two separate display devices designed to provide isolated display for each eye (see Figure 6.27; note that there are HMDs made of only one device that extract two channels of display for each eye through the use of optics). Two separate (synchronized) images (for the right and left eye, respectively) are generated and fed into the respective display channel to create the stereo effect. The display isolation also creates the feeling of immersion aside from the stereoscopic effect, another important factor in creating effective VR applications. Unlike large displays such as monitors or projectors, HMDs are worn on the head (in order to provide isolated images to the eyes). As for the display device itself, miniature LCDs or CRTs are used. The small images that appear on these LCDs or CRTs are magnified through the use of optics.

Simple magnifiers (Figure 6.25) are problematic because the magnifying lens often cannot be placed close to the image to produce a wide FOV due to other image-enhancing modules. The eyes must be positioned quite closely at a certain spot from the magnifying lens in order receive a bright-enough image. This can cause strain on the eyes even though the exit pupil (see below) is quite forgiving. Instead, a compound microscope HMD design is often used as shown in Figure 6.26. A second lens is used to produce an intermediate image. This combination produces a small range of distance (called the exit pupil) at which the eyes can be positioned to receive most of

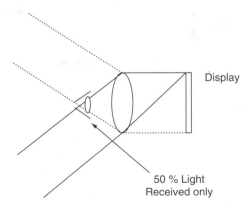

FIGURE 6.25. A simple magnifier design for HMD Design.

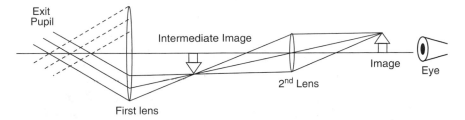

Figure 6.26. The compound microscope HMD design.

the images. To be precise, the exit pupil (or eye motion box) is the area where the eye can be placed in order to see the full display. If the eye is outside the exit pupil then the full display will not be visible. The use of the second lens also allows for a wider realizable FOV as the second lens can be placed very close to the intermediate image.

The lens close to the eye is usually adjustable so that the exit pupil can be adjusted to the position of the eyes for user convenience. The exit pupil formed in this way is usually located farther than the sweet spot of the simple magnifiers, thus causing less eyestrain. However, the exit pupil is not so forgiving and the right positioning of the eye becomes more important. On the other hand, to allow users with glasses to use the HMD, there must be enough distance between the eye and the closest optical element from the eye. This distance is called the *eye relief*. An eye relief of 25 mm is usually known be the minimum for use with eyeglasses. (If the HMD is focusable such that eyeglasses are not required, then the eye relief can be less.) Generally the greater the eye relief, the smaller the exit pupil will be [CRL04].

HMDs are nice because they provide images "isolated" from the external world (the eyes only see the images and not the outside world) and are often coupled with head-tracking to provide viewpoint-dependent display. This results in a much higher sense of immersion and presence. However, most HMDs suffer from narrow fields of view and heavy weight (not to mention being tethered to the computer). Combined with the fundamental problem of how stereo display systems cause inconsistency between the eye's accommodation and convergence, it poses a big human factors problem. Other problems with the HMD include the imprecise location of the eye that changes during the period of user wearing (with respect to the exit pupil and eye relief). In addition, the eyes may not be positioned in the center with respect to the image planes (screens) nor their direction perpendicular to them.

HMDs come in two varieties: see-through and nonsee-through. The nonsee-through ones allow the user only to see the images on the display devices, however, the see-through HMDs allow users to "see through" the display and see the outside world (e.g., images are shown by half-mirrors). This way, the computer-generated images and outside real-world images can be shown together for augmented reality applications. See Figure 6.27.

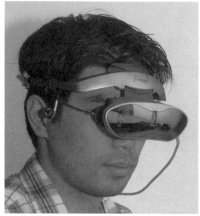

FIGURE 6.27. Various HMDs. Left: Non-see through, Right: See through.

Implementation

In all major types of display systems we have described, the generation of stereo effect requires generation of appropriate images for the left and right eye (see Figure 6.28). For instance, one simple method to create a pair of left and right images is to take two photos or two movies in which the camera positions for the respective images are separated by an approximation of the InterPupiliary Distance (IPD) (because different people have different IPDs, an average value (∼6.5 cm) is normally used). Graphic rendering can be made based on two view volumes set up as shown in Figure 6.14, likewise separated by the average IPD in the x-direction of the camera coordinate system. As for the computer-generated images, the IPD value can be a variable in the system, thus customizing the view volume model according to the respective user.

Other Display Systems

There is a variety of standard display systems designed to promote higher immersion or customized for particular tasks. One natural variation is using large or multiple screens to offer a wide field of view. Figure 6.29 shows a system originally conceived at University of Illinois, Chicago (called the CAVE) in the early 1990s [Cru93]. Ideally, a small cubical room is constructed with each of the sides serving as a large projection screen. The user is literally totally immersed in 360 degrees. Both passive and active stereo systems can be employed. Due to the high cost of building such systems (a six-sided CAVE with passive stereo would normally require 12 projectors and mirrors), only a few sides are sometimes used (e.g., just four for right, center, left, and the bottom; see Figure 6.29).

Rather than using multiple tiles of rectangular and upright screens, specially made large spherical or cylindrical screens can be used also. Most often multiple projectors are used because one projector is not enough to cover the whole area. Because the projection surface is curved, the image is *pre-distorted* or warped so that it appears correct on the curved display surface. Note that as the screen gets larger, the viewing distance must become larger to keep the whole surface in view. Such display systems are often used for large-scale displays for a large group of people, for instance, in a theaterlike setting, in which immersive viewing is the primary purpose (with minimal interaction).

Figure 6.30 shows the workbench type of display where one projection surface is used in a tablelike manner using a mirror underneath. Such table displays are very suitable for tasks such as painting, surgery, operation

```
int main (int argc, char *argv[ ]) {
    ...
    /* set up views */

    left = pfNewChan(p);
    right = pfNewChan(p);
    pfSetVec3(hprOffsets, -eyeAngle, 0.f, 0.f);
    pfSetVec3(xyzOffsets, -Iod/2.f, 0.f, 0.f);
    pfChanViewOffsets(left, xyzOffsets, hprOffsets);
    pfSetVec3(hprOffsets, eyeAngle, 0.f, 0.f);
    pfSetVec3(xyzOffsets, Iod/2.f, 0.f, 0.f);
    pfChanViewOffsets(right, xyzOffsets, hprOffsets);
    ... }

static void DrawChannel(pfChannel *channel, void *left)
{
    ...

    /* draw and switch between views */
    if(Shared->stereo) {
        if(*(int*)left) {
            glDrawBuffer(GL_BACK_LEFT);   }
        else {
            glDrawBuffer(GL_BACK_RIGHT);   }
    }
    ...
}
```

(a)

FIGURE 6.28a. Example code fragments for setting up stereoscopic display rendering using Performer[2]: (a) time multiplexed;

---

[2] Performer is a registered trademark of SGI Corporation.

```
Int main (intargc, char *argv[])
{
    ...
    /* set up views */
    for (loop=0; loop < 2; loop++)
    {
        chan[loop] = pfNewChan(p);
        pfChanTravFunc(chan[loop], PFTRAV_DRAW, DrawChannel);
        pfChanScene(chan[loop], scene);
        pfChanNearFar(chan[loop], 1.0f, 10.0f * bsphere.radius);
        pfChanFOV(chan[loop], 45.0f, 0.0f);

        fstats= pfGetChanFStats(chan[loop]);
        pfFStatsClass(fstats, PFSTATS_ENGFX, PFSTATS_ON);
    }
    pfSetVec3(xyz, 2.0f, 0.0f, 0.0f);
    pfChanViewOffsets(chan[0], xyz, hpr);
    pfSetVec3(xyz, -2.0f, 0.0f, 0.0f);
    pfChanViewOffsets(chan[1], xyz, hpr);
    pfChanViewport(chan[0], 0.0, 0.5, 0.0, 1.0);
    pfChanViewport(chan[1], 0.5, 1.0, 0.0, 1.0);

    /* display to two view channels */
    for (loop=0; loop < 2; loop++)
    {   pfChanView(chan[loop], view.xyz, view.hpr);     }
    ...
}
```

(b)

FIGURE 6.28b. *Continued* (b) HMD.

planning, and so on. Compared to the large-scale spherical or cylindrical displays, CAVE or workbenches are most suitable when close-range interaction is required.

Figure 6.31 shows a display system for a flight simulator setup. The flight simulator creates a unique situation where most objects in the display are far away. A special optic system can be created where the distance from the magnifying glass to the image is equal to the focal length of the magnifying lens. This way the image is felt as being at infinity. Such an image is called a *collimated* image. In this scheme, the need for binocular stereoscopy is not significant because its effect is not significant for objects far away.

Human Aural System

The principle in designing (setting the configuration of) a visual display can be applied equally to an aural display. That is, one must have a basic understanding of how human aural systems work, and what important

```
int main(intargc,char**argv) {   ...
    glutDisplayFunc(HandleDisplay);
    ... }

void HandleDisplay(void) {   ...
    glColorMask(GL_TRUE,GL_TRUE,GL_TRUE,GL_TRUE);
    switch (glassestype) {
    case REDBLUE:
    case REDGREEN:

    /* Mask Definition */
    case REDCYAN:
        glColorMask(GL_TRUE,GL_FALSE,GL_FALSE,GL_TRUE);
        break;
    case BLUERED:
        glColorMask(GL_FALSE,GL_FALSE,GL_TRUE,GL_TRUE);
        break;
    case GREENRED:
        glColorMask(GL_FALSE,GL_TRUE,GL_FALSE,GL_TRUE);
                            break;
    case CYANRED:
        glColorMask(GL_FALSE,GL_TRUE,GL_TRUE,GL_TRUE);
        break;     }

    /* Camera Setting Left Eye */
    gluLookAt(camera.vp.x-right.x,
              camera.vp.y-right.y,
              camera.vp.z-right.z,
              focus.x,focus.y,focus.z,
              camera.vu.x,camera.vu.y,camera.vu.z);
        CreateWorld();
        glFlush();
```

```
    /* Mask Definition */
    glColorMask(GL_TRUE,GL_TRUE,GL_TRUE,GL_TRUE);
        switch (glassestype) {
    case REDBLUE:
        glColorMask(GL_FALSE,GL_FALSE,GL_TRUE,GL_TRUE);
        break;
    case REDGREEN:
        glColorMask(GL_FALSE,GL_TRUE,GL_FALSE,GL_TRUE);
        break;
    case REDCYAN:
        glColorMask(GL_FALSE,GL_TRUE,GL_TRUE,GL_TRUE);
        break;
    case BLUERED:
    case GREENRED:
    case CYANRED:
        glColorMask(GL_TRUE,GL_FALSE,GL_FALSE,GL_TRUE);
        break;     }

    /* Camera Setting Right Eye */
    gluLookAt(camera.vp.x+ right.x,
              camera.vp.y+ right.y,
              camera.vp.z+ right.z,
              focus.x,focus.y,focus.z,
              camera.vu.x,camera.vu.y,camera.vu.z);
        CreateWorld();
        glFlush();
        ... }
```

(c)

FIGURE 6.28c. *Continued* (c) passive. (See companion CD for more details; courtesy of Namgyu Kim.)

parameters there are in order to match them as closely as possible with the aural display system. Figure 6.32 shows the anatomy of the human ear.

Sound waves cause the tympanic membrane (eardrum) to vibrate. The three bones in the ear (malleus, incus, stapes) pass these vibrations on to the cochlea. The cochlea is a snail-shaped, fluid-filled structure in the inner ear. Hair cells are located on the basilar membrane of the cochlea. When the hair cells are excited by vibration, a nerve impulse is generated in the auditory nerve. These impulses are then sent to the brain.

The next question is how humans perceive 3D sound or directionality of sound. The brain uses three major properties of the sound in order to locate its direction of origin. At first, it used to be thought that the loudness of the sound (its amplitude) played the most important role in sound localization. However, it was found that the increase and decrease in the cycle of a single vibration of a sound (its phase difference) also played an important role. That is, the sound wave heard by the right ear will be slightly different in timing, compared to that heard by the left ear (akin to binocular disparity). This slight difference in timing (or phase) helps humans to locate the origin of the sound. This observation brought the invention of stereo sound (two speakers with a phase-controlled sound source) and surround sound systems (multiple speakers with a phase-controlled sound source). Note that two persons who hear the same sound would interpret the sound a bit differently

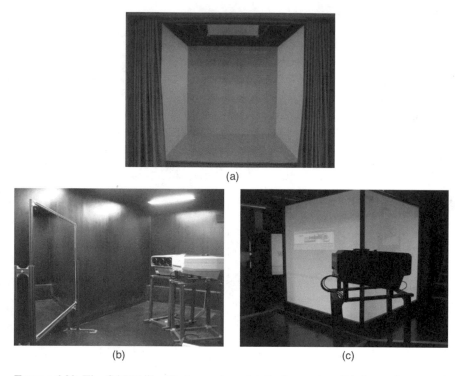

FIGURE 6.29. The CAVE-like display system: (a) the front view; (b) the projector and mirror in the back; (c) another view of the projector and mirror in the back. (Courtesy of Bo H. Cho.)

as the phase differences felt by the two ears will be different due to differences in the shapes of their ears reflecting the sound wave into their ears.

Later, a more refined theory of 3D sound perception was found. According to this theory, 3D sound perception is based on the difference in energy distribution in the frequency domain of the sound waves [Kra01]. This sparked the invention of a function (or concept) called the *Head-Related Transfer Function* (HRTF) and the HRTF-based technology that produces spatial sound with new energy distributions according to the (possibly varying) locations of the sound sources (for the right and left ear; see Figure 6.33). To be precise, to find the sound pressure that an arbitrary source $x(t)$ produces at the eardrum, we can physically measure the "impulse response," $h(t)$, from the source to the eardrum. This is called the Head-Related Impulse Response (HRIR), and its Fourier transform $H(f)$, is the head-related transfer function. The HRTF captures the energy distribution in the frequency domain of the sound from a particular location, and it can be used to reproduce or synthesize binaural signals from a monaural source (for the right and left ear). Note that the HRTF is a function of the location of

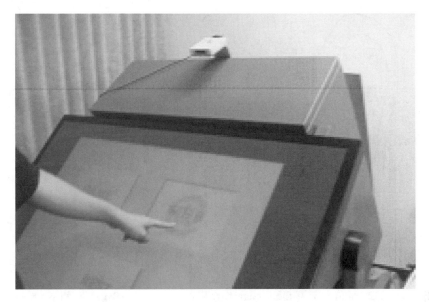

FIGURE 6.30. A person closely interacting with a workbench style display system. (Courtesy of J. Hwang.)

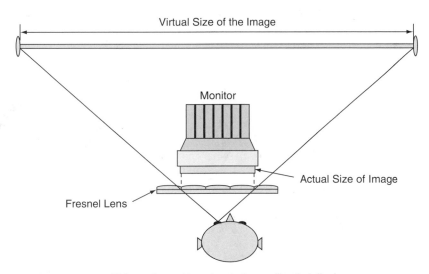

Using a fresnel lens to create a collimated display

FIGURE 6.31. Using a fresnel lens to create a collimated display system for a flight simulator.

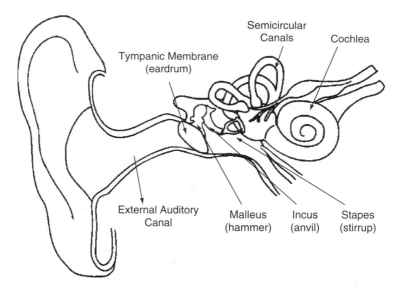

FIGURE 6.32. Anatomy of the human ear. (Adapted from [Ber97] with permission from Houghton Mifflin © 2004.)

the sound source. Thus, for a faithful reproduction of 3D sound the user location must be known or tracked (using separate sensors), and used as input to the sound synthesis system. HRTF approach would also suffer from the fact that each person has different ear shapes that will distort the energy distribution (that is, one HRTF that works for one person will ever so slightly not work for another). Thus, HRTF is obtained in laboratories, in

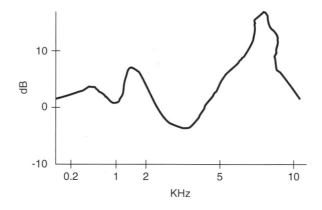

FIGURE 6.33. 3D sound systems use a frequency response function synthesized from the head-related transfer functions. It is used to modify the energy distribution so that sound from the speakers is perceived as coming from the virtual source. (Adapted from [Kra01] with permission from IEEE © 2004.)

addition for different locations, for different population and age groups so as to personalize the 3D sound system as much as possible [Dud00].

The sounds generated with the help of the HRTF would be played directly to the ears of the human using a headphone (two speakers are enough to simulate the 3D sound using HRTFs for the right and the left ears), producing the 3D localization cue. The 3D sound quality produced from the general-purpose sound cards is best heard with the use of a headphone instead of from a set of speakers. This is because the HRTF functions used in the sound cards are usually sampled with microphones located in the two ears of a dummy head model. This in turn makes the use of multichannel speakers difficult because the synthesized sound is based on two channels. However, using headphones also creates what is known as the Inside-the-Head Localization (IHL) phenomenon, a false impression that a sound is emanating from inside the user's head [Ken95].

Aural Display Systems (3D Sound)

The simplest 3D aural display would be one based on sound amplitude control. This would require two or more speakers and a capability to send synchronized sound streams with different amplitudes. The amplitudes would be adjusted according to the location of the sound with respect to the listener. For instance, the total volume can be set up to diminish linearly according to the distance from the sound source, and the relative volumes (panning) are computed from relative orientations (θ) of other participants according to a cosine function. That is,

$$\text{Right\_Volume} = RightMax/2 + (\cos\theta)^* RightMax/2$$
$$\text{Left\_Volume} = RightMax - \text{Right\_Volume}$$

where *RightMax* is the maximum volume for the right channel and θ is the relative angle between the user and the other sound source (e.g., if there is a sound source at the right side, θ is 0 degrees, if in the front, 90 degrees).

Most sound cards are capable of producing stereo or surround sound. Ideally, stereo or surround sounds require sounds recorded in stereo or surround with two or multiple audio streams that have differences in their phases. Such pre-recorded stereo sound will sound differently when heard at different locations, when speaker locations are different from the original recording settings, and when heard by different people. Stereo alone thus provides only few directional cues. But most often, the usual sound cards do not provide the capability to control the phases of sound streams in an intricate way. In fact, to the author's knowledge, direct low-level programming of the sound cards is nearly impossible for all practical purposes (not open to the general public). Today's PC sound cards (and programming APIs) are equipped with a set of HRTF functions and a capability to deliver HRTF-controlled sound streams for changing locations of sound sources.

Most sound programming libraries offer functionalities to simply play or record sound bites and change some sound characteristics. DirectSound,[3] a part of DirectX[3] available from Microsoft, offers ways to play sounds on PCs (with most sound cards) with very low latency and other sound-related functionalities including 3D sound, multiple sound playing, sound effects such as the Doppler effect, echo, and even recordings. Figure 6.34 shows the three major sound systems for virtual reality. Figure 6.35 shows a code sample for setting up and delivering 3D sound using the DirectSound APIs.

In terms of types of sounds used for display, three broad sound types can be identified. In the most ideal case, the sound display should be as real as possible employing physically based simulated sounds or something recorded from the real world and played back. Iconic sounds are often used for practical purposes instead of the real and natural "as is" sounds. For instance, if an environment has many doors, one might record only one sample of a door opening or closing sound to be used for all the doors (even though each door opening or closing would be slightly different in actuality). Finally, the simplest sound display might employ just a beeplike sound to indicate its presence, while not providing any cue to what it might represent.

---

[3] DirectSound and DirectX are registered trademarks of Microsoft Corporation.

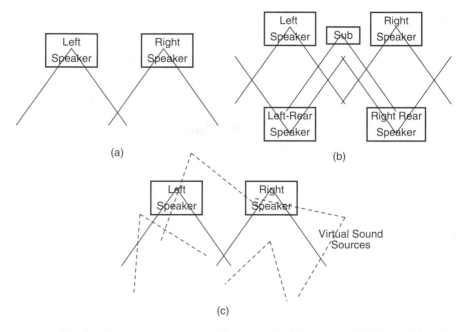

FIGURE 6.34. Various sound systems: (a) stereo; (b) 5.1 surround; (c) HRTF-based 3D sound. (Adapted from [Kra01] with permission from IEEE © 2004.)

```
/* set up sound source */
HRESULT C3DSound::Setup(int env_type, WCHAR *pwsFileName, * pPerformance, IDirectMusicLoader8*
pLoader){
    ...
    m_pLoader->LoadObjectFromFile( CLSID_DirectMusicSegment, IID_IDirectMusicSegment8, pwsFileName,
    (LPVOID*) &m_pSegment)
    m_pPerformance->CreateStandardAudioPath( DMUS_APATH_DYNAMIC_3D, 64, TRUE, &m_p3DAudioPath )
    m_p3DAudioPath->GetObjectInPath( DMUS_PCHANNEL_ALL, DMUS_PATH_BUFFER, 0, GUID_NULL, 0,
    IID_IDirectSound3DBuffer8, (LPVOID*) &m_pDSB)
    m_pPerformance->CreateStandardAudioPath( DMUS_APATH_DYNAMIC_MONO, 64, TRUE, &m_p3DAudioPath )
    m_p3DAudioPath->GetObjectInPath( DMUS_PCHANNEL_ALL, DMUS_PATH_BUFFER, 0, GUID_NULL, 0,
    IID_IDirectSoundBuffer8, (LPVOID*) &m_pDSB)
    ...
}

/* set volume */
void C3DSound::setVolume(longvolume){
    m_p3DAudioPath->SetVolume(volume, 0);
}

/*play */
HRESULT C3DSound::Play(bool bLoop){
    ...
    m_pSegment->SetRepeats( DMUS_SEG_REPEAT_INFINITE )
    m_pPerformance->PlaySegmentEx( m_pSegment, NULL, NULL, DMUS_SEGF_SECONDARY, 0, NULL, NULL,
    m_p3DAudioPath)
    ...
}

/* set position of sound source */
HRESULT C3DSound::setPos(float fX, float fY, float fZ){
    ...
    m_pDSB->SetPosition( fX, fY, fZ, DS3D_IMMEDIATE )
    ...
}

/*set position of listener */
HRESULT C3DSound::setListenerPos(float fX, float fY, float fZ){
    ...
    m_pListener->SetPosition(fX, fY, fZ, DS3D_IMMEDIATE)))
    ...
}

/* set sound direction */
HRESULT C3DSound::setListenerOri(float vx, float vy, float vz, float ux, float uy, float uz) {
    ...
    m_pListener->SetOrientation(vx, vy, vz, ux, uy, uz, DS3D_IMMEDIATE)))
    ...
}
```

FIGURE 6.35. An example of programming with DirectSound® API.

Haptics: Force and Tactile Feedback

The word '*haptics*' refers to the sense of touch, and can be subdivided into two subfields; force (kinesthetic) and tactile feedback. Force feedback displays interact with the muscles and tendons to give the human a sensation of a force being applied. Humans rely on their haptics in exploring environments in which there is poor or no visibility. For instance, pegs can be inserted into a hole by feeling for the surface and the chamfers into the hole. But in most cases, haptics work best when used with other modalities such as the visual and aural display.

Most force feedback devices are in the form of robotic devices, such as high-Degrees Of Freedom (DOF) manipulators and exoskeleton mechanisms, low DOF force feedback joysticks, or motion platforms that can generate and stimulate a user with the various types of forces at the point of interaction (called the virtual proxy). Tactile feedback is explained in the next section.

Haptic devices can also be categorized as active and passive. Active devices generate force feedback to be exerted on the human user (e.g., a manipulator or motion platform). Passive devices provide haptic cues solely

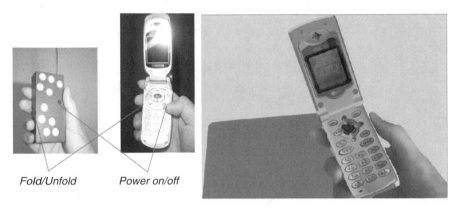

Fold/Unfold   Power on/off

FIGURE 6.36. Example of use of passive haptics (props): (a) the rectangular prop represents the mobile phone. The prop has 10 yellow markers for vision-based registration purpose and two wireless switches for interaction; (b) what is seen by the user through the head-mounted display [LeeSY04]. (Reprinted with permission from IEEE © 2004.)

by their physical existence (see Figure 6.36). That is, humans can obtain "passive" feedback by grabbing or colliding against an inactive object such as in using props and real-life objects as interaction objects. Passive haptics can be an attractive option sometimes, because active haptics employ expensive devices that can clutter the visual display, plus it is relatively safer (no active parts), and easy (metaphorically shaped) to use. Most haptic devices only provide very limited force feedback such as point force feedback (e.g., through the end effector of the manipulator), or low degrees of freedom (no rotational force). To deliver a large amount of force, the device must carry sufficient mass, which makes the device less safe and more cumbersome to use (less mobile, obstructs visual displays). Thus, it is difficult to project if there will ever be a "natural" haptic system as envisioned and portrayed in science fiction (unless we can find a way to directly stimulate and control the sensorimotor system of the brain). To summarize, haptics can find good use in a limited manner for very specific tasks in which force feedback is critical for efficient task completion or virtual experience [Smi04].

Haptic Display and Implementing Haptics

As with any display system, to correctly design a haptic interface the anatomy and physiology of the body must be taken into consideration. The details of such human factors issues and design of ergonomic mechanisms are beyond the scope of this book, and there has only been little work in the ergonomic design of haptic devices. For instance, Figure 6.37a shows the ground-based manipulator type force feedback device. Ground-based

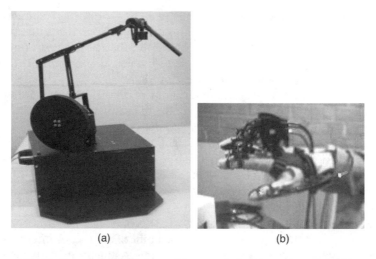

(a)   (b)

FIGURE 6.37. Various haptic displays: (a) grounded; (b) ungrounded. (Courtesy of Kwang H. Ko and Luke Shih.)

devices are solidly connected to the ground, where as ungrounded devices are usually worn on the body like an exoskeleton (see Figure 6.37b). These are basically robotic devices that are actuated by electric motors or hydraulic/pneumatic pumps. The important parameters to consider as the user of the technology would be the output strength of the devices in relation to the capabilities of the human joints. According to Kilchenman [Kil00], for instance, a force output of 3 to 4 N is needed for size discrimination, identification, and object detection.

The degree of freedom is another important parameter. Some robotic manipulators can only deliver three degrees of freedom (for cost reasons) where as human hands and arms can move in more than six degrees of freedom, thus limiting the movement of the human user and creating discomfort. The output strength of robotic devices is related to their mass, and usually the greater the mass, the greater the size. Large-sized haptic devices either clutter the visual display or are heavy to use if worn on the body. Light and small-sized haptic devices can break easily. Note that haptic devices are usually equipped with sensors (e.g., to measure the movements of the haptic device and thus indirectly measure motion of the human action) so that their values can be used as input. The sensors usually sense the linear and/or rotational position, velocity, and even acceleration, and their values are used to compute the correctional force to be applied in the next instant. In fact, generating a "stable"[4] force requires a closed feedback loop that runs at a very high rate (up to 1000 Hz) for 'rendering the force' (i.e., sensing the user

---

[4] According to the system control theory, without sufficient update rate, response force can exhibit oscillation or jitter, or in the worst case, divergence.

motion, simulating/updating the scene (e.g., the object in contact), and generating the force response (the graphic rendering may run at lower rate)). However, it has been reported that a feedback loop operating down to 40 ~ 80 Hz is good enough for simple tasks such as size identification and discrimination, and round corner detection [Kil00].

There are other haptic devices that do not resemble robotic manipulators or exoskeletons, but they mostly operate on similar principles: they use various actuators in different degrees and directions of freedom in conjunction with sensors to generate and regulate the force output. Examples include the force feedback joystick, motion platforms, force-controlled bicycles and stepper machines, and the like. Recently, game pads came out equipped with simple force feedback actuators using electronically controlled mechanical relays that provide a very simple and crude sensation of inertia at the time of (virtual) contact.

Computing for the force feedback at the point of contact or interaction (or virtual proxy) is referred to as haptic rendering. As mentioned above, haptic rendering involves checking for existence and location/direction of collision (as a separate process; see Chapter 9), reading the current values of the sensors, and computing the value of the force feedback to be displayed at the virtual proxy as a response to the collision. Such collision responses may be based on physically based formulations considering the dynamics and kinematic properties of the interaction object and the virtual proxy (e.g., the human hand). In many cases, simplistic models are used, however, to reduce the amount of computation (note that this computation must be done ideally at a rate of 1000 Hz which is much higher than the visual update rate of ~25 Hz). One of the simplest models calculates the reactive force as a value proportional to the collision velocity with its direction directly opposite to the colliding direction. Figure 6.38 illustrates the model. Chapter 10 covers some of the basics of physical simulation and generating collision response effects.

Stimulation of Other Modalities I

Tactile Feedback

Sensation of touch (e.g., texture of objects) can be important for certain explorative manipulation tasks such as medical palpation, where physicians locate hidden anatomical structures and evaluate tissue properties using their hands [How02]. Tactile display devices stimulate the user's skin (usually constrained to be the fingertip) to generate these sensations of various types of contact. The skin responds to several distributed physical quantities; the most important are perhaps high-frequency vibrations (that can be provided using, e.g., small vibratory motors, piezo-electric materials; see Figure 6.39), small-scale shape or pressure distribution (can be provided

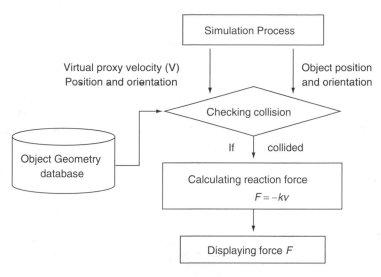

FIGURE 6.38. A simple haptic rendering procedure.

e.g., by using an array of small moving pins), and thermal properties [How02].

However, most tactile display systems are still in the research stage, and cannot be used effectively for a VR system yet. The devices, similarly to haptic devices, tend to be large (and thus immobile) in their sizes and only provide sensations to a very small area (fingertip). A number of companies have come out with a mouse that can provide a limited amount of tactile

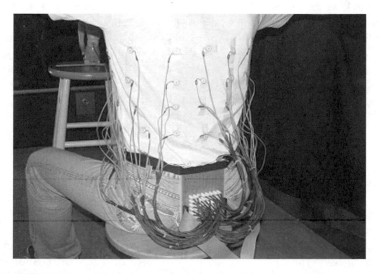

FIGURE 6.39. Vibratory tactile feedback device [Jan02].

sensation [Vir04] and SONY is working on computer screens (LCD) that can provide tactile sensations using special solid-state devices [Pou02].

Although most research on tactile feedback systems has focused on techniques to exactly recreate the texture of virtual surfaces using special devices and materials, there also have been proposals to use tactile feedback (usually using vibration) as an abstract information channel in several application contexts. Typically, to effectively convey certain information, such tactile feedback systems are applied to a larger skin area (e.g., abdominal region), and thus are often in a wearable form. The U.S. Navy has developed a system called the TSAS (Tactile Situation Awareness System), a tactile vest to help pilots' situation awareness in aerial navigation and combat [Tat00].

Proprioception

Proprioception refers to sensations obtained from receptors in our muscles, tendons, and joints. With signals from these organs, we, for instance, are aware of the positions of our arms and legs even with our eyes closed. In addition to positions, we can accurately sense the speeds, directions of movements, and forces of our limbs as well. The sense of proprioception creates a *body image*, a vivid sense of different body parts occupying space [Ber00]. Proprioceptive feedback is important for enacting natural interaction and task performance/learning (because we usually move our body parts to interact and carry out tasks), and spatial perception. When we turn our heads, we use the proprioceptive feedback from the neck joint to encode the space around us. However, there is no external device that can directly stimulate our proprioceptive receptors (they would have to be connected directly to our nerves). Instead, if possible, a VR system should employ head-tracking and view-dependent scenes in as many directions as possible and also strive to implement whole-body interaction that utilizes as many body limbs as possible for close-range 3D interaction. This helps the user to build a better perception of space and feel the higher presence in the virtual environment.

Vestibular Sense

The vestibular sense is the sense of acceleration and balance. The vestibular organ is the semicircular canal located within the inner ear which is filled with fluid that moves under acceleration or deceleration (but not under constant velocity). That fluid movement provides the cues for perceptions about gravity, acceleration, and balance. Similarly to proprioception, it is difficult to provide the right vestibular sense externally consistent with what happens in the virtual environment (one has actually to run, walk, make sudden moves, or tilt one's body on one's own). Rather, the fact that humans possess this vestibular sense is a source of discomfort. Similarly to the phenomenon where humans feel discomfort from the inconsistency between convergence and accommodation when looking at (artificial) stereoscopic images, the coupling between the vestibular and visual sense is very strong. One of the typical sicknesses induced in a VR setting often happens in virtual navigation where the user receives cues of moving through the virtual environment through the visual channel, whereas in reality, one is standing still in the physical real world (thus having no vestibular sense of moving). Such inconsistency creates sickness and discomfort that are very difficult to get around. Ironically, making the VR system induce higher presence (e.g., by using more immersive displays, rich interaction, and so forth) is known to make this problem worse. On the other hand, it is possible to reduce the effect of such sicknesses by making the user pay attention to certain tasks or to a storyline (although it is not clear what the after-effects might be). Motion platforms that generate sudden accelerated motions can deliver limited stimulation to the vestibular sense and add to the creation of compelling virtual navigation.

Stimulation of Other Modalities II: Olfactory, Wind, Thermal, Taste

No practical sensory display systems or devices exist for simulating the effects of smell, wind, taste, and other more "exotic" human sensory modalities. For instance, very little work, commercial or research, has been done on olfactory display systems. Unlike color, it is not possible to compose a new scent from the basic component scents and once a scent is diffused into air, a problem of quickly removing the residuals remains. Researchers at the University of Central Florida [Mor03] are working on a scent-specific technology with objectives to deliver a specific odor at a specific time. Their system, the "ScentKiosk" is PC-controlled and provides three different scents in small amounts near the user's nose for quick detection without residual room odors (see Figure 6.40). Another system by the same group, called the "ScentDome" can provide 20 scents dispersed by a small fan. Researchers at the Institute of Creative Technologies (ICT) are working on a concept the "Scent Release Necklace" (see Figure 6.41) that uses several scent cartridges controlled by a wireless interface. At the recent IEEE Virtual Reality conference, Yanagida et al. presented a novel olfactory display system called the 'Air Cannon'. The Air Cannon, detached from the user by some distance, tracks the location of the nose by a camera, and "shoots" a portion of a small scent packet using an aerodynamic pump system so that the portion arrives near the nose of the user [Yan04].

The sensing of the wind or air flow can be an important presence-promoting factor by providing a cue or medium that bridges the virtual and physical worlds. Moon et al. have developed an interface that simulates the effect of wind using 16 small computer-controlled fans [Moo04]. They reported that the interface along with the visual feedback improved the user-felt presence significantly (see Figure 6.42).

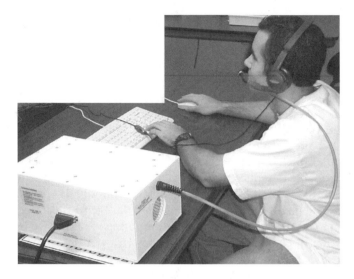

FIGURE 6.40. The ScentKiosk that provides several odors directly to the user's nose. (Reprinted with permission from the ScentAir Technologies © 2004.)

FIGURE 6.41. The Scent Collar[5] under development by ICT [Mor03]. (Reprinted with courtesy and permission from J. Morrie and the ICT © 2004.)

---

[5] The Scent Collar is a development effort between USC's Institute for Creative Technologies and Anthrotronix, Inc. The Scent Collar development is sponsored by the U.S. Army Research, Development, and Engineering Command (RDECOM); however, the content of the information pertaining to the collar does not necessarily reflect the position or the policy of the government, and no official endorsement should be inferred.

FIGURE 6.42. The wind interface developed by Moon et al. [Moo04]. (Reprinted with permission from the ACM © 2004.)

Although work is in progress, no "practical" displays for simulating the effects of smell, wind, taste, and other "exotic" modalities that humans possess exist at the time of writing this book. However, ingenuity can go a long way to overcome the problem sometimes. Sensorama, perhaps the very first virtual reality system, created by M. Heilig in the late 1950s, included a fan device to simulate the wind drag effect of motorcycle ride and a one-shot simple device to reproduce the foul smell of New York City alleyways [Sen61]. Dinh et al. studied the effects of multimodality on the participants' sense of presence in a virtual environment and on their memory for the environment and the objects in that environment. In their study, they used a coffeemaker to produce the effect of the smell, a small electric fan for the effect of the wind, and a high-energy light bulb for the thermal effect [Din99].

Summary

Multimodal interaction is one of the defining characteristics of a true VR system. To design an effective multimodal display, once must first understand how the human perceptual system works, and try to match the display capabilities to those of the human. In addition, the type of the task to be carried out must be considered as well. Although humans possess five major senses, it is the "big three" modalities of the visual, aural, and haptic that are taken advantage of in today's usual VR system. Although display systems for other modalities are still in the research stages, special-purpose devices can sometimes accomplish the desired effect.

Pondering Points

- Imagine a projective display system of 2 m × 3 m with the user 2 m away from the middle of the screen. Assuming 20/20 vision of the user, calculate the required resolution, FOV, and pitch size.
- Take the HMD in your lab (or look one up on the Web), and jot down the important parameter values such as the FOV, resolution, exit pupil, and eye relief.
- Most HMDs today suffer from a narrow field of view. Suggest a way to overcome this problem.

Chapter 7
Sensors and Input Processing

The last chapter examined various display systems for different human sensory modalities used as output devices in virtual reality systems. In this chapter, we examine typical sensors used as input devices. Like the display systems, using or wearing sensors raises human factors issues and it is important to understand their capabilities and working principles to design the right interface (see Chapter 8 also).

The sensors can be largely divided into three styles: continuous, discrete, and combined [Bow05]. Continuous input devices are hardware devices that sample certain physical properties or quantities of the real world such as a position, orientation, acceleration, velocity, pressure, and so on. The discrete input hardware devices generate one event at a time upon the user's designated action, such as pressing a button or making a pinch action. Continuous input devices are usually used in combination with discrete input devices (as with a mouse), and in conjunction with event-generating recognition software (such as recognition of gestures, voice commands, body movements, etc.).

In order to reflect the user's intention back to the virtual world as soon as possible, the sensors must have as low latency as possible. Latency refers to the time from capturing certain data and delivering them to the system. This includes the time of capture, certain processing (which may include the recognition process if required), and time for delivery to the system. Usually, the bottleneck is on the processing part, especially if it has to be done in software (e.g., format conversion, recognition into a discrete meaningful event). Apart from latency, a sensor's capability will be bounded by its update (or sampling) rate. This is the rate at which the sensors "sample" the world to produce the sensor data. The higher the update rate, the better temporal resolution of the world data will be obtained. However, if the latency is too large, the high update rate would be of little value. Too much latency or very low update rate can introduce noticeable lag in using virtual reality systems. In addition, sensors can introduce sizable inherent error and distortion and require a calibration process to minimize such effects.

Sensors must also be carefully 'registered' into the virtual world, meaning that the relationship between their coordinate systems must be established correctly. Matching this unitless quantity to the real requires a mapping process. That is, depending on the display devices used, when moving by 100 in virtual space, how much it amounts to the real-world quantity will have to be measured separately to establish such mapping and this mapping will be different for different display systems and sensors.

Trackers

The most important (continuous) input device used for virtual reality systems is the tracker that senses and tracks a designated position or orientation in the 3D space. Trackers are important because tracking 3D position and orientation is essential in realizing natural interaction. For desktop systems, we use the mouse to track positions in the (limited) 2D space. Trackers come in many different flavors according to how they work (which is related to the accuracy and amount of possible distortion), whether they are wired, degrees of freedom, and operating range. Table 7.1 summarizes the various types of trackers and categorizes them according to these characteristics.

Magnetic trackers are composed of a source that emits a low-frequency magnetic field and sensors that determine their position and orientation relative to the magnetic field. They are relatively inexpensive with reasonable operating range and accuracy, but suffer from significant distortion with metal objects in the environment. Acoustic trackers use sound waves and their travel distance in unit time to triangulate the position and orientation of the sensor. Due to its operating principle, the line of sight between the sensor and the sound wave source must be clear. Acoustic trackers are inexpensive but usually have low accuracy and limited range.

Mechanical trackers rely on sensing the joint movements of mechanisms, such as in a manipulatorlike robot, and thus are highly accurate. Depending on the mechanism used, it can be difficult to control. For instance, the Spaceball[1] and the Magellan[2] (see Figure 7.1) are what are called isometric devices and may require a relatively large amount of force of twisting or pushing to move a small distance. Inertial trackers are based on computing (integrating) distances or orientation traveled (from a known reference point) with acceleration values obtained from gyros or accelerometers. Due to the nature of integration, after some time of operation, errors start to accumulate (drift errors) and the system must be reset again.

Most devices described above must tethered by nature, or making them untethered is an expensive option, however, vision-based tracking offers an inexpensive option with wireless convenience. Vision-based tracking used to

---

[1] Spaceball is a registered trademark of 3DConnexion, Inc.
[2] Magellan is a registered trademark of Logitech Corporation.

TABLE 7.1. Various trackers used in VR systems

Type by working principles		Accuracy (in the order of)	Tethered or not	Degrees of freedom	Op. range (up to)	Reliability
Magnetic		High (0.1 in / 0.1 deg)	Both	6	Long (up to 30 ft.)	Distortion with metal objects in environment
Ultrasonic / acoustic		Medium (1 cm / 1 deg.)	Tethered	6	Short (< 2 m)	Occlusion problem
Mechanical	Spaceball	High	Tethered	6	Medium (2~4 m)	Hard to control
	Robotic	High	Tethered	6	Short	
	Magellan	High	Tethered	6	Medium	Hard to control
Inertial		High	Both	3	Medium	Orientation only (drift error)
Vision based	Marker / color	Medium (1 cm)	Wireless	2.5/3	Medium	Occlusion / lighting problem
	Without marker	Low	Wireless	2.5/3	Medium	Occlusion / calibration problem

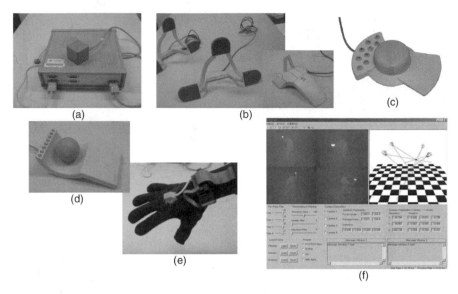

FIGURE 7.1. Various tracking sensors: (a) magnetic trackers, (b) ultrasonic 3D mouse; (c) Magellan; (d) Spaceball 3D mouse (cursor position moves in six degrees of freedom by controlling the isotonic ball; (e) finger trackers (glove); and (f) vision-based trackers (four cameras tracking a marker worn by the user). (Pictures: Courtesy of Bo H. Cho.)

be impractical due to the high computational load, but it is becoming popular because of the increased capabilities and reduced costs of the PC and associated hardware such as digital signal processing and even graphics boards. Vision-based tracking still has relatively low accuracy, unless markers or a known static background is used. There are also special-purpose devices for tracking gaze, fingers (e.g., glovelike device), body postures, and human limbs.

Event Generators

There is a variety of discrete event generators used for virtual reality systems. From the viewpoint of interaction, we describe them by the parts of the body used to initiate the events. The most typical interaction is carried out through the hand. Button devices (typically mounted on trackers as "hybrid" devices) are the most common hand- or finger-activated event generators (see Figure 7.2). Another possibility is to use pressure sensors mounted on fingertips on gloves, and use the finger pinch actions to generate many different events. Hand (motion) gestures are also used often. However, recognition of hand gestures is generally difficult because hand/finger posture/movements need to be tracked either by vision-based techniques which

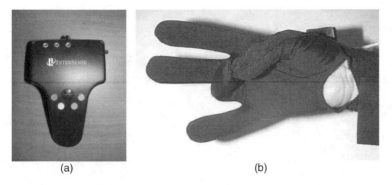

FIGURE 7.2. Hand/finger activated (hybrid) button devices: (a) 3D mouse; (b) pinch glove.[3]

usually require a certain background (e.g., static background scene) or high processing power, or by mechanical sensors that are difficult to use ergonomically. Furthermore, this is all on top of the difficulty in unambiguous recognition of gestures from continuous finger or joint data or hand position. This problem is further exacerbated by the need to segmentize out the data that correspond to the gesture and those that do not (i.e., where does the gesture start and end, and which portion is the neutral/meaningless pose?).

The foot has been used primarily for interaction control for navigation. Custom-made buttons or pressure-based sensors mounted on mats or floors (or even stepper machines) have been used to detect footsteps and are interpreted for navigation control (e.g., direction and speed; see Figure 7.3). These devices can be combined with rotational tables to add orientation and direction control as well.

Voice and speech recognition represents another natural method for interaction in virtual reality systems as humans do use speech every day in conjunction with other modalities. The technology is advancing rapidly, but voice and speech recognition is only at a level to be used for isolated word recognition. It is still speaker-dependent (requires training) and suffers from low recognition rate if there is significant ambient noise (might require special microphones). To avoid recognition errors, contextual information can help (e.g., the "up" command is only recognized when the menu is present). Because most recognition algorithms are based on statistical similarity, it is recommended to use short keywords that are as distinct from each other as possible (e.g., "right" vs. "light"). In fact, most speech interfaces are used for keyword recognition with fairly low word counts. Even so, using voice/speech recognition with other types of input method has been demonstrated to be very useful [Bol80].

---

[3] Pinch Glove is a registered trademark of Fakespace Corporation.

FIGURE 7.3. The "Walk-in-Place" metaphor used for navigation interface. The walking gesture of the user is recognized to control navigation in the virtual environment. The enactment of the walking enhances the user-felt presence [Sla95]. (Courtesy of Seok H. Jeon.)

Sensor Errors and Calibration

VR systems employ a number of input sensors to realize 3D multimodal interfaces as described in this chapter (see Figure 7.4). Among them (as is the mouse for the 2D desktop interface) 3D trackers play a very important role in VR systems. However, due to the various operating principles and external conditions, they exhibit a large amount of error that results in an incorrect reflection of user input and distorted output, thus make it difficult for the user to accomplish a given task and also cause user discomfort. For instance, magnetic trackers are one of the most common VR devices for their wide operating range, high degrees of freedom (6D), low latency, and relatively low cost. However, they suffer from quite a significant output distortion when there are interferences from common electromagnetic devices in the environment such as monitors, power cables, metal objects, and the like. Moreover, the underlying working principles make the errors more apparent as the sensors are farther away from the magnetic sensor source. One of the ways to battle such intrinsic sensor errors is to calibrate them, correcting the sensor output by adjusting it to match or conform to a dependably known and unvarying measure. That is, we sample the output values, throughout the operating space, at known locations and orientations

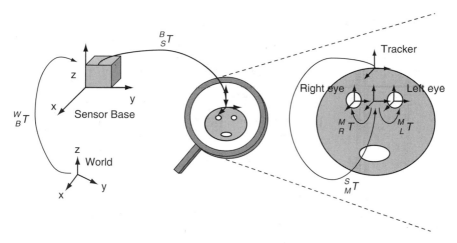

FIGURE 7.4. Setting up coordinate systems in virtual space with (tracking) sensors.

and record the error values to build a large table of error values indexed by the designated positions and orientations. From the table, we can estimate the relationship between the positions/orientations and the error values using a high-order polynomial function (usually second or third), and the function enables us to estimate the errors at positions and orientations that were not sampled in the first place, and correct the raw data by software. However, such a calibration process requires tedious data collection, and whenever the environment changes it must be carried out again.

Summary

Sensors are equally important as display systems: they allow the user to convey her intention to control and access the virtual world. After all, interaction is a two-way street. To effectively use sensors, their operating principles and working characteristics must be understood. A calibration is often needed to compensate for their inherent errors and distortion.

Pondering Points

- Imagine that you are building a virtual running machine. Describe the most effective and natural sensor system to acquire various possible types of user intentions and actions.
- As in desktop environments, menus are often used in virtual environments. Describe various ways to use the menu system (e.g., pull-up menu, select and confirm, close menu). What kind of sensors or input methods would you use? What kind of feedback (upon input) would you use? Explain your answer.

Chapter 8
3D Multimodal Interaction Design

Why Go 3D Multimodal?

One of the goals and ways to realize virtual reality is through using 3D multimodal interfaces. Unlike the usual desktop interaction in which we use the mouse and keyboard to click and type on a small 2D canvas to carry out various tasks, three dimensions and multimodality are important for virtual reality because humans do live and operate in a three-dimensional world employing various sensory and motor organs. Thus, it is fair to assume that 3D multimodal interfaces will be natural for human users for many tasks, as they leverage the motor and sensory skills that we use every day.

This does not mean that 3D multimodal interfaces will always be "better" than the traditional desktop 2D interface. Equally, there might be tasks that are best accomplished in a seemingly "unnatural" way. The way humans carry out tasks in the real world may be assumed to be natural, but bounded by various physical constraints. In the virtual world, where operating constraints are different, the physical constraints of the real world may be nullified to some extent. Only human ergonomics would constrain the interaction design. That is, it may be possible, for certain tasks, to devise "magical" interaction methods that are only possible in the virtual world, yet more efficient. Humans, with their great adaptive capability can often quickly learn such new interfaces. Thus, naturalness is not a necessary condition for interaction efficiency. However, natural and ergonomic (suited to human evolution) interfaces are generally easy to use and learn.

It has also been suggested that natural or ergonomically designed interactions contribute to a higher sense of presence. Badly designed interaction models and interfaces cause distractions and fatigue to the user, and lower the sense of presence. 3D multimodal interaction design is further complicated by the fact that the devices and computational resources required by the nature of the given task are not usually immediately available and "satisificing" (satisfy + sacrifice) solutions must be often made (e.g., high efficiency but low sense of presence or vice versa).

Structured Approach to the Interaction / Interface Design

In discussing 3D multimodal interaction, we first make an important distinction between two terminologies: interaction and interface. Interaction is an abstract model that describes how a user accomplishes some tasks. Interface is a specialized choice of hardware and software through which a user communicates with the computer system (a particular implementation of the interaction model; see Figure 8.1).

The key to a good interaction design is to carefully model the given task, and propose a set of interfaces that satisfice the multidimensional criteria of presence, naturalness, and efficiency. As with any design, interaction design also goes through the iterative phases of synthesis/modification and evaluation, for the lack of established design methodology (compared to the maturity for the 2D interface counterpart). This is partly because the sensor and display technologies (and their cost) are continually changing and the goals of interaction design are often conflicting. Moreover, the evaluation criteria are often loosely defined. Although for interaction efficiency, quantitative measures of task performance such as the completion time and error rate can be used, presence, user preference, and naturalness are quite subjective, and correct evaluation of interaction design with respect to these subjective criteria would ideally require a usability experiment with a large number of subjects. This is often practically an impossible thing to do in an iterative design process. There is no complete established methodology in 3D multimodal interaction design, however, a few guidelines from prior and ongoing research do exist [Bow05] and they can be applied effectively to reduce the trial-and-error cycles and overcome the dependence on sole experience.

Although the basic goal of any interaction design is to have the user accomplish a certain task, the designer must prioritize the possibly conflicting goals such as task performance efficiency, presence, ease of use, learnability,

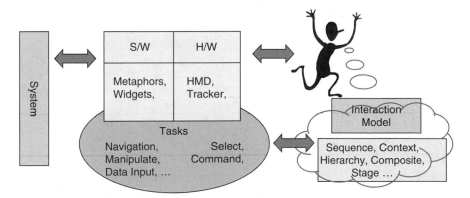

FIGURE 8.1. Interaction model and interface implementation.

and so on. With this in mind, the first guideline in interaction design is to carry out an analysis of the interactive task. This involves first identifying the user and considering the human factor requirements.

For instance, items of consideration can include the age, gender, experience with computers and games, eye strength, and so on. The heart of task analysis is the decomposition of the high-level task into smaller ones. When faced with a multidimensional task, such as moving an object in three-dimensional space, studies at the University of North Carolina at Chapel Hill have shown that users usually break the task into a series of lower-dimensional (1 or 2D) problems [Bro77]. For instance, the task can be characterized as moving the object in the xy-plane before moving it into its final position by moving in the z-direction. Tasks may simply be decomposed into subtasks based on their characteristics. Certain tasks may need to be carried out one after another, and some may be done concurrently. There exist formal approaches to task analysis via decomposition such as the GOMS approach that is based on the human problem-solving model [Car80]. The task decomposition produces a hierarchy of tasks and sub-tasks as shown in Figure 8.2. The subtasks at the bottom of the hierarchy that cannot be decomposed any further are called *primitive* tasks. Typical primitive tasks include those such as object selection, object manipulation, navigation, and system control [Bow05]. In many cases, the high-level tasks can be designed as the collections and combinations of these primitive tasks (*composite* tasks). Figure 8.3 shows a specific example of a task hierarchy.

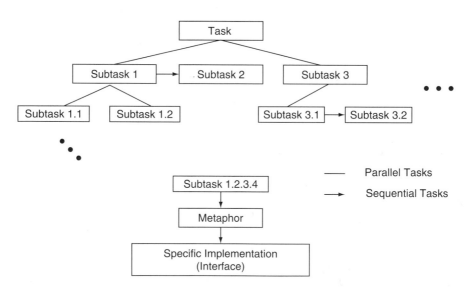

FIGURE 8.2. Task analysis for interaction/interface design.

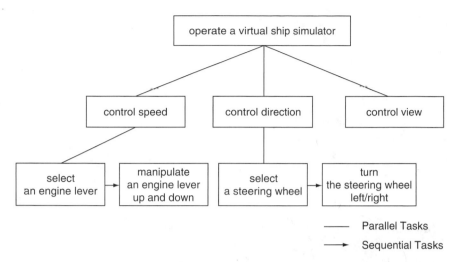

FIGURE 8.3. An example of a task hierarchy (the Ship Simulator case).

Metaphors

Once the primitive tasks are identified, an interface can be designed with a specific choice of hardware devices and software components (e.g., graphic feedback, sound effects, speech recognition, etc.). Metaphors are often used in designing an interface for a given task. Metaphors, in the context of human–computer interaction, are entities that are deliberately designed to be easily manipulable (for its familiarity, concreteness, down-to-earthness, abstraction, etc.) for a more intuitive control of a certain task. Metaphors we use every day are mostly visual (e.g., icons), although other modalities such as textual, aural, and even haptic would be possible. Metaphors help users build a mental model of computer systems by tapping into the knowledge about a familiar domain that is mapped on the unfamiliar domain or task. The successful use of metaphors hinges upon the degrees of matching user expectation to what the interface object should and should not do [Pre94]. Note that metaphors can be implemented in both hardware and software. Figure 8.4 shows several metaphors designed for the primitive task of navigation. In fact, many different metaphors and interface designs have been proposed for the four representative primitive tasks (i.e., selection, manipulation, navigation, and system control) over the years [Bow05]. Many of them have also been tested for their usability as well. We give an overview of them in the next section. However, before we do so, we discuss various issues in integrating different modalities for 3D and natural interaction.

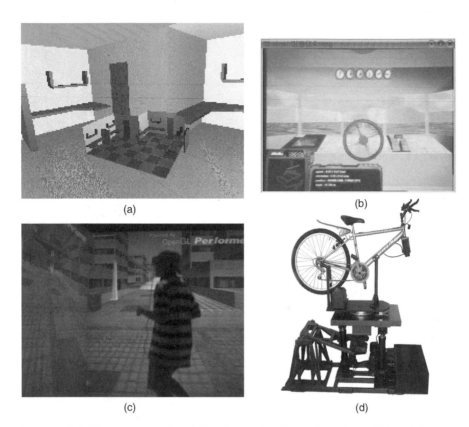

FIGURE 8.4. Various metaphors for the navigation task: (a) world-in-miniature: navigate by moving in the mini-map [Sto95] (Reprinted with permission from ACM © 2004.); (b) shiplike navigation; (c) navigation by natural motion (running); (d) navigation with bicycling action [Kwo01]. (Reprinted with permission from IEEE (c) 2004.)

Interface Design

The first thing to remember in interaction/interface design is that interaction is a closed-loop task with the human user as a part of it. There are aspects of both input and output. The input is driven and guided by what is displayed to the user, and the display is affected by the user input. The parameters that the user controls would be determined through the task analysis and the most ergonomic hardware/software choice must be made with the given resource. The user-controlled parameter must be reflected "immediately" as a matched display output in the most intuitive and natural fashion. Again, what is intuitive and natural depends on the task at hand and although there do exist established methods for certain tasks, this aspect is subject to running experiments and going through some trial-and-error processes.

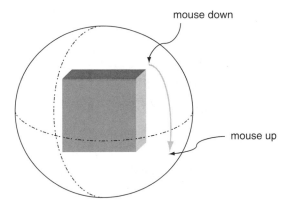

FIGURE 8.5. The Arcball metaphor for object rotation [Sho92].

For instance, rotating objects as part of a manipulation task can be metaphorically represented through a virtual ball. When attempting to rotate a selected object, a spherelike semi-transparent template would be superimposed on the target object, and by rotating the sphere, the target object would rotate accordingly. The Arcball [Sho92] is agreeably a natural metaphor for representing the act of rotation, and is simple enough (computationally) to be implemented so that the applied rotation is immediately (unnoticeable delay) reflected upon the target object (see Figure 8.5). The relationship between the applied rotation to the amount actually reflected to the target object can be adjusted, but it should be kept within reasonable bounds to be intuitive and natural.

One of the aspects of usability is the human factor. As explained in Chapter 6, the interfaces that we design must conform to our sensory and motor organs as much as possible. For instance, we must consider visual, aural, or kinesthetic (or any other modal) capacity of humans such as the effects and fatigue from using stereoscopic displays, the minimum or sufficient image resolution (in both lateral direction and depth), maximum tolerable audio intensity or quality, the minimum update rates for haptic rendering, tolerance for flickering, and so on.

Although it is beyond the scope of this book to fully investigate the process involved in designing ergonomic tools and devices for humans, one ergonomic principle, called Fitt's law [Fit54], is important to remember. Fitt's law was originally formulated in the context of real-world use, but should be applicable for operations in the virtual world as well. Fitt's law states that the time to reach (which is related to the overall task performance) a target object, whose width is W and is at distance A from the user, is logarithmically related to A/W (see Figure 8.6). Thus, this law can be used to place and properly size virtual tools, 3D widgets, and menus with respect to users.

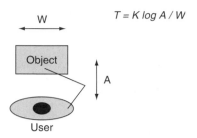

$$T = K \log A / W$$

FIGURE 8.6. Fitt's law: the task performance time is related to the width of the interaction object and the interaction distance in a logarithmic way [Fit54].

The information content in the display must be informative so that the interface is easy to use and drives the user to make as few mistakes as possible (e.g., by constraining the choices that can be made or by providing rich environment information, immediacy, and intuitive correspondence). For instance, in the Arcball example, we can augment the Arcball with graphics or text indicating the current rotation direction, or an ability to freeze certain rotational degrees of freedom. Another example is in the use of gestures for input. Many studies have concentrated on gesture recognition itself, rather than on the design of gestures. Many gestures do not have any relevance to the task at hand (no metaphorical connection). A typical case might be using various hand gestures or pinch codes to make system commands or invoke tasks. It is recommended that "natural" gestures be used whose motion profile or gesture configuration is abstracted from the actual in the geometric sense [Chu01]. Obscure gestures are difficult to recall, similar to voice/speech recognition systems with many keywords to remember. Making an interface amounts to reducing the cognitive load put on the user. This brings back the point that the type of user must be considered, for instance, in terms of cognitive maturity and capability. The "magic number" of 7 is often referred to as the approximate limit for our short-term memory [Mil56].

Multimodality

The whole premise behind multimodality is that by adding an "independent" input channel, the amount of information that is processed by the brain is increased. The increase in information reduces the error and time taken to complete a task. It also reduces the energy consumption and the magnitudes of contact forces used in a teleoperation situation [Smi04].

Physiologically, as emphasized throughout Chapter 5, the most usable (within the resource constraint) input/output device that matches our sensory capabilities must be used. However, the most important issue pertinent to *multi*modality is the issue of consistency. In fact, note that multimodal interfaces can be either simultaneous or sequential [Ovi03]. In the simultaneous interface, different modalities would be used as input or output methods at the same time. In the sequential one, different modalities are used one after another. In the former, when more than two modalities are used at the same time, maintaining the consistency among them is very important. We have already described the fundamental problem with the stereoscopic display that has to do with the inconsistency between accommodation and convergence cues that cause discomfort and sickness. The same goes for any multimodal input/output combination. For instance, it has been reported that humans will perceive a graphic and audio event to be different if separated at about 180 msec [Min98]. Humans are particularly sensitive to the discrepancy between the visual and vestibular sense. Virtual navigation often suffers from this problem, because visual feedback creates the sense of movement while not actually moving (called the vection). This is fundamentally difficult to overcome due to the very objective of virtual navigation. Incorporating an attentive task is believed to lower the sickness caused by such multimodal inconsistencies.

It is sometimes difficult to achieve complete consistency among the different modalities, however, the use of multimodal interaction itself can enrich the virtual experience and even create synergistic effects by one modality compensating for the others. It is generally accepted that multisensory feedback is beneficial to both presence and task performance in the context of virtual reality systems [Kam02; Sal01]. This is only true provided that the feedback from each modality is consistent with another [Ovi03], and the multisensory feedback (or input) is configured appropriately for the task at hand [Ovi99]. The modality appropriateness hypothesis postulates that the modality that is most appropriate or reliable with respect to a given task is the modality that dominates the perception in the context of that task [Shi01]. Vision has higher spatial resolution, hence its dominance in spatial tasks, and audition has a higher temporal resolution, hence its dominance in temporal tasks [Shi01]. The visual cue typically overpowers the haptic cue. This fact could help solve simulation of the meeting of a virtual object with a hard immovable object. If the user is presented with a visual cue that the virtual effector has reached a hard surface, even though the haptic interface does not give the force of a hard stiff surface, but rather a linear Hooke's law approximation, the user can still be fooled into thinking the virtual wall is rigid [Smi04]. Many synergistic multimodal interaction systems have been devised and studied that employed gestures [Bol80], voice [Cor02], proprioception [Min97], speech/audio [Gra98; Min98], force feedback [Ric94; Sal01], and even smell, thermal [Din99], wind [Sen61], and biosignal feedback [Mit93].

On the other hand, multisensory interactions can also modify user perception, as illustrated by the famous McGurk effect. The McGurk effect is a perceptual phenomenon in which vision alters speech perception [McG76]. Simple visual tricks can easily alter the body image that is created by the proprioceptive sense [Ram98]. In the study of Yang et al., for instance, it has been reported that the use of proprioception and tactility in addition to visual feedback make it possible to increase the effective field of view (or Geometric Field of View, GFOV[1]) to make the scene more visible without introducing any negative effects (such as distorted size perception) [Yan04]. Burdea et al. reported that multimodal interaction involving stereoscopic display, audio, and haptic feedback increased task efficiency significantly [Ric96]. When active haptics is not feasible, passive haptics and the use of props (along with visual feedback) can produce very good effects.

Although the best-known cross-modal effects are those of vision influencing other modalities, visual perception can also be altered by other modalities as well [Wal99]. In particular, the perception of distance is due to a combination of visual and motor input (muscles of the eyes, neck, and other body parts), and therefore proprioception plays a major role in spatial perception [Ber00]. We already pointed out that proprioception is also important in creating a body image and thus in promoting self-presence, one of the main goals of any virtual reality system. Slater et al. have reported that higher presence was achieved when one's own body was shown (through an HMD) as a way of matching the proprioceptive sense to that of the visual [Sla97]. Another work by Slater and his colleagues has shown that employing a proprioceptive interface involving physical motion resulted in a higher user-felt presence, for instance, the "walk-in-place" metaphor for navigation versus simply pressing mouse buttons [Sla95].

Cases of Interaction/Interface Design

In this section, we present several cases of interaction and interface design for various applications. Each case illustrates the domain customization and the process of trade-offs among different issues depending on the goal of the application. These interesting issues include multimodality, tangibility, generic and commonly used interfaces, limited device capabilities, task analysis, human factors, presence, alphanumeric input, and so on.

a. Case Study 1: Ship Simulator

Figure 8.2 showed the task decomposition for the Ship Simulator used in the earlier part of this book. The functions of the Ship Simulator can be mainly

---

[1] The GFOV differs from the actual physical FOV in that it refers to the angle encompassing a given scene (in its original scale). For instance, a 100% GFOV coincides with that of the physical FOV, and 200% GFOV would allow one to see twice as much angularwise (or physical FOV, and 200% GFOV would allow one to see twice as much angularwise (or the scene is reduced in half angularwise).

FIGURE 8.7. A trainee user interacting with the Ship Simulator to control the steering handle and the engine lever. (Courtesy of J. Seo.)

divided into two concurrently applicable functionalities: operating the ship (initiated by the trainee) and setting the training environment and situation (available to the trainer through separate control point). The ship operation, which is basically a navigation task, is further decomposed into three subtasks of ship speed control, direction control, and view control. The primitive tasks such as selection and manipulation, and certain metaphors (in this case, no metaphors are used) of selection and manipulation are needed to realize navigation control. As for the trainer, the task of setting up the training situation or environment is further refined into several subtasks, such as introducing (or removing) additional (existing) ships and environment objects, changing ship engine parameters, and environment conditions (e.g., day or night, weather). We can judge that, for the trainee interface, implementing it with 3D multimodality will be useful for the transfer of training to the real ship maneuvering situation (see Figure 8.7), whereas for the trainer, a desktop interface using the keyboard and mouse would be sufficient.

b. Case Study 2: Immersive Authoring [LeeG04]

Suppose we would like to construct an interactive content, such as the famous story of the hare and the tortoise, in an immersive manner. To realize this story as a VR-based content, several subtasks will be required. The objects must be modeled (i.e., geometric shape and configuration) according to the details required by their functions. For instance, the hare's running perhaps requires modeling of the legs and a rhythmic motion/sound associated with the legs. The initial scenes must be put in place. Specific details need to be filled in for the object's behavior such as timing, motion profiles, conditions, triggering events, and the like. The director (i.e., user) should be able to insert special effects, sound tracks, and change the lighting condition into the behavioral time line. All of these important modeling subtasks may be repeated and rehearsed as the content develops and matures, during which time the director take notes, adjust parameters, try different versions, replay and review, and even act out the object's role. The director will also constantly require various types of information to make decisions and carry out these tasks. Many of these tasks can benefit from what 3D interaction. Table 8.1 shows a possible task hierarchy and interface proposal. One of the key interaction requirements will be to provide the feeling of "concreteness" so that less tech-savvy people, such as artists and producers, can quickly learn and use the authoring system. More detailed descriptions of possible choices for

TABLE 8.1. Possible subtasks and interfaces for immersive authoring.

Subtask Hierarchy			Possible/Proposed Interface
Objects (actors) specification	Form specification	Geometric modeling	Direct Manipulation/2D GUI
		Object placement/rotation	Direct manipulation/props
		Shape modification (scaling)	Direct manipulation/props
		Attribute setting	2D GUI/props
	Function specification	Motion specification	PBD/props
		Scripting/programming	Keyboard (virtual/real)
		Adaptation	N/A
	Behavior specification/ user interaction	Scripting/programming	Keyboard (virtual/real)
		Model-based specification	PBD/2D GUI props
		Spatial constraints	
		Events	
		Actions	
		Routes	
		Synchronization of two objects	Two-hand tracking
		Synchronization of multiple (> 2) object behaviors	Mixture
		Role playing (object control)	Mixture
		Deployment	Direct manipulation in 3D
		Adaptation	Mixture
Scenewide operations	Inserting effects	Sound	2D GUI
		Lighting/camera	World in miniature [Sto95] Direct manipulation in 3D
	Reviewing	Navigation	2D GUI/button
Information gathering and retrieval	Note taking		Keyboard
	Information request	Behavior/timing	2D Graphics/text
		Object-specific	2D Graphics/text
		Scene-specific	2D Graphics/text
Version management	Save/replay		2D GUI
	Compositing		2D GUI

metaphor and interface design are treated in the second part of the case studies.

To develop an immersive authoring system with a reasonably comprehensive set of functionalities and the associated interactions, the various interaction models and proposed interfaces must be consolidated into a manageable set with usability and device constraints in mind (see Figure 8.8). Table 8.2 shows the consolidated interface design with three main interaction models: direct manipulation using a virtual hand (or through props with a real hand when the see-through option is used) for most important authoring tasks, conventional programming through alphanumeric input using the real keyboard, and the use of 2D GUI within the 3D space for other system controls.

Thinking over that scenes of stories are usually similar to the real world environment, and because most of the participants will be naïve users (e.g., children), a virtual hand is chosen for the interaction method. Two hands must be tracked to realize both the multiple object motion/behavior coordination and the keyboard-based alphanumeric input. In contrast with the execution environment, the authoring environment needs many more interaction techniques and modes of modeling tasks. Therefore, a menu system is necessary to organize these various interaction techniques and modeling tasks. Under this requirement, an iconic menu is presented for the user at a fixed position relative to the view parameters. Using a 3D manipulation with a virtual hand for the menu system is the most consistent way with the

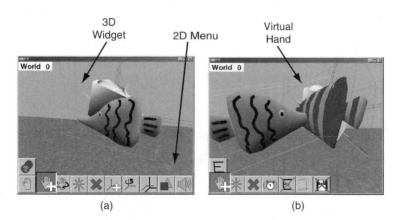

FIGURE 8.8. A possible interface for immersive authoring. A user immersed in the virtual space can specify form, function, and behavior of virtual objects and execute and test them, by directly interacting with virtual objects in a concrete manner: (a) the user selecting a virtual fish with a virtual hand and scaling it using a 3D widget; (b) the user demonstrating a collision event by grabbing one virtual fish (blue) and moving it toward the other (yellow) [LeeG02]. (Reprinted with permission from the ACM © 2004.)

TABLE 8.2. Consolidated interface design for PiP

Chosen interface	Subtasks	Devices needed
Direct manipulation (virtual hand)/ Props (real hand)	Object placement/rotation/scaling Motion specification Attribute setting/viewing Deployment Navigation/camera control (world in miniature) Behavior coordination Model-based behavior specification	Two trackers for two hands, camera, props, button device
Keyboard/button	Scripting/programming Note taking Role playing (object control)	Two trackers for two hands, keyboard, button device
2D GUI/menus	Discrete attribute setting/viewing Version management System control/effects	Tracker, button device

execution environment. Navigating through a lot of menu items using a virtual hand might bring more fatigue to the participants' arms. In addition, continuously moving their hands between a virtual object and the menu system is quite inefficient, whereas it would be more efficient if menu items are selected in another way and the participants' hands stayed with the virtual object being manipulated. Concerning this problem, an additional interface is introduced for the menu selection. Users hold a three-button prop on their nondominant hand and select menu items by pressing the buttons on it (e.g., left, right, select). The final set of interaction devices needed to realize these interactions/interfaces are two 6DOF motion trackers and two buttoned devices for the direct manipulation tasks and 2D GUI interaction. Figure 8.9 shows the VR devices used in this immersive authoring system: a head-mounted display, 6DOF tracker for tracking head and hand positions and orientations, and a 3-buttoned prop for menu selection.

c. Case Study 3: Tabletop Computing

Interaction modeling and interface design are not only applicable to VR systems. Figure 8.10 shows a platform for computing and interaction based on a tabletop environment (similar to a workbench style of display system). One can envision a particular set of applications (e.g., three or four family members playing a board game) and common interactions/interfaces required in such an environment by the same task analysis process. Figure 8.11 shows a simple task analysis for several possible suitable applications on the tabletop environment. The common primitive subtasks are identified to form a basis for developing a unified consistent form of interface. Note that a few different styles of interfaces may be employed for one task depending on the application. However, the number of different options should be

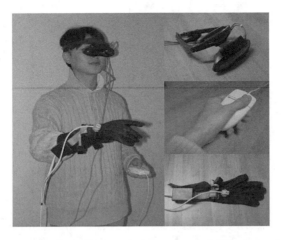

FIGURE 8.9. Interaction and display devices proposed for the task of immersive authoring: a head-mounted display, button device, tracker, and a glove (for simple gesture input) [LeeG02]. (Reprinted with permission from the ACM © 2004.)

minimized as much as possible to create a generic computing platform. As a form of generic computing environment, emphasis should be put on overall usability and consistency rather than on VR-related concepts as experience and presence.

An important part of designing the appropriate interfaces for tabletop computing is the selection of the tracking technology. We might consider two possible choices that are wireless and device- or marker-free: using a touchscreen and using a camera-based hand (or fingertip) tracking system.

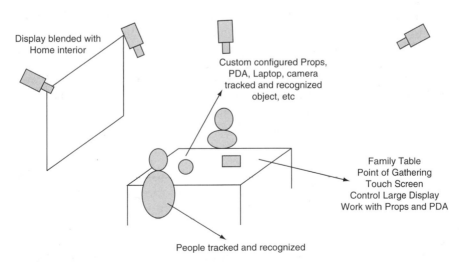

FIGURE 8.10. A hypothetical tabletop computing environment.

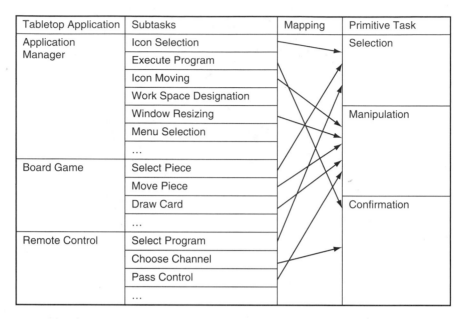

Tabletop Application	Subtasks	Mapping	Primitive Task
Application Manager	Icon Selection		Selection
	Execute Program		
	Icon Moving		
	Work Space Designation		
	Window Resizing		Manipulation
	Menu Selection		
	...		
Board Game	Select Piece		
	Move Piece		
	Draw Card		Confirmation
	...		
Remote Control	Select Program		
	Choose Channel		
	Pass Control		
	...		

FIGURE 8.11. Extracting common primitive subtasks from several applications.

The touchscreen system provides stable tracking whereas camera-based hand tracking can be rather unstable due to slight variations in skin colors, environment lighting, jitter due to the constantly changing shape of the hand blob, and so on. However, due to the relatively low height yet large area, touching the screen, especially for the far part of the table, can be ergonomically difficult. A simple application of Fitt's law is illustrated in Figure 8.12.

With smaller icons or objects, the task time will generally increase, although it is possible to pack more items within the limited table area. In addition, in order for the hand-tracking camera to cover the whole tabletop space, it must be installed high above the table, and depending on the capability of the camera, the effective accuracy might prevent the icons or objects from being too small. Thus, a compromised solution might be to use both touchscreen and camera-based hand tracking for the space immediately near the user, and hand tracking only for space relatively far from the user. This way, for far objects, the user can select and manipulate objects through a cursor drawn by extending the line between the user's assumed head (or body position) and the tracked hand tip to the surface of table. The size of the objects or icons can be set at a medium size ($\sim$5 cm), and varied dynamically according to the distance from the user. Aside from tracking the hands, an additional interface such as voice or gesture recognition may be considered. For instance, a selection confirmation might be made based on time passage, that is, the cursor staying for an extended period of time above a particular interactable button might trigger the "push" action. Or, it

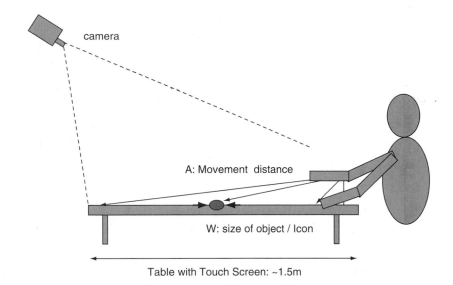

FIGURE 8.12. Using Fitt's law to compare the projected task time between when having to touch the table screen and when using camera-based hand tracking so that the user can interact above the table. The object size must change to maintain the theoretical bound on task performance time.

might be more efficient to employ a simple voice command and recognition (e.g., upon selection, user says, "Push"). Ideally, the final choice of the interface should be determined after an extensive usability study comparing different aspects (task performance, preference, fatigue, etc.). As for the primitive tasks such as selection, manipulation, navigation, and system control, many possible interface designs have been proposed and studied extensively including their task analysis (although simple) and taxonomy [Bow05]. We introduce them in the next few sections.

d. Case Study 5: Selection and Manipulation

According to Bowman et al. [Bow05], *selection* is the task of acquiring or identifying a particular object from the entire set of available objects. The task of selection is one of the most important tasks in any interaction because it is needed in virtually any application. Manipulation is also a very common task and usually involves positioning and rotation in 3D space. Note that selection must usually precede manipulation. Thus, the tasks of selection and manipulation are discussed together.

Figure 8.13 shows a classification of various selection techniques by task decomposition [Bow05]. The task of selection mainly involves these sub-tasks: (1) indication of the object to be selected, (2) confirmation of the selection, and (3) providing feedback. Each of these subtasks may be realized

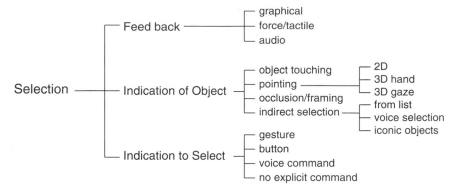

FIGURE 8.13. The selection task decomposed into subtasks [Bow05]. (Reprinted by permission of Pearson Education, Inc., as Pearson Addison-Wesley © 2005.)

by various interfaces. For instance, the indication of the target object may be done by a direct touch, by voice, laser point like picking (also called virtual raycasting) from hand (or by gaze), flashlight/spotlightlike picking (see Figures 8.14 through 8.16), and so on. Selection confirmation may be realized by a discrete event (such as a button press), simple gesture, voice command, passage of time, and so on. The feedback after a selection is made is also important in that the user is immediately notified as to the result of the action. It may be visual (e.g., highlighting the object), aural (e.g., simple beep), or even haptic/tactile.

Figure 8.17 shows a similar task hierarchy for object manipulation [Pou98]. Manipulation is divided into the major tasks of (1) attaching the target object to a control medium for manipulation (which practically amounts to object selection); (2) actual positioning; and/or (3) actual orient-

FIGURE 8.14. Virtual hand selecting an object by collision or direct touch.

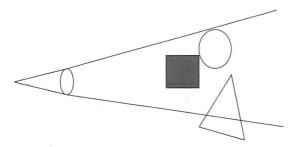

FIGURE 8.15. Spotlight selection metaphor [Lia94]. The closest object among the objects within the cone is selected.

ing; and (4) producing feedback indicating whether the task has been carried out successfully. Similarly, many different interfaces are possible. For instance, the object may be attached to the control medium simply by direct selection with the virtual hand with which the manipulation would be carried out. Note that the medium for selection and manipulation need not be the same, although they usually are as in the previous example. The object may be attached to various types of control media such as the virtual hand, teleoperated cursor, widget, or virtual tool, gaze line (a line connecting the assumed position of the eyes and the target object), and so on.

Once the object is selected and attached to the control medium, the actual positioning and orienting subtasks can be carried out and the fashion in which they are carried out depends on the way the object is selected. For instance, an object selected with a virtual hand and attached to a virtual hand can be manipulated, again by direct hand movement. The mapping between the actual hand movement and the virtual object movement may be

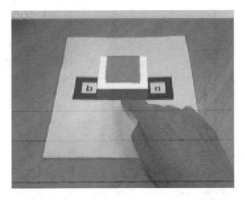

FIGURE 8.16. Occlusion-based selection for augmented reality applications. When a marker is occluded for a predetermined period of time, the corresponding object is selected and rendered in the view. (Courtesy of Gun Lee.)

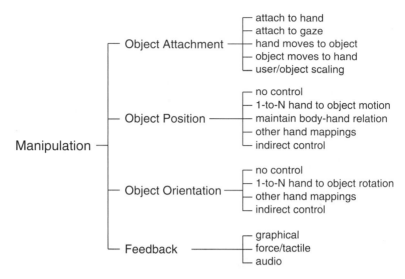

adjusted and controlled. If an object was selected with a virtual ray, then the object can be moved or rotated according to the movement of the hand that controls the direction and orientation of the ray. Manipulating objects from a far distance using a virtual ray tends to be difficult. One way to alleviate this problem is to select the objects far from the user and "bring" them within close range so that the object can be manipulated directly. Then the manipulated object is put back into the original place. However, the task of putting back the object can be nontrivial. The method called the scaled world grab scales down the entire virtual environment around the user's viewpoint to a convenient size so the user can manipulate the object once it is selected [Min97]. This has the same effect of bringing the (far) object to the user for manipulation without the worrying about how to put it back. That is, after manipulation, the world is scaled back to its original size, thereby taking the object back to its intended position and orientation (see Figure 8.18).

Another way to overcome this problem, called the Go-Go/Homer technique, was proposed by Poupyrev et al. [Pou96]. The Go-Go technique combines the intuitiveness of direct selection by virtual hand for objects beyond the user's reach (see Figure 8.19). For objects that are far away, the user can extend the virtual arm or hand (like the Go-Go gadget) to reach the target object, and the rate of the growth is exponential with respect to the distance of the target object (it grows faster as the hand extends and reaches the object). Once the object is selected this way, it can be manipulated as if it were grabbed by the hand. To allow the user to position virtual objects

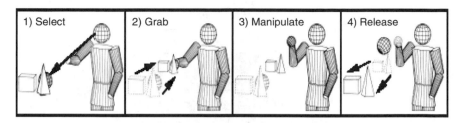

FIGURE 8.18. Scaled world grab. The scene is scaled down and in the process brought into the space reachable by the user. The user manipulates the objects in his personal space and scales it back to normal size [Min97]. (Reprinted with permission from ACM © 2004.)

within a large manipulation range, the technique linearly scales the user reaching distance (or user motion) within the user-centered coordinate system. Although operationally it is similar to a virtual raycast and remote manipulation, and by the mere fact that it "seems" as if the object is actually grabbed by the hand, it preserves the intuitiveness offered by the original direct manipulation with the virtual hand.

In the approach called the World-in-Miniature by Stoakley [Sto95], a 3D mini-map of the entire world is given to the user for selection, manipulation, and even navigation purposes (See Figure 8.20). The mini-map represents the actual virtual world that the user is immersed in, and thus by selecting and manipulating the mini-objects in the 3D mini-replica, actual corresponding objects can be selected and manipulated. As one of the objects in

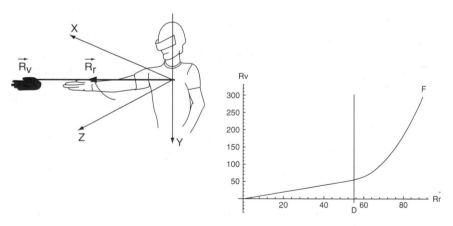

FIGURE 8.19. The Go-Go technique for selection. The function maps the user movement to the extension of the virtual arm [Pou96]. (Reprinted with permission from ACM © 2004.)

FIGURE 8.20. World-in-Miniature [Sto95]. (Reprinted with permission from ACM © 2004.)

the 3D mini-replica includes the user, selecting and manipulating it amounts to navigation (changing the position and orientation of the user).

In order to move and orient an object in 3D space, six degrees of freedom are needed. However, allowing all six degrees of freedom can hamper exact positioning and orienting. Thus, it can be useful to limit the degrees of freedom, or consider only few degrees of freedom at a time using constrained movement or rotation.

e. Case Study 5: Navigation

Navigation, as already mentioned, is also a very commonly required task in any virtual environment. Figure 8.21 shows the major subtasks for navigation and possible interfaces for them. The first subtask is to select the direction or the target to which the user wants to move. Then the second optional task may be to select the amount of the velocity (or even acceleration). The third task (which could be combined with the first task) is the actual command to move toward the selected direction. This command will vary in input conditions, for example, whether a long move requires a repeated application of small moves, or just commands for start and stop, or other more sophisticated control (with acceleration and deceleration control).

For instance, the direction of travel may be determined by the gaze direction, 3D pointing, discrete (e.g., arrow keys) or continuous (e.g., steering wheel) event devices, voice commands, body gestures (e.g., leaning to the right or left), and even through haptic interaction. Note that although gaze-directed travel can be less tiring and efficient, it restricts the users from viewing the environment not in the direction of the movement. The styles

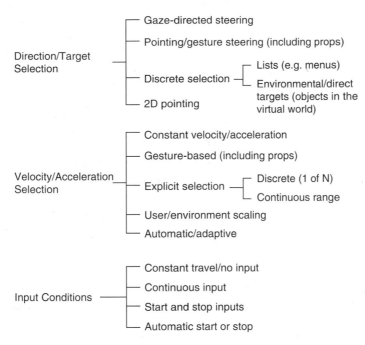

FIGURE 8.21. Navigation task hierarchy and possible interface styles [Bow99]. (Reprinted with permission from MIT Press © 2004.)

of interfaces for these subtasks are often designed after a selected metaphor. Examples include driving a car, flying an airplane, flying a helicopter, walking, navigating a spaceship, and the like. Many metaphors are real-life inspired, but "magical" navigations are certainly possible such as in the World-in-Miniature approach.

The task of navigation can occur in several different contexts, whether it is for an open exploration (just looking around without a specific destination), exploration following a path, searching without a path, training to learn the spatial layout, and so on. Aside from designing the most appropriate interface for the navigation task itself, it can be helpful to use landmarks, signs, and maps to achieve higher task efficiency (e.g., help the user find something faster). Without such aids, virtual navigation often results in users getting lost and becoming disoriented.

f. Case Study 6: Menu Selection and Invocation (System Control) [KimN00]

Another important and commonly required interaction task in any application is system control. System control refers to the way of making a command to the system to perform a particular function that is usually not

3D-related. There may be a sizable number of functions available and often they are organized in a hierarchical manner. A menu system is quite suitable to serve as a means for system control, whether driven by a mouse and keyboard, by voice, or even by 3D interaction. The menu system is also the most familiar 2D computer interface that we know of, and it would be beneficial for computer users to have it extended in the immersive 3D environments. In this section, we analyze some of the ways a menu system can be realized in the context of providing system control for 3D virtual worlds.

In 3D environments, unlike in 2D, we must first carefully consider where to locate the menu system within the world, which in turn, will determine the user's viewing direction to the menu (see Figure 8.22). There are some simple possibilities we might consider.

1. World Fixed (WF). The menu system resides at a fixed location in a "strategic" world location.
2. View Fixed (VF). The menu system is attached at and viewed from a fixed offset from the user (thus it moves with the head-tracked user).

WF allows a relatively comprehensive display of the overall menu structure and menu selection history (because it is located at a strategic location away from where the task is being carried out), whereas with VF, a more compact menu display must be used so as not to block the task area. This is especially true in an immersive environment where head-mounted displays are used, as most HMDs suffer from low resolution and narrow fields of view.

Aside from location, the following are variants of menu display methods (see Figure 8.23).

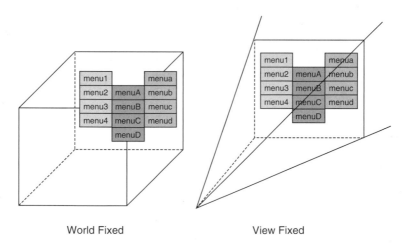

World Fixed   View Fixed

FIGURE 8.22. Menu style by location [KimN00]. (Reprinted with permission from IEEE © 2004.)

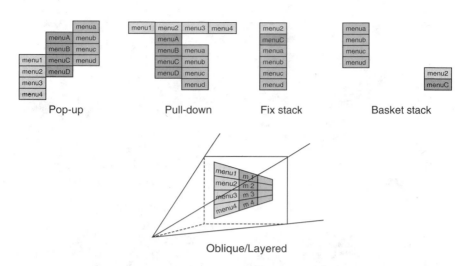

FIGURE 8.23. Variants of VE menu display by items [KimN00]. (Reprinted with permission from IEEE © 2004.)

1. Pull-down (PD). The usual pull-down menu that displays the highest level menu items, and show its branches only during the selection task.
2. Pop-up (PU). The usual pop-up menu that disappears once the selection is made. The menu structure associated with the particular menu selection path is shown only on the user's invocation.
3. Stack Menu. A menu system that persistently displays the selection path either at the top portion of the popup menu (disappears once the selection is done), thus called the Fixed Stack (FS), or at a separate location (e.g., at the corner of the screen), thus called the Basket.
4. Stack (BS). Only the menu options selectable at a given level are shown.
5. Oblique/Layered (OL). This is a flat menu presentation displayed in an oblique fashion, or its structure organized and displayed by layers.

Here, we consider some possible menu designs, which are listed below and illustrated in Figure 8.24.

1. WF-PD: World Fixed, Pull-down
2. WF-PU: World Fixed, Popup
3. VF-FS: View Fixed, Fixed Stack
4. VF-BS: View Fixed, Basket Stack
5. VF-OL: View Fixed, Oblique/Layered

Given the various ways the visual aspect of the menu system can be designed in a virtual environment for system control, the next design issue is to decide upon the way the item is selected and confirmed. Table 8.3 can be drawn classifying various combinations among methods for positioning and making the final confirmation command. For positioning, tracking, gesture,

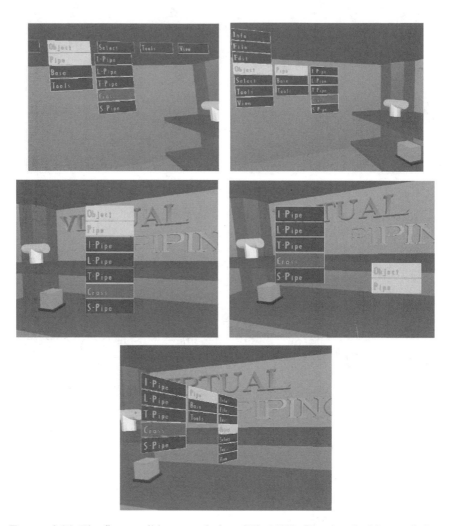

FIGURE 8.24. The five possible menu designs [KimN00]. (Reprinted with permission from IEEE © 2004.)

and voice were considered, and for making a command, button input, gesture, and voice were considered to signal the final yes or no decision. Tracking simply tracks to user-hand or a metaphorical object to designate a desired menu item and is considered a continuous event-driven modality. However, voice and gesture recognition, which allows users to directly speak of the menu item (e.g., start, enter, escape) or make positioning or commands (e.g., next, previous) has a discrete event-driven modality. The "X" marks in the table show the infeasible combinations for the selection task. For instance, tracking and voice combination under the column of zero hand is simply impossible (i.e., one hand used). The enumeration of various ways

TABLE 8.3. Combinations of Input Methods Possible by Modalities (3D Tracking, Gesture, and Voice) and Number of Hands Used.

		Positioning					
		Tracking		Gesture		Voice	
Num of Hands used		1	2	1	2	0	1
Making a command	Button	TB1	TB2	GB1	GB2	X	VB1
	Gesture	TG1	TG2	GG1	GG2	X	VG1
	Voice	TV1	X	GV1	X	VV0	X

[KimN00]. Reprinted with permission from IEEE © 2004.

of designing a menu system and modality choices illustrates the enormity of the design space with 3D UI design.

g. Case Study 7: Whole Body Interaction

Training has been considered as one of the most natural application areas of virtual reality. Here, we describe the interface for a VR-based motion/dance training system called "CloneMotion" [Yan01]. CloneMotion is an excellent example of naturally employing a whole body interface for a more complete VR experience. The usual way of learning dance is to observe the teacher, follow, and correct the motion. An ideal VR-based dance training might require accurate sensing for many of the limbs of the body (e.g., full-body motion capture) and an on- or offline evaluation module. As a full-body motion capture is impractical for an entertainment system, a low-cost marker-based tracker based on infrared cameras was developed for approximately tracking the important body positions (wrists, ankles, and belly) of the trainee wearing five reflective markers at the respective positions (see Figure 8.25).

The evaluation module compares the original motion data to that of the trainees (obtained by the motion tracking module) frame by frame. At pre-designated "key posture" frames, a scoring system provides an indication to the user of how well one followed that particular posture using graphic special effects (e.g., explosion at the coincided body positions, and textual remarks such as "Excellent," "OK," etc.). The frame-by-frame scores are tabulated, summed with appropriate weights, and averaged for a final score.

Thus, the user is to follow a character dancing with pre-captured motion data, and the tracked motion data of the user is compared to the original for evaluation. In order to help the user follow the dancing character better and be able to correct himself in real-time (rather than after the dance sequence is over), a concept of a sliding ghost was used that shows the discrete freeze-frames of the next imminent postures along with the continuous dance motion. As the trainee tries to follow the character on the screen, one is given a feel for how well one is following with the evaluations and corre-sponding special effects at the key posture frames, and a final score at the

FIGURE 8.25. A user trying to follow the dancing character. The dancing character is shown with successive freeze-frames of the postures so that the user can see and expect what kind of motion to follow moment by moment.

end. The interface development process for CloneMotion well illustrates how the trade-off among cost, usability, whole body experience, and evaluation accuracy is made.

h. Case Study 8: Tangible Interface for Product Evaluation

Recently, "immersive" virtual reality systems have been proposed as a more effective platform for effective analysis of an evolving design because of, among other things, the natural style of interaction they offer when examining the product, such as the use of direct and proprioceptive interaction, head-tracking and first-person viewpoint, and multimodality, compared to a desktop graphic rendering.

It goes without saying that the foremost requirement of any effective analysis virtual system would be to provide sufficient visual realism, especially for the product itself (vs. the scene that is included). Another related requirement is to have the virtual product match the real one in terms of the size. This is especially important for small-sized products such as the mobile phone. The third probable requirement for effective evaluation of small-sized handheld products is direct interaction. A related requirement to direct interaction is the provision of tactile/haptic modality in addition to the usual and relatively easy to provide visual and aural interaction.

The popular ground-based systems, such as the Phantom[2] manipulators, can only simulate forces and texture surfaces at point contact. The exoskeleton glove device such as the CyberGrasp[3] system is very expensive and

---

[2] Phantom is a registered trademark of Sensable Technologies Inc.
[3] CyberGrasp is a registered trademark of Immersion Corporation.

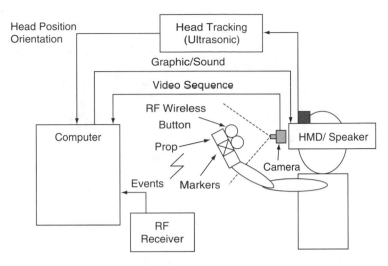

FIGURE 8.26. To track the prop and segment the image of the hand/fingers holding the prop. In order to track the prop using computer vision, 10 yellow markers are put on the blue-colored rectangular prop [LeeSY04]. (Reprinted with permission from IEEE © 2004.)

inconvenient to use. An alternative approach is to use a *prop*. A prop is an interaction device that represents the virtual object (to be interacted with), and whose shape and/or appearance matches that of the actual physical object. Props can be spatially registered with virtual objects providing inexpensive physical feedback to the user.

Props allow us to add inexpensive physical and tactile feedback, significantly increasing presence for immersive environments and establishing a common frame of reference between the device and desktop 3D user interfaces. The introduction of tactile augmentation allows us to explicitly control the realism of virtual environments. The disadvantages of props are that each prop only represents one object. In light of this, designing a prop (or interaction device) that looks exactly like the actual phone (to be tested) is not only restrictive in its applicability, but also defeats the very purpose of using virtual products (that is, we would like to eliminate the need of building physical mockups or prototypes as much as possible). Instead it would be possible to design a "reconfigurable" prop that represents a family of products. For instance, as for mobile phones, the designed prop is just a flat rectangular box (as most mobile phones are roughly rectangular) with push-button switches on it. Figure 8.27 shows a prop with two button switches for a few simple functions. The tracked prop appears in the virtual space as various mobile phones.

The use of a "representative" prop (i.e., one that only represents the actual object, but not the actual object) necessitates the use of a head-mounted

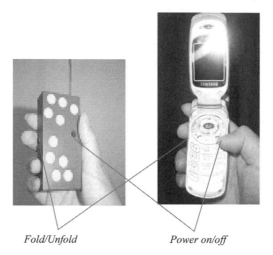

Fold/Unfold   *Power on/off*

FIGURE 8.27. The rectangular prop representing the mobile phone. The prop has 10 yellow markers for vision-based registration purpose and two wireless switches for interaction [LeeSY04]. (Reprinted with permission from IEEE © 2004.)

display (rather than a desktop or projection display) so that the virtual product (or mobile phone) can be rendered at the position of prop in the virtual space without distraction. This is more inconvenient for the user and makes the overall system more expensive.

A problem with using the HMD is that, in the virtual space, the users have to interact with the target product using virtual hands, and this is expected to drop the feeling of directness and realism. A VR interface is designed that can show the real hands, segmented out from the real scene captured by the camera, and drawn by using a computer-vision technique (see Figures 8.26 to 8.28).

i. Case Study 9: Alphanumeric Input

Even in virtual environments, there are occasions when alphanumeric input is required. The most typical and simplest method of enabling alphanumeric input in a VR setting is through the virtual terminal using a virtual keyboard. A virtual terminal refers to a virtual object, functioning as computer terminals do in the real world. Virtual terminals may have similar appearances to real-world terminals (i.e., having a display device, keyboard, mouse, and other items). Users may interact with virtual terminals in the same way in which they use them for programming in the real world. It could be represented with just a single flat virtual panel showing texts and 2D diagrams. Users may interact with it by handwriting, gestures, voice recognition, or any other methods to give input to the virtual terminal. Figure 8.29 shows the virtual keyboard registered with the real hand, and a note-taking application overlaid on the virtual environment.

FIGURE 8.28. What is seen by the user through the HMD, while holding the prop to interact with the virtual mobile phone. Note the seam between the image-captured hand and the virtual cell phone [LeeSY04]. (Reprinted with permission from IEEE © 2004.)

Virtual keyboards are often used for information kiosks, PDAs with touchscreens, and even when the physical keyboard is present to expand the range of input characters. For VR systems, the approach to alphanumeric input can be categorized by whether they are mobile and wearable and whether they provide tactility and/or haptics. The mobile/wearable keyboards are compact and reduced in size (for wearability), thus they usually have different key layouts from conventional keyboards. For instance, Matias' Halfkeyboard [Mat04] is a wearable keyboard worn on the forearm with only 22 keys sized at about $146 \times 80 \times 18$ mm and 125 g. The Visual Panel [Zha01] overlays the virtual key layout on a tracked tablet, held by one hand, on which users can use fingers from the other hand to select letters in the virtual space. The Finger Joint Gesture Wearable Keypad [Gol99] uses 12 button switches (laid out as the telephone keypad) attached on the finger joints and the typing is performed by pressing on them with the

FIGURE 8.29. The virtual keyboard registered with the real hand in a virtual environment.

thumb using the Thumbcode. Although these devices provide the tactility and/or haptics (which enhances typing performance as indicated earlier), they are difficult to use (e.g., device wearing) or learn (e.g., type with one hand only), and not appropriate for a large amount of text input.

The Fingering and Acceleration Glove [Fuk97] and Vtype [Eva] are special devices for tracking the movements of the user's fingers. The fingers are tracked and tested for collision with the virtual keyboard. These approaches use the conventional keyboard layout (that users are most familiar with), however, they suffer from device usability and lack of haptics/tactility. The importance of leveraging the tactility and conventional typing skill for the successful deployment of an alphanumeric input method is well illustrated in the approach by VKB [VKB04] who recently unveiled the Projection keyboard (even though not designed for a VR setting). The Projection keyboard uses an optical device to project a "conventional" keyboard layout on any flat surface and a separate vision-based module track and interprets the finger "tapping" movements to enable near-natural typing.

Another natural method for alphanumeric input is to use voice/speech recognition, or combine it with some of the methods described above. The pioneering work of the "Put that there" system by Bolt et al. demonstrated the usefulness of such multimodal interaction [Bol80]. However, voice recognition is still not practical enough for something other than recognition of a small set of keywords.

Summary

Designing an easy to use, natural, and efficient interface is a difficult problem. In most cases, all the design goals cannot be met. Interface design must be preceded with a task analysis producing an interaction model. Interfaces are proposed and tried based on the interaction model. Employing a multimodal interface is an effective way to produce a natural (with high user-felt presence) and at the same time efficient interface. However, it is vital to carefully maintain the multimodal consistency.

Pondering Points

- Imagine an environment where the user must select various objects far or close. Is it better to employ one way of selecting the object far or close, or employ two different modes, one for selecting a close object (e.g., direct touch) and one for the far (e.g., virtual ray)? Explain your answer.
- Can a person, in general, listen to music and solve a math problem at the same time? How about reading a book while listening to music? What does this tell us about applying multimodality in interaction design?

Chapter 9
Simulation I: Collision Detection

So far we have covered several important topics for virtual reality. We first covered the systematic process for designing the basic structure of a virtual reality system. Then, we considered the need and problem of designing 3D multimodal interaction for naturalness, efficiency, and presence. It goes without saying that using realistic-looking geometric models and objects contributes positively to increasing the sense of presence, and the same goes for dynamics and behaviors of objects. Objects exhibit many different behaviors, and we cannot possibly cover all of them as to how to formulate and implement them. However, we discuss three important classes of object simulation. They are collision detection, physical-based motion, and handling collision response (which uses the former two).

Handling Collision

There are largely three things to consider in handling collision: detection of collision, determining the location of collision (let's call this collision determination for the lack of better shorthand), and generating a response to a collision. The accuracy and methods as to finding the location of the collision on the respective objects depends on what kind of scheme is used to detect the collision in the first place (e.g., it may be possible to merely detect the incident of collision (fast), but not be able to determine the exact location of collision). Once we know there was a collision, and the locations and directions of the collision on the involved objects are known, a response must be simulated. The way the responses are calculated and simulated can be based on a complex physical model or on a simple heuristic formula. We defer the explanation of the response computation in later part of chapter 10 after introducing the simulation of physics-based motion. In this chapter, we first look at different ways to detect collision, and in some cases, determine collision.

As we already know, geometric models used in 3D graphics or VR systems are made of polygons. The most naïve way, thus, to detect and determine

The Simulation Loop

1. Read any external input.

2. Compute simulation and update the objects and scene graph.

2.1 Check for any collision and generate response.

3. Update thecamera position/orientation.

4. Redraw thescene.

5. Go back to 1.

FIGURE 9.1. The overall computation model for VR program.

collision, is to perform a pairwise "piercing" test between all the polygons in the scene (see Figure 9.2). In the simpler case, the polygons might be all triangles. If there are n moving objects and m nonmoving static objects in the scene, we are looking at $(n * m + {_n}C_2)$ object combinations (that can possibly be in collision), and for each object combination, with objects with maximum k polygons, there are k^2 polygon pairs to check for collision (or piercing each other). In total, there are $(n^*m + {_n}C_2) * k^2$ polygon piercing tests. The collision testing and response generation is to be done at every tick in the simulation loop (or at the minimum refresh rate of 15 Hz) upon small amounts updated in the scene (see Figure 9.1). This is, even for a moderately populated virtual scene, computationally heavy to handle in real-time (in a fraction of the one simulation tick). Also note that for an object that moves so fast it passes through another object during one simulation tick, the collision would not be detected. Still, the polygon-level piercing test is a good enough approximation of the location of the collision (i.e., we only know which triangles pierce each other, but not exactly where within the triangle; see Figure 9.2). To further find the exact collision locations "on" the respective polygon surfaces, further calculations would be required.

Thus, the challenge is to reduce the amount of computation as much as possible yet provide the appropriate and right amount of information about the collisions for a given application. One way to accomplish this is to filter out the unreasonable pairwise (objects and/or polygons) testing possibilities (reduce the numbers in the first part of complexity equation, n and m). This requires knowledge or assumptions about the environment, for instance, knowing that certain objects will never collide with each other, or knowing in advance the region of interest of the user (i.e., do not care about correct collision simulation in other parts of the scene). The other way is to reduce the number of polygons to test for by reducing the numbers in the second part of the complexity equation k^2 by using bounding volumes. A bounding volume of an object is a simplified geometric object representing (and containing) the original with much fewer polygons. Naturally, when only bounding volumes are used, the exact location of the collision cannot be

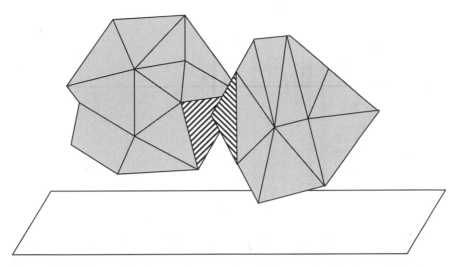

FIGURE 9.2. Polygon piercing test between two objects made of polygons/triangles.

determined. The overall process can further be made efficient by using a hierarchical object structure. We can intelligently search and test for parts of the two objects most likely to collide first. This reduces the overall average computational complexity dramatically.

As we explain the different approaches to collision detection and determination, we go over the necessary basic geometric calculation required to realize these approaches.

Collision Detection with Line Segment(s)

In certain cases, for practical purposes, it suffices to approximate an object with short line segment(s). For instance, a car may be, for all practical purposes, augmented with two short line segments emanating from the bottom of its wheels in the direction perpendicular to the horizontal plane of the body (see Figure 9.3). The collision checking between these segments and the terrain polygons can be used to make sure and render the car right above the ground (and prevent it from hovering over or penetrating underneath an irregularly shaped terrain).

Line segments can be used on the virtual hands or fingers for object selection. The virtual hand might look like a hand with its index finger pointed out, where a "line" of contact is defined (usually, only one sensor is used to track some representative position of the hand such as the index fingertip). Here we can put a virtual line segment on (or along) the index finger and test collision between the segment and the target object. The objects would be selected or object interaction can be initiated by

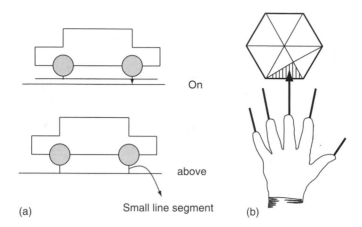

FIGURE 9.3. Collision detection with objects approximated with line segments: (a) car on a terrain; (b) virtual hand.

approximately detecting the collision between the hand (or actually the line) and the target object.

Line Segment (Ray) Versus Triangle [Moo88]

Suppose that, in the above example, we want to check if the line segments from the car are in collision with the subset of polygons from the terrain. Further suppose the polygons are all triangles. The lowest-level test procedure we need is to check if the line segment penetrates a triangle, or more precisely, to compute the distance of the point toward the triangle (i.e. penetration distance) in the direction of the ray. A point on a triangle can be represented by the following formula, where $v0$, $v1$, $v2$ are the three points of the triangle and u, v are the barycentric[1] coordinates of the point (with respect to the given triangle).

$$A \text{ point on triangle} = (1 - u - v) * v0 + u * v1 + v * v2$$

A line segment (or interchangeably a ray) is represented by an equation: $o + td$, where o is the origin of the ray, t is a real number, and d is the unit

---

[1] Barycentric coordinates are coordinates formed by expressing a point in $(n-1)$-dimensional space with respect to n designated points that forms the $(n-1)$ dimensional space. For instance, two designated points define a line (one-dimensional space) and by a weighted sum of these two designated points, a point on the line can be specified, and similarly for three designated points on two-dimensional triangle, and four points on a three-dimensional tetrahedron. The weights must sum to one to represent a point within the respective space (line, triangle, tetrahedron, etc.).

direction vector of the line. The range of t defines the bounds of the line segment ($t \geq 0$, and less than length of the segment). We equate the two equations (point on triangle and the ray).

$$o + t * d = (1 - u - v) * v0 + u * v1 + v * v2$$

After rearranging the terms, we get a set of linear equations and can solve for the values u, v, and t. By formulation, t must be greater than 0, and $u + v$ is less than or equal to 1 to be specifying a point within (on) the triangle (otherwise, the ray does not cross the interior of the triangle). Once t is known, the distance between the origin of the ray and the point on the triangle where the ray would hit can be computed easily and a threshold value can be used to invoke a collision event (see Figure 9.4).

Ray Versus Polygon [Mol02]

Suppose the polygons were not all triangles. Then, we need a more general formulation. Given a ray and a polygon, we first compute if the ray passes through the infinite plane formed by the polygon (infinite plane that coincides with the polygon surface). Let's denote n_p as the normal of the infinite plane (this can be computed from the vertices of the polygon). Then, the plane equation can be set up as

$$n_p \cdot x = D$$

where x is a point on the plane and D is the perpendicular distance from the origin to the plane (see Figure 9.5). We substitute the line equation into x and solve for a valid t (t that is within the range):

$$n_p \cdot (o + t * d) = D$$

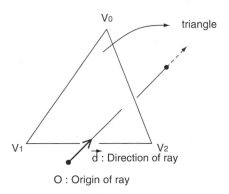

FIGURE 9.4. A ray and a triangle.

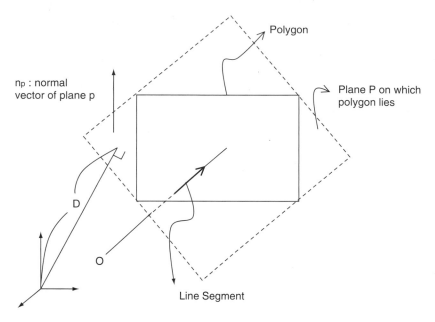

FIGURE 9.5. A ray and a polygon.

where o is the origin of the ray and d is the unit direction vector of the ray. If $|n_p \cdot d|$ is less than a pre-set threshold (near zero), then the ray is (or nearly is) parallel to the polygon and does not cross the polygon. Otherwise, we need to find the value of t and use t to find the point p (the point the ray would hit on the infinite plane), and see if p lies within the polygon.

In order to do this, we project all the vertices onto the two-dimensional plane (xy or yz plane, whichever maximizes the area) by simply dropping the z- or x-coordinate value. To determine if p is within the polygon, we apply the Jordan curve theorem that states, informally, that when we shoot a ray from p to the positive x-direction and if we count the number of crossings across the lines formed by the polygon and it comes out to be an odd number, that means the point lies within the polygon (see Figure 9.6).

To apply the Jordan curve theorem, we translate the point p into a new coordinate system where p serves as the origin. Then, we perform a line versus ray (originating from p and going in the positive x-direction) intersection test for each edge of the polygon (note that vertices are likewise translated accordingly). The algorithm can be made simpler by ruling out some simple cases, as shown in Figure 9.7.

An intersection test between an infinite ray and an edge (last part of algorithm) can be done simply by equating the two line equations.

$$o1 + s * d1 = o2 + t * d2$$

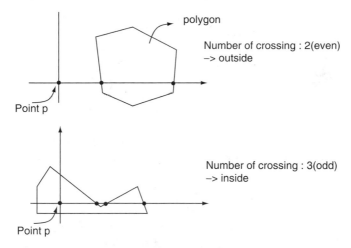

FIGURE 9.6. The Jordan curve theorem for checking insideness.

One vertex on the segment is $o1$, and the other is $o1 + s^*d1$ with a known s. $d2$ is in the $+x$-direction and $o2$ is the origin where p has translated. t, greater than zero, can be found easily.

To summarize, the ray versus triangle (or polygon test) would have to be applied in a pairwise fashion to all the potentially intersecting pairs. This is still a lot of computation even though slightly less than pairwise polygon–polygon testing. Reducing one object down to a couple of rays is an efficient

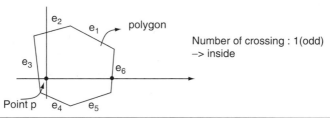

```
c = 0      /* c is the number of crossing */
For each edge,
    /* check the y coordinates of vertices */
    If same sign, Then cannot cross      /* edges e1, e2, e4, e5 in the figure*/
    Else
    /* check the x coordinates of vertices */
    If both positive Then c = c+ 1      /* edge e6 in the figure */
    Else if both negative Then cannot cross      /* edge e3 in the figure */
        Else      /* x coordinates differ in sign */
        Compute infinite ray ( x axis) vs. edge intersection and update c value
```

FIGURE 9.7. A fast algorithm for implementing the Jordan curve theorem.

method to go, however, another avenue for improvement would be to reduce the set of potentially intersecting pairs. Although possible, simplifying both objects in the potentially intersecting pairs to rays is rare. Rather, there usually is a key active object reduced as a ray (such as the moving finger in the object selection example) for which intersection with other objects (or its bounding volume) is tested.

Polygonal Objects Versus Polygonal Objects (Collision Detection Only) [Can86]

It is not possible to simplify an object as a ray all the time, for various reasons, for instance, for a more accurate collision detection and determination (and thus to produce a more realistic response also). Given two potentially moving convex polygonal models A and B, Canny et al. [Can86] observed there can be mainly these cases of collision-related events that can occur between A and B (also see Figure 9.8).

1. Some vertices of B are penetrating faces of A.
2. Some vertices of A are penetrating faces of B.
3. The edges of A and B meet at a point.

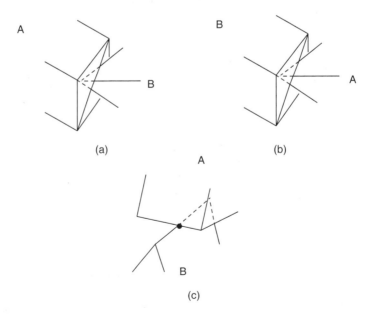

FIGURE 9.8. Three major cases of collision events between two convex polygonal objects. (Adapted from [Can86] with permission from IEEE © 2004.)

For Cases 1 and 2, we need to check if any vertices of B (or A) are penetrating the faces of A (or B). If the purpose is just to check for the penetration, the simple piercing test can be used as follows. Given a vertex, we can decide if the vertex v is on one side (inside) or on the other (outside) by the following test.

$$n_p \cdot v = d \ (n_p \text{ is the normal vector of polygon})$$

If $d = 0$, then v is on the surface of the polygon

If $d < 0$, then v is inside the surface of the polygon

(interior of the polygonal model)

If $d > 0$, then v is outside the surface of the polygon

(exterior of the polygonal model)

The piercing test can be applied for one vertex against all polygons of the other object, and if any one vertex is on the other side of all polygons of the other object, then the vertex has penetrated the other object and the collision is detected.

If the test does not find that the objects are either in Case 1 or 2, then the final test for the third case is checked by an equation:

$$(p_a - p_b) \cdot (e_a \times e_b)$$

where e_a is the edge of A, e_b is the edge of B, and p_a and p_b are any positions on e_a and e_b. The equation checks that the edges e_a and e_b are coplanar (thus meet at a point).

Although the above three cases cover most of the relative spatial configuration of two objects at a given instant of time, note that the list is not complete. For instance, the rare cases illustrated in Figure 9.9 is not detected by the three cases above.

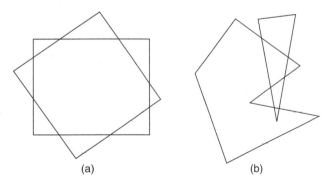

(a)   (b)

FIGURE 9.9. Interfering configurations not covered by the three conditions in Figure 9.8 (illustrated in 2D for simplicity): (a) none of the vertices of A or B penetrates another, yet they are in collision; (b) the condition of collision put forth by Canny does not work for concave objects.

Triangularized Objects Versus Triangularized Objects: The Interval Overlap Method [Mol02]

For two "triangularized" objects, we can certainly apply the above polygonal model versus polygonal model approach. Or, we can test if triangles of two objects are piercing each other pair by pair, instead of Canny's method that pairs polygons/triangles and vertices, testing if any vertex of one triangularized polyhedron is on the other side of all the other "closed" triangularized polyhedra (we later compare the algorithmic complexities between the two methods). Now, we must devise a simple method of testing (or determining) collision between two triangles (triangle vs. triangle piercing test). Suppose that triangle $t1$ is on infinite plane π_1, and t2 on π_2 (see Figure 9.10).

$$\pi_1: \quad n1 \cdot x + d1 = 0$$
$$\pi_2: \quad n2 \cdot x + d2 = 0$$

where $n1$, $n2$ are obtained easily from vertices of $t1$ and $t2$.

We try to compute the signed distance from vertices of $t1$ to π_2. Suppose that vertices of $t1$ are denoted as u_i (where $i = 1, 1, 2$).

$$n2 \cdot u_i + d2 = d_{ui} \qquad (i = 0, 1, 2)$$

Thus, d_{ui} denotes the signed distance from each vertex of $t1$ to π_2. (Note that this is the same as Canny's "other side test" (or vertex piercing) using the dot product.) If all three signed distances are not equal to zero and have the same signs, then there is no overlap (the triangle lies on the other side of the other). If they are all zero, then the triangle lies on the same plane, and their overlap can be tested using the segment versus segment test and point containment test (see previous sections). So far, this is mostly equivalent to Canny's

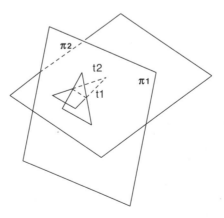

FIGURE 9.10. Testing for overlap of two triangles on the same plane.

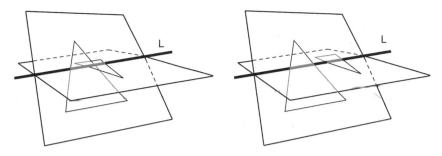

FIGURE 9.11. Two triangles may be in collision or not. Two infinite planes meet at the line L [Mol02]. (Reprinted with permission from A. K. Peters © 2004.)

method. When the signs are different among the three signed distances, the triangles may be piercing or may not be (see Figure 9.11).

If the signs are different among the three signed distances, then π_1 and π_2 intersect at a line (see Figure 9.11). Let's call that line $l = o + t * d$ where d is the direction vector easily obtained by $n1 \times n2$. We compute the portion of each triangle that overlaps on this line, and carry out an interval test to see if those portions overlap. If these portions do overlap, then the two triangles pierce through each other. The portion of one triangle that overlaps on the line l is illustrated in Figure 9.12 as a segment between $t1$ and $t2$. In order to obtain the values $t1$ and $t2$, we use the Similar Triangle theorem and compare the distance d_{u0} and d_{u1} to $\overline{p_{u0}t1}$ and $\overline{t1p_{u1}}$. And, p_{u0} is the point u_0 projected on the line l, and so similarly is p_{u1}. Also, p_{u0} is obtained by a simple dot product between d and $(u_0 - 0)$, and similarly for p_{u1}. The similar triangle holds between triangle $\Delta u_0 bk_0$ and $\Delta u_1 bk_1$, thus the following equation holds.

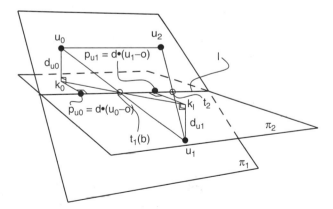

FIGURE 9.12. Computing the interval the triangle overlaps on line l (the geometric situation) [Mol02]. (Reprinted with permission from A. K. Peters © 2004.)

$$(p_{u1} - t1):(t1 - p_{u0}) = d_{u1}:-d_{u0}$$
$$t1 \ d_{u1} - p_{u0} \ d_{u1} - d_{u0} \ t1 = -p_{u1} \ d_{u0}$$
$$t1 = (p_{u0} \ d_{u1} - p_{u1} \ d_{u0})/(d_{u1} - d_{u0})$$

We can get $t2$ in a similar way, and get the other ts for the other triangle (let's call them $t3$ and $t4$). If there is an overlap segment formed by $t1$ and $t2$, and by $t3$ and $t4$, the two triangles overlap.

An exact comparison of this method to that of Canny is difficult, because of the different assumptions made. In Canny's method, a simple dot product test is carried out for all vertices of A against all polygons of B to test for the first case, until any vertex of B that is contained in A is found. Suppose a polyhedron is composed of k polygons, m vertices, and n edges. On the average, the total pairwise tests amount to two $(k * m)/2$ tests (for Case 1 and 2) plus n (for Case 3); thus, $O(k * m + n)$. As for the one-by-one triangle piercing test, $O(k * k)$ comparisons have to be made on the average (if objects are made of k triangles). For low-count polyhedra, the one-by-one triangle piercing tests can be carried out faster than Canny's method plus it does the collision determination. Such a situation can arise if we compare two hierarchically organized bounding volumes where the low-level primitive (triangle piercing) test was done between two very low-count polygonal entities. Note that the collision determination for two polygons would involve much more computation (not derived in this book).

Polygonal Objects Versus Polygonal Objects II [Moo88]

A slightly different method of polygon versus polygon was proposed by Moore and Wilhelm [Moo88] that tests if the edges of one polyhedron pierce through the faces of the other. Given polyhedra P and Q, we check if edge $v_i v_j$ of Q intersects with infinite planes that contain the faces of P. If the perpendicular distances from v_i and v_j to the infinite plane change sign, then the edge pierces through the infinite plane, and that point along the edge can be computed as follows.

u_k: vertex of the polygon p (which would be on the infinite plane)

$d_i = (v_i - u_k) \cdot n_k$ (plane equation with respect to v_i)

$d_j = (v_j - u_k) \cdot n_k$ (plane equation with respect to v_j)

Point on line: $x = v_j + t(v_i - v_j)$

$t = |d_i|/(|d_i| + |d_j|)$

Thus, according to the above formulation, we would obtain a series of ts for one edge against the number of infinite planes. Any values beyond 0 and 1 should be discarded, and the mid-point of the intersections (represented by the ts) is checked for insideness (using the dot product; see Figure 9.13).

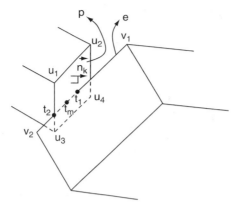

FIGURE 9.13. An edge piercing through a polyhedron.

Voronoi Region Method [Lin95]

A method called the Voronoi region method was proposed by [Lin95]. It has been implemented as a public domain package called the V-Clip collision detection/determination (it has been evolved and optimized over the years since it was first available in 1994). This is known to be one of the fastest methods (almost constant time on the average) of collision detection/determination, but because of the mathematical complexity of the algorithm, we only sketch the principle of how it works, "the closest pair of features." In this method, the concept of a Voronoi region of a feature is used. A feature of a polyhedron refers to the vertex, edge, and face of the polyhedron. A Voronoi region of a given feature refers to the set of points that are closer to the feature than any other feature of the polyhedron. In Figure 9.14, for instance, the space formed by the infinite planes around the edge e of the cuboid object constitutes the Voronoi region for feature e. The Voronoi region for the vertex v of the pyramidal object is also illustrated in the figure. There is a mathematical theorem that states that if the Voronoi regions of two features of two objects overlap, then they must be the closest features between the two objects. Thus, in Figure 9.14, the edge e of the cuboid and the vertex v of the pyramid must be the closest features between the two. Once this is known, the interference between the two objects is a matter of checking the "distance" between the two closest features.

   Thus, the algorithm must first start searching for the closest pair of features between two polyhedra, and at the worst case, this involves a full pairwise test among the features and checking for the overlappings of their Voronoi regions. But usually heuristics can be used to make good guesses and they can be found quite fast. Once a closest feature is found, assuming that the objects move relatively by small increment with respect to the simulation tick and with respect to each other, it can be assumed that the

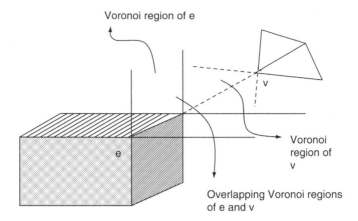

Voronoi region of e

v

Voronoi region of v

Overlapping Voronoi regions of e and v

"Edge e and vertex v are closest feature"

FIGURE 9.14. Overlapping Voronoi regions of two polyhedra.

closest features will not change abruptly. In the case where the closest feature pair is no longer valid, the new closest feature pair should involve features in the close neighborhood, and thus can be found very fast (see Figure 9.15).

Bounding Volumes

A bounding volume (BV) of an object is another object that completely encloses the given object. In the context of collision detection and determination, bounding volumes are usually simple geometric solids, such as rectangular boxes and spheres, that would have much fewer polygons than the object they represent. Thus bounding volumes approximate the shape (or spatial occupation) of a given object so that the needed number of low-level

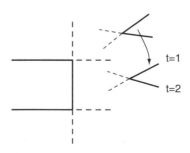

t=1

t=2

FIGURE 9.15. Changing closest feature pair as the objects move.

primitive tests (e.g., polygon vs. polygon, triangle vs. triangle, etc.) is reduced (see Figure 9.16).

This might work for many applications where inexact collision detection suffices. However, for more intricate manipulation of objects and motion representation, this would be an overapproximation. A better, yet not so computationally burdening, method would be to organize the object as a hierarchy of bounding volumes (see Figure 9.17). With hierarchically organized bounding volumes, two objects can be checked for intersection in a recursive manner, either to reject the possibility of the interference quickly or to zoom down quickly to a local portion of the respective objects and then

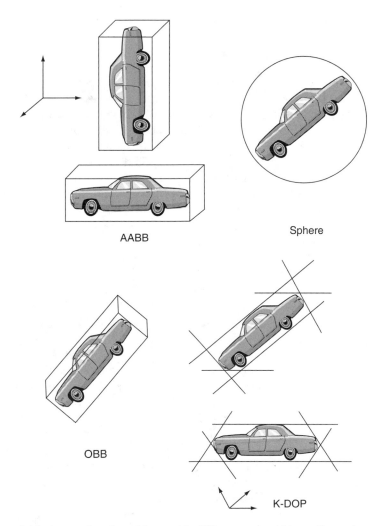

FIGURE 9.16. Approximating objects with different styles of bounding volumes.

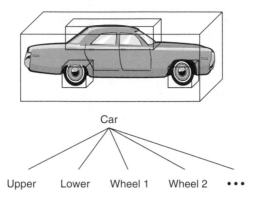

FIGURE 9.17. Approximating objects with bounding volume hierarchy.

test for exact collision determination between the respective regions of interests.

For instance, given two objects A and B, which are represented by a hierarchy of bounding volumes, we first check if the topmost bounding volume intersects (let's call this A_{bv0} and B_{bv0}). If these bounding volumes do not intersect, then there is no way the objects they represent can interfere with another by the definition of bounding volumes (BVs always completely contain the objects). If the volumes intersect each other, there is a possibility that the objects may intersect, and we go down the hierarchy for further checks. We check interference between the BV of one of the objects (for instance, A_{bv0}) against the children BVs (B_{bv1i}, $i = 1, 2, \ldots, n$) of the BV of the other object (B_{bv0}). One of these n children of B (i.e. $B_{bv11} \sim B_{bv1n}$) must intersect with the topmost BV of the object A (A_{bv0}). This way, the part of B that might intersect with A is identified (let's call it B_{bv1k}, where k is between 1 and n). This child BV of the object B (B_{bv1k}) can be tested for the part of A (one of the children BVs of object A, A_{bv1i}) in collision with object B. This is done by checking for interference between the child BV of object B (i.e., B_{bv1k}) and children BVs of A (i.e., A_{bv1i}, $i = 1, 2, \ldots, n$). This process continues either until there is no interference found among the child BVs, or until the tree exhausts its leaf nodes. The leaf node of the object represents part of the object that might be in collision, but cannot be decomposed to any further subbounding volumes. Thus, if two leaf nodes are interfering with each other, one final test remains: applying the interference test among the primitives (such as triangles or polygons) contained in each of the leaf node bounding volumes. The process is illustrated in Figure 9.18. We can readily see that between two objects with k polygons, the computational complexity comes down from $O(k * k)$ (pairwise test) to $O (\log k + 1 * 1)$, where 1 is the number of polygons contained in a leaf node, a very low number, much less than k).

Object Collide (A, B)

  If (not bv-overlap(Abv, Bbv) return false

  Else if (isLeaf(A))

    If (isLeaf(B))

      For each triangle pair between contained in A and B

        If (pierce(Ta, Tb) return true

        return false /* if no triangles pierce */

    Else /* B is not a le */

      For each child Cb of B

        ObjectCollide (A. Cb)

  Else /* A is not a leaf */)

    For each child Ca of A

      ObjectCollide (Ca, B)

  return false

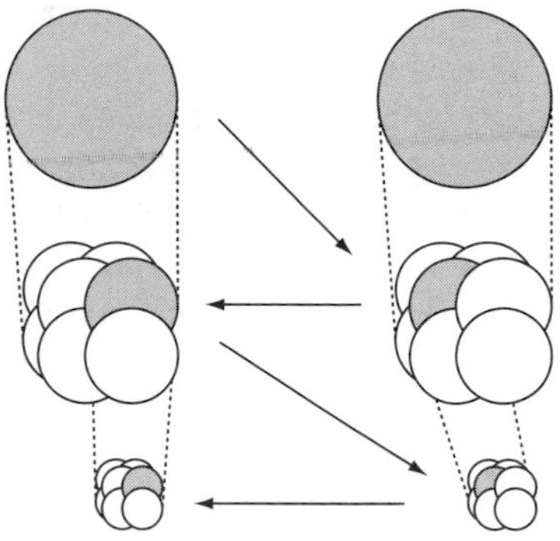

FIGURE 9.18. The recursive algorithm for collision detection/determination with hierarchy of bounding volumes. (Adapted from [Pal95].)

With this basic formulation, we now look at the three remaining issues in implementing a collision detection/determination procedure based on hierarchical bounding volumes. The first issue is how to build various types of bounding volumes for a given object, the second, how to construct the hierarchy of bounding volumes for a given object, and finally, how to test interference among the bounding volumes (before reaching the leaf node, or *overlap* (A_{bv}, B_{bv}) in Figure 9.18).

Building a Bounding Volume

There are many types of bounding volumes. The popular ones are the axis-aligned bounding box (AABB), spheres, oriented bounding box (OBB), and K-DOPs. AABBs are boxes whose faces have normals that coincide with the standard basis (e.g., world coordinate axis). OBBs are boxes whose faces have normals that are pairwise orthogonal (but oriented properly to give a tight fitting), and K-DOPs are geometric entities made of a $K/2$ set of slab pairs (e.g., parallel plates with pre-fixed directions; see Figure 9.16).

AABBs can be constructed easily by identifying the extreme values (minimum and maximum) in the respective directions of the basis vectors, x_{max}, x_{min}, y_{min}, y_{max}, z_{min}, and z_{max}, and building the box with eight vertices. AABBs are simple and can be made quickly on the fly (whenever the object changes its orientation, or in the worst case, at every simulation tick), but because the orientation of the box is fixed, it may not be very tight fitting. This can cause inexactness (if only one bounding box was used) or waste of computation time (if a hierarchical AABB was used) in the collision detection/determination procedure. As shown later, checking for collision among two AABBs is also quite simple and fast.

Spheres also present a similar case. A bounding sphere can be defined with radius value such that the sphere encloses the AABB of the object. Finding the appropriate[2] center/radius takes a bit more calculation than just computing for an AABB. However, checking for two spheres in collision is very simple (measure the distance between two centers of spheres), and spheres do not need to be reconstructed as objects change their orientation. Spheres are in general even less tight fitting than AABBs, and thus introduce further inexactness or waste of computation.

The normals (or orientations) of the faces of the OBBs are determined by the shape of the object in order to find a tight-fitting box around the object. Thus, it is more difficult and time consuming to construct it, however, once constructed, it is not necessary to build it again (whenever the object moves or rotates, the OBBs follow). Because it has a tighter fit, it causes less inexactness (if only one OBB was used) or less waste in computation time (if a hierarchy of OBB was used) in the collision detection/determination procedure. However, checking for collision among two OBBs is a bit more time consuming than that of AABBs.

To construct an OBB of a given object, we must find three local orthogonal axes that constitute the orientations of the faces of the OBB, and reasonably tight-fit the object (see Figure 9.19). A good candidate is the eigenvectors of the covariance matrix of the vertices of the object. Computing for the covariance matrix yields the direction along which x-, y-, and z-coordinates most often tend to vary together (i.e., the direction along which

---

[2] The center might be computed as the average of the vertices of the object, and the radius may be set by finding the sphere that just encloses the AABB.

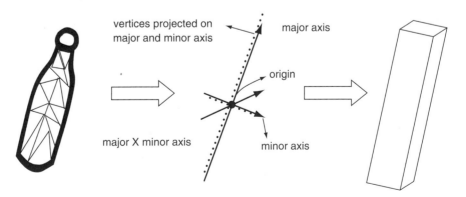

FIGURE 9.19. Constructing an OBB.

x, y, z are most correlated). At the same time it reveals the direction along which axes are least correlated (which is perpendicular to the first). These directions represent the directions of the most and least elongation of the object [Got96]. To reduce the unnecessary influence of concave vertices (if the object was concave) toward computing the elongation directions, we can compute the convex hull[3] of the vertices of the triangles. This takes $O(n \log n)$ time.

Now let the ith triangle of the convex hull have the vertices p_i, q_i, and r_i, the number of triangles in the convex hull n, and the area of the ith triangle A_i. A_H is the surface area of the convex hull, which is just the sum of all areas of the triangular facets of the convex hull.

$$A_i = 1/2|(p_i - q_i) \times (p_i - r_i)| \qquad A_H = \sum_i A_i$$

The centroid of the ith triangle m_i, and the centroid of the entire convex hull m_H, are given by

$$m_i = (p_i + q_i + r_i)/3 \qquad m_H = \sum_i A_i m_i / A_H$$

The entries of the covariance matrix C_{ij} is given by the following formula (for details, see [Got96]).

$$C_{ij} = \sum_i^n (A_i/12A_H)[9m_i^k m_j^k + p_i^k p_j^k + q_i^k q_j^k + r_i^k r_j^k] - m_i m_j$$

The eigenvectors of the covariance matrix C are orthogonal, and form the axes of the OBB.

Once the axis vectors are known, we can compute the maximum and minimum extents of the original triangle set along each axis and obtain the vertices of the OBB similarly to constructing the AABB. The computation of the covariance matrix C takes at most linear time, and getting the eigenvectors from C is a constant time operation. Computing the box coordinates is also a linear time operation. So, the convex hull operation dominates the overall procedure, which is $O(n \log n)$ time [Got96]. The procedure can be made faster by skipping the convex hull step, and just using the triangles in the original triangle set, resulting in a linear time procedure, but this yields boxes that can have very bad fits.

K-DOPs are a generalization of the AABB. The directions of K-DOP faces are fixed but do not necessarily coincide with those of the principal axis, and there may be more than three directions for the faces (thus it is not necessarily a box any more but $2n$-sided volumes, where n is kept reasonably low). A K-DOP of an object can be defined with the normal directions of the faces and the extreme points (min and max) along those directions where the

---

[3] Informally, a convex hull of an object is the smallest convex polyhedron that encloses the object. Algorithms for finding a convex hull can be found in the introductory text books for computational geometry.

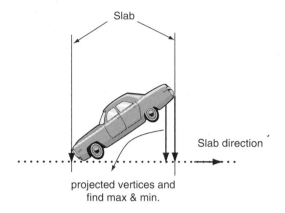

FIGURE 9.20. Constructing a K-DOP.

faces will lie. The extreme points are found easily by projecting the vertices of the object onto the respective normal direction of the faces n_i, and looking for the minimum $d_{i\,min}$, and the maximum $d_{i\,max}$ for $i = 0$ to $K/2$ (each face set or slabs as they are called; see Figure 9.20). The AABB would be a special case of a 6-DOP. K-DOPs offer tighter fit than AABBs, but require more calculation to construct, plus like AABBs, they must be reconstructed whenever the object changes its location or orientation.

Building a Bounding Volume Hierarchy

Building a hierarchy of bounding volumes follows these basic steps in a recursive manner.

1. Build a BV of the given object.
2. If the BV contains more than a preset threshold of geometric primitives (such as triangles, polygons, vertices), split the BV into k children by some criterion. Recurse above for each child BV. Otherwise, stop.

The most straightforward criterion for the way the split is made is to split the bounding volume in half (or into n equal subspaces). The only requirement would be that the k subspaces collected together entirely encompass the original object, and preferably not overlap each other too much (to avoid redundancy). Figures 9.21 and 9.22 show the hierarchy construction process. For symmetric bounding volumes such as the spheres, boxes, and ellipsoids, it is easy to decompose the volume into half or n equal subspaces. For irregularly shaped bounding volumes such as the K-DOPs, a heuristic criterion often used is cutting in half along the x-, y-, or z-axis (the principal axis), whichever

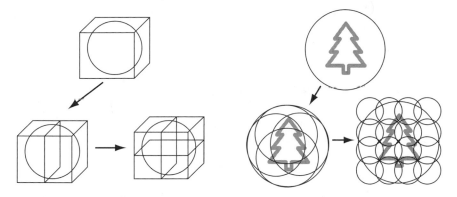

FIGURE 9.21. Constructing an AABB tree and a sphere tree.

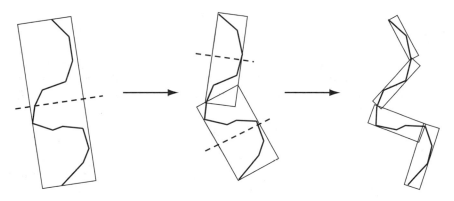

FIGURE 9.22. Constructing an OBB tree [Got96]. (Reprinted with permission from the ACM © 2004.)

minimizes the sum of the subvolumes, or cut along one of the slab directions whose distribution of projected vertices is the largest [Mol02].

Testing Interference Among Bounding Volumes

Ray Versus Spherical BV

Between a spherical bounding volume and a ray, we can make a figure such as that shown in Figure 9.23. The ray may meet with a sphere at zero, one, or two points. The radius of the sphere is equated to the distance between the intersection point and the center:

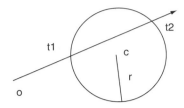

FIGURE 9.23. Ray versus sphere and its application.

$$R2 = |o + td - c|$$

This results in a simple quadratic equation and can be solved for the values of t. If there is no real valued solution for t, then the ray does not meet with the sphere.

Ray Versus Box (or Slab) [Mol02]

To check intersection between a ray and a box (or a slab), we check the intersection between an infinite slab (composed of two infinite and parallel planes that comprise one dimension of the box) and a ray (see Figure 9.24). The two infinite planes are represented by

$$a_u \cdot x = d1 \quad \text{and} \quad a_u \cdot x = d1 + L,$$

where L represents the (perpendicular) distance between the slab and a_u is the normal vector of the slab. We can re-represent the same equations with the origin translated to a_c, where a_c is the centroid of the box, as

$$a_u \cdot x' = L/2 \qquad a_u \cdot x' = -L/2$$

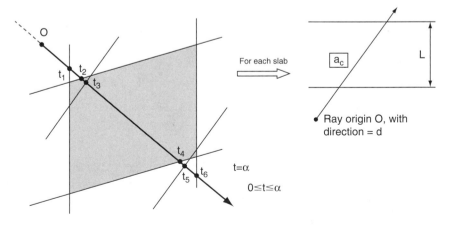

FIGURE 9.24. Ray versus slab.

We equate with x', the equation of the ray, but represented with the origin translated to a_c. Thus the equation of the ray becomes $o + td + p$, where $p = a_c - o$, and thus, $a_c + td$.

$$a_u \cdot (a_c + td) = L/2, \quad a_u \cdot (a_c + td) = -L/2 \quad \text{and} \quad t_{1,2} = (a_u \cdot a_c \pm L/2)/a_u \cdot d$$

Once you find the values of t with respect to all the dimensions of the box/slabs against the ray, they can be checked against the valid range that defines the original line segment to finally determine whether the line segment penetrates the slab volume.

Sphere Versus Sphere

Checking interference between two spheres is simple: we compare the distance between the two centers ($c2 - c1$) to the sum of their radii ($r1 + r2$). If the former is greater, then there is no overlap.

Sphere Versus Box

Although rare, one might have a set of objects that are made of different types of bounding volumes, for instance, one with sphere(s) and the other with box(es). To test interference between a sphere and an AABB, the following simple steps can be used.

1. Test if the center of the sphere is within the AABB bounds (i.e., test if r_i is between $a_{i\min}$ and $a_{i\max}$ for all i, where $i = x,y,z$).
2. If the center is inside the AABB, there is collision, otherwise calculate the distance from the center of sphere to the x-, y-, and z-axis. If they are all less than the radius of the sphere, then there is interference. Otherwise, there is no interference.

AABB Versus AABB

Checking for interference between two AABBs is also quite simple, requiring few comparisons among the extreme points of the respective AABB (see Figure 9.25). Given two AABBs of object A and B, let's call a_i the coordinate value of AABB of A in direction i, and similarly for b_i. For the two AABBs to be disjoint, it suffices to check if $a_{i\min}$ is greater $b_{i\max}$ or $b_{i\min}$ is greater than $a_{i\max}$ for any $i = x,y,z$. If the above condition is true for any i, then the AABBs are disjoint, and otherwise, there is an overlap.

OBB Versus OBB [Got96]

The interference checking among two OBBs is more involved and complicated, however, it requires a relatively small amount of computation. It uses something called the separating axis theorem [Got96]. The separating axis

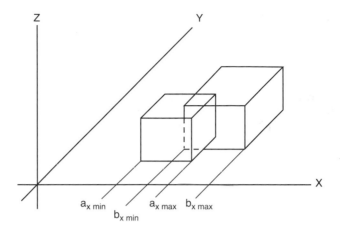

FIGURE 9.25. AABB versus AABB.

theorem states that for any two arbitrary convex disjoint polyhedra A and B, there exists a "separating" axis on which projection of the polyhedras, which form intervals that are also disjoint.

Furthermore, it implies that, if A and B are disjoint, then they can be "separated" by an axis that is orthogonal to faces of A, faces of B, or edges from each polyhedron (see Figure 9.26). For three-dimension OBBs, there is

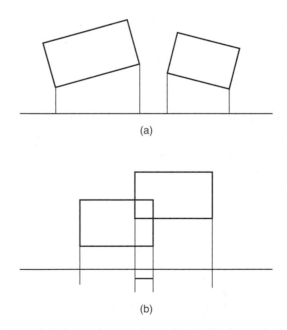

FIGURE 9.26. Two polyhedra and separating axis: (a) disjoint and (b) overlapped.

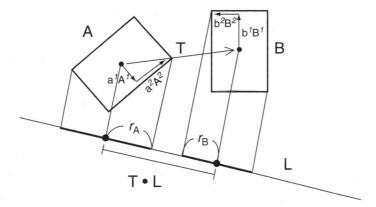

FIGURE 9.27. Checking for overlap between two OBBs. L is given (one of the 15 possible directions of separating axes to check for), T is the vector between the centroid of the two boxes, and T·L is projection of T onto L. What needs to computed are r_A and r_B. r_B is the projection of a^1A^1 and a^2A^2 onto L and likewise for r_B. a^i is the half length of box A in the ith direction of the box, A^i. A check is made to see if r_A and r_B overlaps.(Reprinted from [Got96] with permission from ACM © 2004.)

a total of 15 cases to test for: 3 separating axes that are orthogonal to faces of A, 3 that are orthogonal to faces of B, and 9 that are orthogonal to edges whose directions are determined by the cross product between one edge direction from A and the other from B (total 3×3 combinations). If, among the 15 cases, a disjointness is found on the projection of the polyhedras, we can conclude that the polyhedra themselves are disjoint also. The formulations necessary to test these are shown in Figure 9.27.

KDOP Versus KDOP

As K-DOPs are a generalization of the AABBs, so are the tests for overlap. For all pairs of slabs between K-DOPs A and B, S_{iA} and S_{iB} (i is the direction of the slabs and goes from 1 to $K/2$), if at any time, the intervals of S_{iA} and S_{iB} do not overlap, then the whole K-DOPs A and B are disjoint.

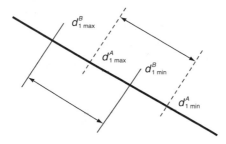

FIGURE 9.28. Interval testing in one direction i between two slabs.

In other words, for each i that belongs to (1 to $K/2$), if $d^B_{i\min}$ is greater than $d^A_{i\max}$ or $d^A_{i\min}$ is greater than $d^B_{i\max}$, then the objects are disjoint. d^i_j is the coordinate of the slab i in the direction perpendicular to slab direction j. If there are interval overlaps for all the directions i, then there is an overlap between the two K-DOPs (see Figure 9.28).

Summary

As illustrated in the various methods, one must consider the nature of the virtual environment to choose the most suitable collision detection method in terms of desired accuracy and available computational resource. In general, the total cost of the collision detection process can be represented as

$$T = n_V * c_V + n_P * c_P + n_U * c_U$$

where n_V, n_P, n_U represent the number of bounding volumes, polygons, and bounding volume updates required in a given method, and "c"'s represent the respective costs for testing or updates. We have seen that reducing n_V, for instance, generally may increase n_P, or eliminating n_U (by choosing spherical bounding volumes) can increase n_V. Different styles of bounding volumes have different costs for tests and updates as well. Thus, it is neither meaningful nor possible to rate which method is the best.

Pondering Points

- Try to make a more detailed comparison between the interval method and Canny's method for collision detection between two triangularized objects. Note that for triangularized objects $m = 3$.
- How can we modify the method of vertex piercing (Canny's method) to consider collision between concave objects also?
- Propose a way to estimate the point of collision. For instance, if there is one vertex that penetrated a particular face, that vertex position might be used as an approximation of the contact position assuming that it is not too far penetrated from the colliding surface. What if there were two or multiple numbers of penetrations? What about face-to-face contacts?
- Although this is part of the collision response problem, how can we determine the bounce direction upon collision? One simple method is to compute the reflecting direction of the incoming object moving direction.

Chapter 10
Simulation II: Physics-Based Motion and Collision Response

In this chapter, we cover the basic knowledge required to implement realistic motion simulation of virtual objects based on simple physics. Realistic motion constitutes a big part of object behaviors and its realism affects the user-felt presence. Motion simulation is also essential in implementing collision response behaviors.

The study of motion starts with the recognition that motion is generally categorized into two types: linear and rotational. Likewise the motion profiles are dependent on two inherent properties of the object: its *mass* and *moment of inertia*. Mass is the measure of the object's body's resistance to linear motion, and the mass moment of inertia is the measure of the body's resistance to rotational motion. Mathematically, mass is the material density multiplied by the infinitesimal volume over the whole object ($m = \int_v \rho \, dv$). Usually these properties must be known in advance to make any motion-related computation. It may be necessary to recompute the moment of inertia for different rotational axens, or due to changing composure of the object (the object being composed of moving subobjects; see examples later).

Center of Gravity (COG)

For the sake of simplicity, objects are often treated as point mass, and the point in the object that represents the concentration of the object's mass is called the center of gravity (or centroid, center of mass). Usually the center of gravity is contained within the object, but there are exceptional cases. The Center of Gravity (COG) is computed as follows. For instance, the x-coordinate of the COG is computed as the sum of the multiples of COGs of each constituent subobject and its masses, divided by the total mass. The total mass is simply the sum of all masses of the subobjects (or constituent objects) making up the whole object. The formula is similar for the y- and z-coordinates of the COG (note that the COGs and mass properties of the subobjects would have to be provided).

$$COG = [\sum_i (cg_i)m_i]/m_t$$

where cg_i and m_i are center of gravity and the mass of the ith constituent object respectively, and m_t is the total mass. If the object was not represented as a collection of smaller objects, then computing its COG involves the use of a formula which is the generalization of the above concept in the continuous domain. The formula integrates over the whole volume of the object. If the object's shape is rather complex and not well represented, the computation would be difficult. For simple-looking symmetric geometries, COGs can be computed easily from the existing formulas [You00]. Also note that the COG is a property local to the object and if the object moved or rotated, its global coordinates would change.

Moment of Inertia

To compute the moment of inertia, one needs to take the second moment of each subobject mass making up the body about each coordinate axis. The second moment is the product of the mass and the perpendicular distance from the subobject mass centroid to the rotational axis, squared. In general, we can draw a figure as shown in Figure 10.1, where O is the COG of the object, and n is the rotational axis.

$$I = \Sigma m_i (R_i)^2 = \Sigma m_i (|r_i| \sin \theta_i)^2$$
$$= I_{xx} \cos^2 \alpha + I_{yy} \cos^2 \beta + I_{zz} \cos^2 \sigma + 2 I_{xy} \cos \alpha \cos \beta + 2 I_{yz} \cos \beta \cos \sigma$$
$$+ 2 I_{zx} \cos \sigma \cos \alpha$$

where α, β, σ are angles made between $r_i = (x_i, y_i, z_i)$ and the x-, y-, and z-axes, and

$$I_{xx} = \Sigma(y_i^2 + z_i^2)^*(m_i)$$
$$I_{yy} = \Sigma(x_i^2 + z_i^2)^*(m_i)$$
$$I_{zz} = \Sigma(x_i^2 + y_i^2)^*(m_i)$$

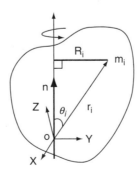

FIGURE 10.1. Calculating the rotational moment of inertia.

and

$$I_{xy} = I_{yx} = -\Sigma(x_i y_i)^*(m_i)$$
$$I_{xz} = I_{zx} = -\Sigma(x_i z_i)^*(m_i)$$
$$I_{yz} = I_{zy} = -\Sigma(z_i y_i)^*(m_i)$$

For instance, the moment of inertia with respect to the x-axis would be just (because the $\alpha = 0$, $\beta = 90$, $\sigma = 90$):

$$I = I_{xx} = \Sigma(y_i^2 + z_i^2)^*(m_i)$$

However, if the rotational axis was an arbitrary vector going through the COG, computing the I would involve all six components, namely, I_{xx}, I_{yy}, I_{zz}, I_{xy}, I_{yz}, and I_{zx}. We can conveniently represent the inertia with its components in a 3×3 symmetric matrix form, and this is called the inertia matrix.

$$\begin{bmatrix} I_{xx} & I_{xy} & I_{xz} \\ I_{yx} & I_{yy} & I_{yz} \\ I_{zx} & I_{zy} & I_{zz} \end{bmatrix}$$

Computing the moment of inertia will require information about the mass properties of the subobjects. Again, similar to the case with computing the COG, if the object was not represented as a collection of smaller objects (i.e., just a single object), then computing its COG would be more complicated. A continuous integral must be solved over the whole volume of the object and if the object shape is complex and not well represented, the computation will be difficult. For several simple-looking symmetric geometries, simple formulas for the mass moment of inertia exist (the product of inertia terms such as I_{xy}, I_{yz}, and I_{zx} go to zero) [You00]. Also note that the moment of inertia is a property local to the object and relative to the designated axis of rotation. Assuming that the axis of rotation goes through the COG of the object and the local coordinate system is also placed at the COG, the local inertia matrix will remain constant. However, as the object moves and changes its location and orientation, the global inertia matrix (i.e., inertia matrix computed with respect to the global coordinate system) will change. In fact, the global inertia matrix only changes with object rotation (not translation). Initially, assuming that the global coordinate system and the local coordinate system's orientations coincide, the global and local inertia matrices are also the same. The relationship is expressed as follows.

$$^W I(t) = {}^W R_O(t) \, {}^O I \, {}^W R_O(t)^T$$

where $^W R_o(t)$ is the orientation matrix between the fixed-world coordinate system and the moving object coordinate system.

We illustrate the use of the formulas with the following example. A car is composed of several subobjects; a body, driver, and four wheels with the

TABLE 10.1. Mass Properties of the Subobjects of the Car

	Body	Driver	Wheel 1	Wheel 2	Wheel 3	Wheel 4
Length	120	10	8	8	8	8
Width	50	10	3	3	3	3
Height	40	20	8	8	8	8
Weight (kg)	1000	60	5	5	5	5
Centroid	150,125,20	180,125,20	100,150,0	200,150,0	100,100,0	200,100,0

following physical properties (see Table 10.1). All the subobject's shapes are approximated as rectangular boxes (see Figures 10.2 and 10.3). Here the objective is to compute the total moment of inertia of the composite object around its z-axis on its centroid.

First, we compute the COG of the car from the six subobjects.

$$m_t = 1000 + 60 + 5 + 5 + 5 + 5 = 1080$$

$$^W\text{COG}_{\text{car}} = \Sigma(cg_i)m_i/m_t = (151.7,\ 125,\ 19.63)$$

Note that the COG of the car just computed is in global coordinates. Assuming that the global and the local coordinate systems of the subobjects are aligned, the local COGs of the subobjects (relative to the local coordinate system of the car) are computed easily by subtracting the global COG of the car from the global COGs of the subobjects (as listed in the table).

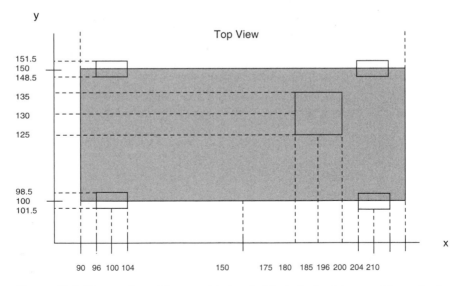

FIGURE 10.2. The top view of the car with six subobjects; body, driver, and four wheels.

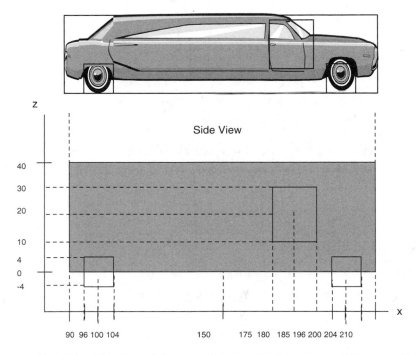

FIGURE 10.3. The side view of the car with six subobjects; body, driver, and four wheels.

$$\text{Body's local COG:} \quad {}^{car}(-1.67\ 0.0\ 0.37)$$

$$\text{Driver's local COG:} \quad {}^{car}(28.3\ 0.0\ 0.37)$$

$$\text{W1's local COG:} \quad {}^{car}(-51.67\ 25.0 - 19.63)$$

$$\text{W2's local COG:} \quad {}^{car}(48.33\ 25.0 - 19.63)$$

$$\text{W3's local COG:} \quad {}^{car}(-51.67 - 25.0 - 19.63)$$

$$\text{W4's local COG:} \quad {}^{car}(48.3333 - 25.0 - 19.63)$$

Now, we can compute the moment of inertia matrix. For instance,

$$
\begin{aligned}
{}^{car}I_{xx} &= \Sigma(y_i^2 + z_i^2)^*(m_i) \\
&= (0^2 + 0.37^2)^*1000 + (0^2 + 0.37^2)^*60 + [(25^2 + 19.63^2)^*5]^*4 \\
&= 20352
\end{aligned}
$$

And, because initially, the global and local axes are aligned (assumption; i.e., $^{W}R(t)_O = I$), the global inertia matrix and local inertia matrix are the same.

$$
{}^{car}I_{xx} = {}^{W}I_{xx}
$$

Similarly,

$$^{car}I_{yy} = {}^{W}I_{yy} = 108852$$
$$^{car}I_{zz} = {}^{W}I_{zz} = 113500$$
$$^{car}I_{xy} = {}^{car}I_{yx} = {}^{W}I_{xy} = {}^{W}I_{yx} = 0$$
$$^{car}I_{yz} = {}^{car}I_{zy} = {}^{W}I_{yz} = {}^{W}I_{zy} = 0$$
$$^{car}I_{zx} = {}^{car}I_{zx} = {}^{W}I_{xz} = {}^{W}I_{zx} = 666.67$$

Suppose that the car rotated by 90 degrees with respect to the z-axis of the world coordinate system, and let's say the new position of the car was expressed by

New COG of the body $= R(t)$ (150, 125, 20) $= {}^{W}(-125, 150, 20)$

New COG of the driver $= R(t)$ (180, 140, 20) $= {}^{W}(-125, 180, 20)$

New COG of the wheel 1 $= R(t)$ (100, 150, 0) $= {}^{W}(-150, 100, 0)$

New COG of the wheel 2 $= R(t)$ (200, 150, 0) $= {}^{W}(-150, 200, 0)$

New COG of the wheel 3 $= R(t)$ (100, 100, 0) $= {}^{W}(-100, 100, 0)$

New COG of the wheel 4 $= R(t)$ (200, 100, 0) $= {}^{W}(-100, 200, 0)$

New COG of the car $= R(t)$ (151.6, 125.8) $= {}^{W}(-125, 151.7, 19.63)$

where

$$R(t) = {}^{W}R_O(t) = \begin{bmatrix} 0 & -1 & 0 \\ 1 & 0 & 0 \\ 0 & 0 & 1 \end{bmatrix}.$$

If we recomputed the global moment of inertia for the car with the same formula (the local moment of inertia does not change, as the local coordinates of the COGs of the subobjects do not change with rotation or translation),

$$^{W}I_{yy} = \Sigma(x_i^2 + z_i^2)^*(m_i)$$
$$= (0^2 + 0.37^2)^*1000 + (0^2 + 0.37^2)^*60 + [(25^2 + 19.63^2)^*5]^*4$$
$$= 20352$$
$$\neq {}^{W}I_{yy} \text{ (before rotation)}$$

Similarly,

$$^{W}I_{xx} = 108852$$
$$^{W}I_{zz} = 113500$$
$$^{W}I_{xy} = {}^{W}I_{yx} = 0$$
$$^{W}I_{yz} = {}^{W}I_{zy} = 666.67$$
$$^{W}I_{xz} = {}^{W}I_{zx} = 0$$

You can check whether $^{W}I(t) = {}^{W}R_O(t) \, {}^{O}I \, {}^{W}R_O(t)^T$ holds.

Kinematics

In certain situations, it is possible to express motion without regard to forces acting on the respective body (e.g., when there is no interobject interaction such as collision). Kinematics is the study of motion without regard to the forces acting on the body. We first look at kinematics before we actually apply the laws of motion (see later sections in this chapter) to simulate the dynamics of interobject interaction. In kinematics, we focus on the relationships among the position, velocity, and acceleration and disregard the effects of force (and mass properties of the objects). Kinematics is applied to two major object representations: a rigid body, which is an object we assume to be nondeforming in its motion, and point mass, which is assumed not to occupy any volume (thus rotational effects are ignored).

Linear Velocity and Acceleration

This part is applicable to both rigid body objects and particles. (Later we treat rotational kinematics for rigid body objects.) Here are the elementary kinematic equations of motion.

$$\text{Distance traveled } s$$
$$\text{Speed} \quad v = ds/dt$$
$$\text{Acceleration} \quad a = dv/dt$$

With a constant acceleration (for instance, gravity), the equations can be further expanded (easily) into this form.

$$v_2 = v_1 + a * \Delta t$$
$$v_2^2 = 2 * a * (s_2 - s_1) + v_1^2$$
$$s_2 = s_1 + v_1 * \Delta t + (a/2)^* \Delta t^2$$

With the motion occurring during a short amount of time, say Δt, v_2, s_2 are the new velocity and new value of the total distance traveled after Δt, and v_1, s_1 are the old velocity and old value of the total distance traveled prior to the passage of time duration Δt (see Figure 10.4). In multidimensions, the above equation is usually solved in different component directions (e.g., x, y, and z).

If the acceleration is not constant (e.g., $a = -k * v * t^2$, an acceleration in time), then a differential equation must be solved to derive a new set of equations for the velocity and displacement.

Rotational Kinematics (for Rigid Body Only)

Similar to the linear kinematic equations, here are the relationships among angular displacement, angular velocity, and angular acceleration (about a certain axis).

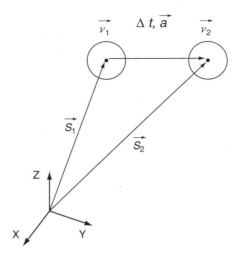

FIGURE 10.4. Linear velocities and accelerations.

$$\omega_2 = \omega_1 + \alpha * \Delta t$$
$$\omega_2^2 = \omega_1^2 + 2^*\alpha^*(\Omega_2 - \Omega_1)$$
$$\Omega_2 = \Omega_1 + \omega_1^*\Delta t + (\alpha/2)^*\Delta t^2$$

Here, the $_1$ and $_2$ are the before and after values of the total angular distance traveled up to that point (in radians). The ω_1 and ω_2 are likewise the before and after values of the angular velocities, and α is the angular acceleration. If we are simulating an object in isolation, we simply need to apply these equations to compute the linear and rotational motion of the object. However, if we were to compute a collision response between two colliding objects, then the resulting motion would be dependent on the contact point of the collision. In other words, the kinetics of the objects will depend on the velocities and accelerations at the point of contact.

A point on an object will move in a circular path around the axis of rotation, when the object rotates (see Figure 10.5). This creates a linear

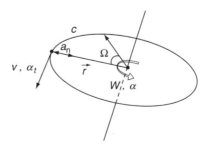

FIGURE 10.5. Rotational kinematics.

motion in addition to the linear motion of the body's center of mass. This traveled distance (arc length) of the point on an object is computed by

$$c = \Omega^* r$$

where r is the distance from the center of rotation to the point and Ω is the angular displacement. Thus the velocity of the point along the path is computed by simply taking the time derivative and it results in:

$$v_t = \omega \times r \quad (\omega^* r \text{ in 2D})$$

Note that ω is a vector with a direction along the axis of rotation. Velocity v, as a vector, is tangent to the circular path swept by the point. Another time derivative gives

$$a_t = \alpha \times r \quad (\alpha^* r \text{ in 2D})$$

When a particle (or point on a mass) rotates, there is another acceleration created called the centripetal acceleration, directed toward the axis of rotation. This acceleration is given by

$$a_n = \omega \times \omega \times r$$

Figure 10.5 shows the whole picture. The total linear velocity (resulting from rotation) and linear motion occurring at the COG of the object is

Total linear velocity: $v_{cg} + v_t = v_{cg} + (\omega \times r)$

Total linear acceleration: $a_{cg} + a_t + a_n = a_{cg} + a_t + (\omega \times \omega \times r)$

The kinematic motion can be created by solving for the incremental linear translation and rotation at regular time intervals (simulation tick) and applying the appropriate translation and rotation matrix to the object for rendering.

Laws of Motion

In order to also consider the effects of forces and torques and create motion with dynamics, we need to first understand the basic laws of motion. Newton's second law states that the resulting acceleration of a body is in the same direction as the resultant force on it,

$$\Sigma F = m^* a$$

The above equation is usually solved in different component directions (e.g., x, y, and z).

$$\Sigma F_x = m^* a_x$$
$$\Sigma F_y = m^* a_y$$
$$\Sigma F_z = m^* a_z$$

Another important equation of motion has to do with the object's momentum G, which equals the mass times velocity. In fact, the rate of change of momentum is equal to the total force exerted on the body. Thus, momentum is conserved: that is, without introduction of new forces, the momentum will stay constant.

$$G = m^*v \qquad dG/dt = m^*a = \Sigma F$$

If the object is composed of subobjects, the momentum at the COG is formulated as the sum of momentum of the subobjects, which equals the total mass times velocity.

$$G = \Sigma m_i^*(dq_i(t)/dt) = m^*v$$

The above equations are valid for translational (or linear) movement $q_i(t)$ stands for the velocity of the ith subobject. As for rotational movement, there is another set of equations. The first relates the total torque on the body to the angular acceleration (analogous to $\Sigma F = m^*a$; see Figure 10.6).

$$\text{Torque about COG} = r \times F$$

$$\text{Total torque} = {}^W\!I(t)^*\alpha$$

where F is the force acting on the body and r is the distance vector from F perpendicular to the line of action of F. ${}^W\!I(t)$ is the inertia matrix (with respect to the world), and α represents the angular acceleration.

The angular momentum L is given as follows, and is also conserved (i.e., it stays constant if no new torque is introduced).

$$L = \Sigma(r_i(t) \times m_i^*(dq_i(t)/dt - v(t)))$$
$$= \Sigma({}^W\!R_O(t)l_i \times m_i^*(\omega(t) \times r_i(t)))$$

and

$$\text{Total torque} = {}^W\!I(t)^*\alpha = dL(t)/dt \qquad \omega(t) = {}^W\!I(t)^{-1}L(t)$$

where

   $x(t)$: COG of the whole object in global coord.

   $v(t)$: Linear velocity of the whole object at the global COG

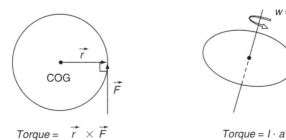

$$\text{Torque} = \vec{r} \times \vec{F} \qquad\qquad \text{Torque} = I \cdot a$$

FIGURE 10.6. Torque $= I^*\alpha = r \times F$.

$q_i(t)$: COG of the ith subobject in global coord.

$^W R_O(t)$: Rot. matrix between global and local coord. of whole object

l_i: Local coordinate of the ith subobject

$\omega(t)$: Angular velocity of the whole object around the rotation axis

$r_i(t)$: Vector from whole object's COG to ith subobject's COG

Also note that

$$q_i(t) = {}^W R_O(t) l_i + x(t)$$
$$dq_i(t)/dt = \omega(t) \times {}^W R_O(t) l_i + v(t)$$
$$r_i(t) = q_i(t) - x(t) = {}^W R_O(t) l_i$$
$$^W I(t) = {}^W R_O(t)^O I {}^W R_O(t)^T$$

Even though the angular momentum is conserved with no new torque introduced to the system, the angular velocity $\omega(t)$ may change due to object rotation (i.e., $^W I(t)$ changes).

These equations are quite complicated. Let us go through the following example to see how these equations of motion are applied for simulating movement. Here is a situation where the car example of Figure 10.1 is "pushed" with an initial linear and rotational momentum (or equivalently given initial linear and angular velocity values). By applying the above equations in an incremental fashion we can compute the car's new location and orientation at each simulation tick (see Figure 10.7).

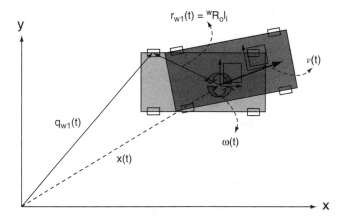

FIGURE 10.7. The car starting to move and rotate with given initial values of linear and angular momentum (equivalent to saying that the car is given an initial linear and angular velocity).

TABLE 10.2. State Data for the Car Object

State Variable	Description	Initial Value
t	Current time (e.g., tick value)	0
$x(t)$	COG of the whole object in global coord.	(151.7, 125, 19.63) From Figure 10.3
$^W R_o(t)$	Rot. matrix between global and local coord. of whole object	Identity matrix (global and local coord. orientations are the same initially)
m_t	Total mass	1080 From Figure 10.3
$^o I$	Local inertia matrix	From p. 184
l_i	Local coords. of subobjects	From p. 183
P	Total linear momentum (stays constant in this example, no new force)	(1000, 0, 0) arbitrarily given, velocity toward x direction
L	Total angular momentum (stays constant in this example, no new torque)	(0, 0, 10000) arbitrarily given, rotation around z axis

For simulation purposes we keep a record representing the state of the whole object (car). The state consists of the information in Table 10.2. The purpose of the simulation is to update the $x(t)$ and $^W R_O(t)$ (the new position and orientation) of the car. Thus, using the equations of motion, at every simulation tick, we compute the state variables listed in Table 10.3. Then, finally, to compute the new $x(t)$ and $^W R_O(t)$, we compute the dx and dR as follows. Here, we use the formula, $dR/dt = w(t) \times {}^W R_O(t)$, that relates the angular velocity (w) to the rotation matrix (R), to compute the incremental change in R.

$$dx = v(t)^* \Delta t$$
$$x(t) = x(t-1) + dx$$
$$dR = [\omega(t) \times {}^W R_O(t-1)]^* \Delta t$$
$$^W R_O(t) = \text{Normalize } ({}^W R_O(t-1) + dR)$$

Note that the results obtained from the incremental update of the $^W R_O$ is normalized columnwise to keep it an orthonormal matrix (by dividing the each column by its norms). Also see Table 10.4.

TABLE 10.3. Other State Variables Derivable (at Each Simulation Tick) from Variables in Table 10.1

What to compute	Description	How to compute
$^W I(t)$	Global inertia matrix	$^W R_O(t-1) {}^o I {}^W R_o(t-1)^T$
F, T	Any new force or torque	For now there is none, but if there were a collision, we need to figure this out
$v(t)$	Global velocity	$P(t-1)/m_t$
$\omega(t)$	Angular velocity	$^W I(t)^{-1} L(t-1)$
$dq_i(t)/dt$	Velocity of ith subobject	$v(t) + \omega(t) \times r_i(t-1)$ $r_i(t-1) = {}^W R_o(t-1) l_i$

TABLE 10.4. Traces of the simulation from $t = 0$ to $t = 3$.

Time	$x(t)$		$^W R_o(t)$		
$t = 0$	(151.7 125.0 19.63)	Row 1	1	0	0
		Row 2	0	1	0
		Row 3	0	0	1
$t = 1$	(152.6 125.0 19.63)	Row 1	0.99	−0.1	0
		Row 2	0.1	0.99	0
		Row 3	0	0	0.99
$t = 2$	(153.5 125.0 19.63)	Row 1	0.98	−0.2	0
		Row 2	0.2	0.98	0
		Row 3	0	0	1.0
$t = 3$	(154.4 125.0 19.63)	Row 1	0.96	−0.26	0
		Row 2	0.26	0.96	0
		Row 3	0	0	1.0

Dynamics

Before incorporating forces into our motion equations (for a more realistic simulation of moving objects), we first should recognize the two major types of forces. One is the *contact force* that is exerted through direct contact (e.g., object collision, holding a book). *Noncontact* forces, the other type of force, acts from force fields on objects without touching the object. The force fields are usually uniformly present throughout a large space (such as gravitational force or magnetic force). Most usually, we only consider contact forces in simulating rotational dynamics. Forces from force fields are assumed to act only on the COM of the object and thus do not cause any rotational dynamics (of course this is not true in reality).

In considering object dynamics, the first line of business is figuring out the major forces acting on the object under consideration. From the information about forces, we derive the acceleration and apply the kinematic equations (if somehow the accelerations are known, then the problem reduces to just the kinematics problem). To summarize, the general procedure for solving object dynamics is as follows.

1. Calculate the body's mass properties (mass, COM, moment of inertia).
2. Identify and quantify all major forces and moments acting on the body (and sum them) and apply $\Sigma F = m^* a$ and ΣM (total torque) $= I^* \alpha$ to solve for the linear and angular accelerations.
3. Integrate with respect to time to obtain velocities and displacements.
4. Check for and handle collision.

Thus, for Step 2, the newly found forces and torques are updated (third row of Table 10.2) and the resulting change in linear and angular momentum is updated in the object state (last two rows of Table 10.1). The rest (Step 3 above) is the same as in computing the kinematics. Thus the major problem in dynamics lies in finding the appropriate forces and torques given information regarding the collision (e.g., collision point).

If there are multiple objects, then they must be treated one by one, and because we are assuming that the above procedure will occur at a very high rate with small simulation tick duration, the order of object consideration will not matter very much.

Ad Hoc Collision Response

A simple nonphysics-based approach may simply generate $v(t+1)$ based on some heuristics (see Figure 10.8). For instance, the direction of $v(t+1)$ may just be in the reflecting direction of the incoming object. The magnitude may be adjusted to simulated energy absorption ($|v(t+1)| = c|v(t)|$, and $0 < c < 1$).

A similar approach is to introduce a new spring force proportional to the amount of penetration upon collision. The direction of the force would be normal to the penetrating polygon surface. This method is similar to the simple haptic rendering introduced in Chapter 6. This approach is illustrated in Figure 10.9.

The Impulse-Momentum Principle [Bou01]

The physics-based collision response computation is based on the Impulse-Momentum principle. Impulse is defined as a force that acts over a very

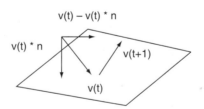

FIGURE 10.8. A nonphysics-based ad hoc approach to collision response.

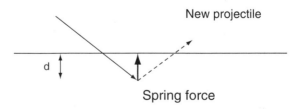

FIGURE 10.9. Introducing spring force normal to penetrated polygon surface.

short period of time. The principle states that (linear) impulse is equal to the change in momentum. For rotational aspect, angular impulse is equal to the change in rotational momentum.

$$\text{Linear Impulse: } m(v^+ - v^-) = \int \Sigma f \, dt,$$

$$\text{Rotational Imuplse: } I(\omega^+ - \omega^-) = \int \Sigma I \, dt,$$

where $v+$, $v-$,$\omega+$, *rmomega*-are linear and rotational velocities after and before the short amount time $(\Delta t = t^+ - t^-)$ the impulse occurs. m is the object mass and I is the inertia matrix. In easier terms:

$$\Sigma f = F = m(v^+ - v^-)/\Delta t$$
$$\Sigma I = M = I(\omega^+ - \omega^-)/\Delta t$$

In addition to this principle, another required law of physics is the conservation of momentum which states that when a system of rigid body collides, momentum is conserved. In an equation,

$$m1^* v1^- + m2^* v2^- = m1^* v1^+ + m2^* v2^+$$

where, m1 and v1 refer to the mass and velocity of object1 along the line of action and vice versa for object2. Note that the velocities used in the calculation must be the velocities (projected) along the line of action. The line of action is the line connecting the COGs of the two objects. Thus if two moving objects collided in an angle, the velocity components in the direction of the line of action can be obtained by simple projection. Thus, note that the "after" velocities computed with the above equation will also be the velocity components projected along the line of action. How do we then find the actual "after" directions of the objects? This is done by using an assumption that there is zero impact along the tangential direction of the collision point (direction perpendicular to the line of action), and the velocity along that line is preserved after the collision. For instance, if two objects collided head on, then the after velocities will be the very opposite (with no tangential components). Therefore, there will be two components of the "after" velocities, one along the line of action and another along the tangential direction. Each of those components can be projected back to the principal axis and summed to obtain the final velocity vector (since we know the angles among the principal axis, the incoming directions and the line of action).

When dealing with rigid bodies that rotate, we have to derive a new equation for impulse that includes the angular effects. We need to recall here that linear velocity is affected by rotation. Figure 10-10 shows the situation. The line of action, when angular effects are considered, becomes the line perpendicular to the colliding surfaces (rather than the line between two COGs). Assuming that the line of action can be found (through the

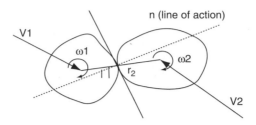

FIGURE 10.10. Incorporating both linear and rotational kinematics.

collision determination process), velocities used in the subsequent equations are component velocities of the actual projected on the line of action.

$$\text{Total linear velocity: } v = v_{cg} + v_t = v_{cg} + \omega \times r$$

where r is the perpendicular distance from the point of contact (where the force is applied) to the COM, and ω is the angular velocity. For convenience, we drop the subscript "cg".

For body 1 and 2, the linear impulses are:

Body 1: $M1^*[(v1^+ + \omega1^+ \times r1) \cdot n - (v1^- + \omega1^- \times r1) \cdot n] = F^* \Delta t = J$

Body 2: $M2^*[(v2^+ + \omega2^+ \times r2) \cdot n - (v2^- + \omega2^- \times r2) \cdot n] = -F^* \Delta t = -J$

For these impulses, there is one contact force, F (over a short time), and from the body 1's perspective, it is F, and from body 2's perspective it is $-F$.

The rotational impulses are:

$$\text{Body 1: } I1(\omega1^+ - \omega1^-) = r1 \times (F^* \Delta t) = r1 \times J$$
$$\text{Body 2: } I2(\omega2^+ - \omega2^-) = r2 \times (-F^* \Delta t) = r2 \times -J$$

In addition to these equations, we can implement a heuristic approach to account for the actual loss of energy when collision occurs. We establish a co-efficient of restitution, e, to represent the degree of "elasticity" of the collision.

$$e = (v1^+ - v2^+)/(v1^- - v2^-)$$

The higher the value of e is, the more elastic the collision is and that means there is no loss of energy in the collision. The lower the value of e is the more inelastic the collision is and that means, at extreme, two objects will simply stick together (and do not bounce off absorbing all incoming energy). Different e values can be used depending on the material properties of the objects in question.

Collision Response

When a collision is detected, the resulting velocities should be updated according to the physical principles that govern the preservation of momentum. They were:

Body 1: $M1^*[(v1^+ + \omega1^+ \times r1) \cdot n - (v1^- + \omega1^- \times r1) \cdot n] = F^*\Delta t = J$
Body 2: $M2^*[(v2^+ + \omega2^+ \times r2) \cdot n - (v2^- + \omega2^- \times r2) \cdot n] = -F^*\Delta t = -Jn$

$$e = (v1^+ - v2^+)/(v1^- - v2^-)$$

Remember that the total velocity equals $v + \omega xr$. Also remember that the equations must be applied along the line of action (denoted as vector n). Disregarding the rotational effects for the time being ($\omega \times r = 0$), upon detection of collision, we compute J as:

$$J = -[(v1^- - v2^-) \cdot n](e + 1)\,(1/M1 + 1/M2)$$
$$v1^+ \cdot n = v1^- \cdot n + J/M1$$
$$v2^+ \cdot n = v2^- \cdot n - J/M2$$

The actual $v1^+$, $v2^+$ are found in the same as explained in the previous section using the assumption that there is zero impact along the tangential direction of the collision point (direction perpendicular to the line of action), and the velocity along that line is preserved after the collision.

If we add the rotational effect, the collision detection module must produce the location of contact, i.e. $r1$ and $r2$ (we will not cover how to do this in this book in detail, although some techniques in the collision detection section can be used to approximate this location), and the impulse J can be computed as (derived from the original set of equations):

$$J = -[(v1^- - v2^-) \cdot n](e + 1)\{1/m1 + 1/m2 + n \cdot [(r1 \times n)/I1] \times r1 + n \cdot [r2 \times n]/I2\} \times r2\}$$

Once J is computed, the v's and ω's after the collision are computed with the formulas presented earlier.

$$v1^+ \cdot n = v1^- \cdot n + J/M1$$
$$v2^+ \cdot n = v2^- \cdot n - J/M2$$
$$\omega1^+ = \omega1^- + (r1 \times J)/I1$$
$$\omega2^+ = \omega2^- + (r2 \times -J)/I2$$

Real-Time Simulation Revisited

Now that we have covered the basic physics model, we turn to how to use it and implement a real-time simulation for virtual reality. Recall that there were two major computational structures for a VR program, one based on a single thread of infinite loop that handles the external input, does the simulation, updates the environment, and renders the scene in sequence, and the other, a distributed approach in which each of those components would run as separate threads in synchrony. Either way, the simulation module applies the physics model, described in the previous sections, once at some small increments of time (simulation tick). Also remember the general procedure for solving object dynamics. Once an acceleration of an object is figured out, the next line of business is to apply integration to obtain object velocity and displacements. This small increment of time (dt) is the basis for our calculation of the object motion that involves differentiation or integration of quantities with respect to time. Note that the Δt will be the current time minus the time stamp of the last time of simulation calculation, thus it must be tracked using a system timekeeping function.

We have already seen this style of motion kinematics simulation in the last part of the kinematics section. As for the motion dynamics, the only difference is to figure out the new acceleration (or velocities) resulting from the collision using the impulse-momentum equations (or ad hoc methods).

Between one increment of small simulation tick, we can write:

$$dv = a \, dt \quad \text{and} \quad v = \int a \, dt \text{(over small time duration } \Delta t)$$

If we replace dt with Δt, then $dv = a^* \Delta t$, and the new velocity is:

$$\text{New velocity: } v(t + \Delta t) = v(t) + a^* \Delta t$$

The new displacement value, after the increment of delta t, will be:

$$s(t + \Delta t) = s(t) + \Delta t^* v(t + \Delta t)$$

Even though the process is simple, it is an approximated way of carrying out the integration of the acceleration over the short period of time to obtain velocity and displacement. This is called Euler's method and is based on the Taylor expansion theorem that states:

$$y(x + \Delta x) = y(x) + \Delta x^* y'(x) + \Delta x^2 y''(x)/2! + \text{high order terms}$$

If we ignore the third and rest of the terms in the right-hand side of the equation and replace y with v, and Δx with Δt, we arrive with the Euler approximation of integration. If we only use up to the second term (one that uses y'), that amounts to an integration in the linear sense, approximating y with a linear motion model. We can certainly choose to include more terms to reduce the error and produce a better approximation of the y. But it requires more computation.

Deformation (As a Result of Collision)

So far, we have assumed that the colliding bodies were rigid, and did not deform upon collision. Here, we illustrate two methods for simulating a simple deformation effect. Deformation of an object modeled as a mesh amounts to moving the vertices near the point of contact. A simple form of deformation is illustrated in Figure 10.11. The upper part of the Figure 10.11 shows the effect of moving one vertex toward the right. Vertices near by are attracted toward the right depending on their distances from the original

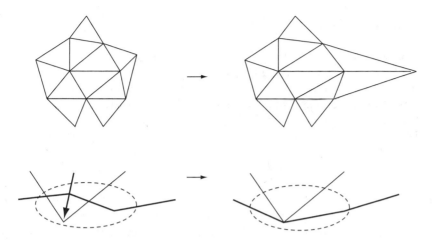

FIGURE 10.11. Deformation by moving a group vertex proportionally. Upon collision the vertices of the colliding objects can be moved in a similar way.

vertex that moved. Thus, when a collision occurs, the vertex near the point of collision can be moved proportional to the penetration distance and the vertices near by can be moved in a similar way.

There are a number of other more elegant methods of handling deformation. For instance, the motions of clothes or drapes are simulated by modeling the clothes as a network grid of particle masses connected by springs and dampers. The motion of the particles can be computed approximately by solving the dynamics equations for each pair of particles in the grid in some predefined order.

Summary

Many typical behaviors of virtual objects are manifested by motion. Thus, modeling motion as realistically as possible can be important in making the virtual environment more believable. The motion simulation realism may also be important for creating the right virtual environment for correct training and education. Physical motion involves both linear and rotational components. However, including rotational components can make the modeling process more difficult and it involves more computation. Depending on the given situation, the rotational effects may be ignored. Most often, full physically based simulation may not be needed as well. Just considering kinematics or ad hoc dynamics methods may suffice, depending on the requirements of the system.

Pondering Points

- One way of estimating the point of contact is just to use the location of the penetrating vertex assuming the penetration is small relative to the size of the penetrated object. How can we estimate the point of contact for other types of collision (e.g., edge going through the face, edge to edge, face to face, etc.)?
- How can we incorporate friction between objects in the dynamics computation?
- What kind of data structure would we need for simulating force fields such as winds, magnetic fields, and artificial force fields?
- It is said that people employ "folk" physics in understanding the world. Your folk physics model can be quite different from what actually happens in the world. You probably have taken a university or high school level physics course some time in your life. Do you really use the knowledge to reason and act in the world? How good is your physical interpretation of the world? How realistic should a virtual environment be in terms of simulating the actual physics of the natural world? Perhaps you can adapt a new "folk" physics in a virtual environment. What would be the minimum requirement for an acceptable "folk" physics?
- Simulate the kinematic motion for ships in the Ship Simulator example. You can follow the exact same process as illustrated in the text with the car example. For the dynamics effect, compute (estimate) the approximate force, acceleration, and the change in momentum to compute the new response motion profile.

Chapter 11
Virtual Characters

One of the most important objects in VR or in digital content is including human (or living/moving) characters. Characters can contribute to making a virtual environment more believable. After all, we do live in a world crowded with eight billion people. Mechanically, human characters can be viewed as an articulated chain of limbs, and in fact, most living creatures or animals can also be modeled as articulated chains. These characters are sometimes referred to as *avatars*, meaning that they are to represent the user(s) in the virtual environment, but strictly speaking, there can be characters or entities that do not represent the users and are acting autonomously (e.g., using AI or scripted behavior). In this chapter, we explain how to model characters (human or animal) as an articulated chain, and how to move the characters (or their limbs and bodily parts) to exhibit certain behavior. Note that the character behaviors can be initiated though user control (avatar) or algorithmically (autonomous agent).

As already explained, as a virtual object, one must consider the aspects of its form, function, and behavior when building a virtual character. Depending on the expected functions or behaviors required, the complexity of the form may be determined or vice versa. In this chapter, we simply illustrate the process of building a humanlike figure with reasonable detail so as to carry out various humanlike functions.

Form of a Character

There are two major things to consider for a form of a character. Like any object, characters (human, animal, or any creatures) are created using the computer-aided modelers and they are eventually converted into polygonal models. Thus, one must consider how much detail is needed depending on the requirements of a given application with respect to the number of polygons for performance sake. For instance, the facial details might not be very important and a simple paste of textures may suffice. It might not be necessary to model the fingers or toes, and the muscular landscape of the body. This mostly has to do with the outer appearance of the character model.

The other modeling issue is related to the functions and behaviors of the character, that is, the determination of the control detail. This refers to the problem of which limbs or parts should be controllable by the user or by the computer. For instance, even though it might be necessary to model the arms (for appearance sake), it might not be necessary to move them. If arms are not to be controlled (moved), then they can be modeled together with the body (torso) as one object. If, on the other hand, the arms must be controlled and moved at the shoulder (but not at the elbows), then, one might consider modeling the whole arm as one subobject.

There are mainly two approaches to modeling a character. One is to construct a single mesh for the whole body of the character. This method ignores the issue of control detail just mentioned above. The outer appearance detail is determined by the application requirements. The control detail is treated separately. Whichever control detail is used, it will become difficult to single out and determine parts of the body (e.g., corresponding limbs) to be controlled from the single structureless mesh.

An alternative approach is to model the character as a composite object, as a hierarchy of separate limbs (see Figure 11.1). The level and the detail of the hierarchy can be set to that of the control detail. This way, controlling the character for movement becomes easier, because we know which model corresponds to the desired limbs to be moved.

Motion Control of a Character (Function and Behavior)

In order to control the motion of the character model (which is a mesh or hierarchy of mesh), instead of moving the model data directly, we indirectly move them via another control structure, called the skeleton (see Figure 11.2). The skeleton is simply a hierarchy of coordinate systems each assigned to a convenient location in the limbs. It is like setting up a virtual bone structure where the coordinate systems are set up at the joints of the bones. Each of these coordinate systems will constitute a local coordinate system for the corresponding limb. To move a limb, we move the corresponding coordinate system with respect to the root coordinate system (usually located at the abdomen) or with respect to its neighboring limb coordinate system (e.g., upper arm moving relative to the shoulder). The part of the mesh that is "bound" to that limb moves together. To summarize the whole modeling process, we must do the following.

1. Model the character as a single mesh or as a hierarchy of limb meshes.
2. Design a skeleton according to the dimensions of the character model.
3. Bind coordinate systems in the skeleton to the character model (at a predetermined pose, such as standing in T form).

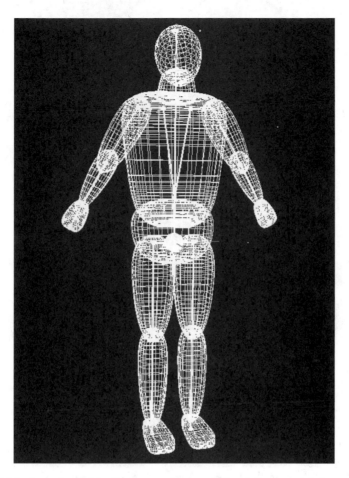

FIGURE 11.1. A mesh model of a human figure with each limb modeled separately.

The binding process amounts to establishing a mapping relationship between a given coordinate system and corresponding vertices in the model. This process is usually done semi-automatically using the modeling tools. The modeling tools allow users to construct a skeleton and the user can locate the skeleton (or hierarchy of the coordinate systems) onto the character model by selecting it with the mouse and moving into and aligning it with the 3D mesh model (see Figure 11.3).

One simple method of binding parts of the mesh to the appropriate coordinate systems is to use a distance-based algorithm. The algorithm classifies the model vertices into different groups based on the "closest" coordinate system. The user then can visualize the mapping and further manually edit and adjust the binding relationships, if necessary (see Figure 11.4). This post-processing is often needed because there are cases where distance alone cannot determine the corresponding limbs correctly. For

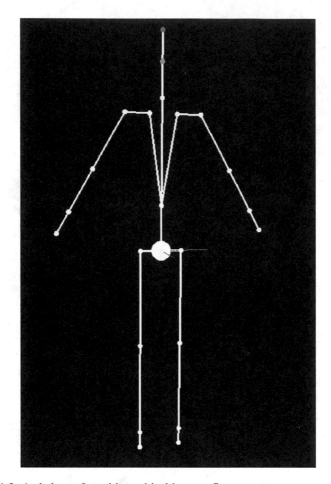

FIGURE 11.2. A skeleton for a hierarchical human figure.

instance, some vertices on the side of the torso can be mapped to the arm instead of the torso (because they are closer).

Using the modeling tools (e.g., 3DSMax[1]), the 3D model is saved together with the skeleton and binding information. However, when using such a model in a VR or 3D graphics engine, such information may not be completely imported and converted into an appropriate internal data structure (it depends on the capabilities of the given engine). For instance, characters built with the 3DSMax can be imported into the DirectX[2] environment with all the relevant information extracted. Even short character animation sequences can be modeled in 3DSMax, saved, and imported into the DirectX

---

[1] 3DSMax is a registered trademark of Discreet, Inc.
[2] DirectX is a registered trademark of Microsoft Corp.

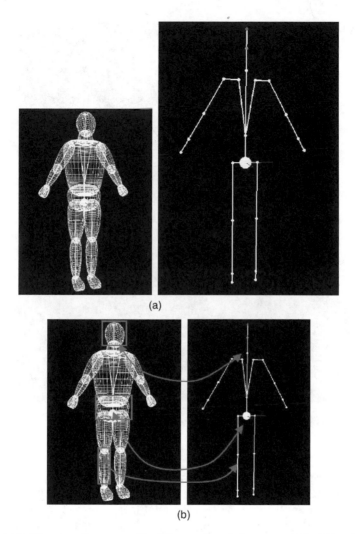

FIGURE 11.3. The overall process of building a virtual character: (a) building the mesh and the skeleton model; (b) scaling/fitting the skeleton to the mesh model and binding parts of the mesh to the skeleton

for easy invocation of later replay. However, the same may not be true for other environments. In many cases, execution environments can only import the model data (vertices and faces) and disregard the skeleton, binding, and animation data. In such a case, the skeleton and binding (and fixed animation) must be specified within the engine by explicit coding.

The binding relationship is important in producing a natural animation of the limbs. The simple "closest coordinate system" algorithm falls short as illustrated in Figure 11.4. In addition, when limbs are moved around the

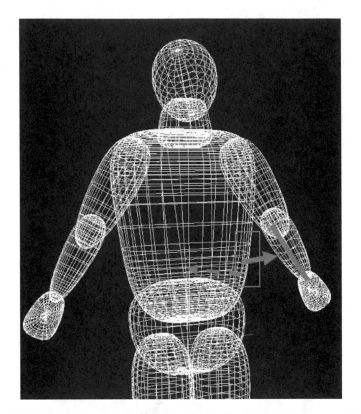

FIGURE 11.4. Wrongly bound vertices. Vertices in the side of the torso are bound to the arm rather than to the spine (because of the short distance to the arm).

joint by a large angle, the limbs can penetrate into the other neighboring limb, or more seriously produce a flattening or tearing effect by extension and elongation on the outer side of the joint (see Figure 11.5). An improved binding relationship can be established using a weighted assignment scheme where vertices are mapped to multiple limbs with different ratios depending on their distance to the joints.

If the hierarchical model is used, the mapping relationship is clear. The mapping can be established using a modeling tool or through explicit coding. When a hierarchy of limbs is used instead of a single mesh, each end of the limbs will overlap and can produce unnatural looks (see Figure 11.6). Different techniques have been developed to overcome these shortcomings [Mae99].

Kinematics

The hierarchical skeleton structure, just like any other composite object, organizes the control structure of the character as a tree (see Figure 11.2),

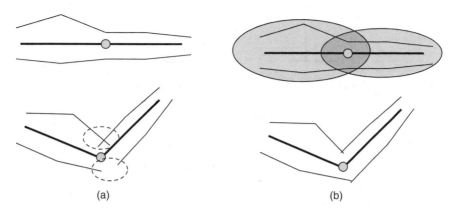

FIGURE 11.5. Pitfalls of direct assignment. Simple direct assignment can cause unnatural self penetration or torn mesh (a). By assigning weights of influence for the vertices near the joints, such situations can be avoided to some degree (b).

where the coordinate systems of the children objects (constituents of the parent object) are defined relative to those of the parent object. When a motion is applied to the parent, all of its children are affected by it as well. In Chapter 2, we examined how to specify two static objects using the 4 × 4 transformation matrix. The same principle applies here. Among two coordinate systems, one parent and the other child, a 4 × 4 transformation matrix

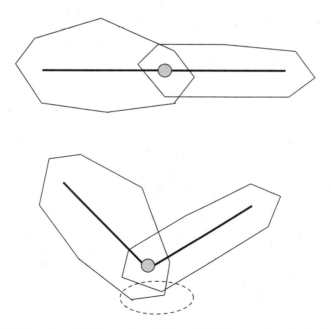

FIGURE 11.6. Elbowing with hierarchy of limbs. Note the unnatural look at the elbow when bent.

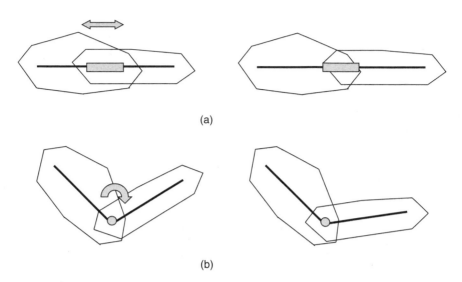

FIGURE 11.7. Two types of joints: (a) prismatic (linear) and (b) revolute (rotary).

can be defined to specify the relative location and orientation between them. The only catch is that they are rotating (or moving) each other around with respect to a "joint." The 4×4 transformation matrix will thus contain a variable that varies according to the angular (or linear) movement with respect to the joint. Note that there are two types of joints, the usual revolute and linear. Figure 11.7 illustrates the differences between revolute and linear (also called the prismatic) joints.

Forward Kinematics

The kinematics (study of motion without regard to forces) of a character motion can be described by the chain of these transformation matrices. In forward kinematics, we are interested in using the joint values and computing the resulting poses of the limbs in the 3D coordinate system (for rendering; see Figure 11.8).

The transformation matrices among the coordinate systems in the skeleton hierarchy can be set up mechanically using the following standard procedure called the Denavit–Hartenberg (D–H) notation [Cra86]. According to D–H notation, we assign the x, y, z-coordinates in a particular way to construct the skeleton. The z-axis is usually placed along the joint axis, and the x-axis is usually placed along the limbs (or links). Figure 11.9 shows the D–H parameters given a joint and two links around it. There are four D–H parameters: the joint angle θ, link length α, offset d, and the twist α. For a revolute joint, θ will be a variable and for a linear joint, the offset d will

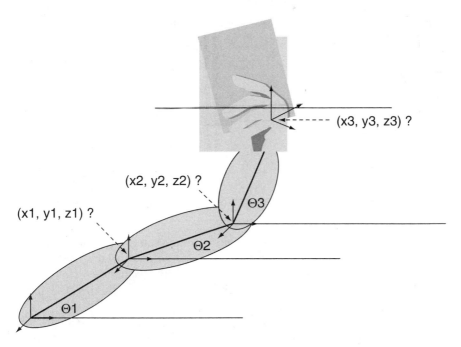

FIGURE 11.8. A pose of an arm with sets of joint angles.

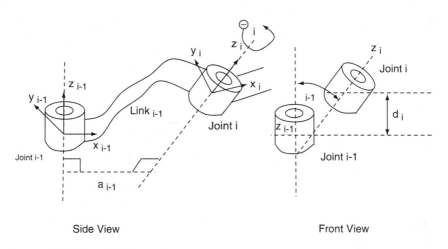

Side View   Front View

FIGURE 11.9. Denavit–Hartenberg parameters.

be the variable instead. The other three parameters are constants according to the geometry of the skeleton. By setting up the coordinate system this way, the 4×4 transformation matrix can be found easily using the following equation and the D–H parameters as shown in Table 11.1.

TABLE 11.1. Denavit–Hartenberg parameters that relate the ith frame and $i + 1$th frame for setting up-$^i T_{i-1}$ [Par02]

Name	Symbol	Description
Link offset	d_i	Distance from x_{i-1} to x_i along z_i
Joint angle	Θ_i	Angle between x_{i-1} and x_i around z_i
Link length	a_{i-1}	Distance from z_{i-1} to z_i along x_{i-1}
Link twist	α_{i-1}	Angle between z_{i-1} to z_i around x_{i-1}

$$
^i T_{i-1} = \begin{bmatrix} \cos \Theta_i & -\sin \Theta_i & 0 & a_{i-1} \\ \sin \Theta_i \cos \alpha_{i-1} & \cos \Theta_i \cos \alpha_{i-1} 1 & -\sin \alpha_{i-1} & -\sin \alpha_{i-1} d_i \\ \sin \Theta_i \sin \alpha_{i-1} & \cos \Theta_i \sin \alpha_{i-1} & \cos \alpha_{i-1} & \cos \alpha_{i-1} d_i \\ 0 & 0 & 0 & 1 \end{bmatrix}
$$

For each joint along the root-to-leaf path in the skeleton hierarchy, a table can be constructed highlighting the values of D–H parameters (as shown in Table 11.2). We can establish a transformation matrix between two coordinate systems (assigned in the joint) easily from Table 11.2, the D-H parameter table, as follows (assume a default initial pose).

Any coordinate along the end of the robot can be converted into the coordinate with respect to the root of the mechanism whose location or orientation is usually known with respect to the World coordinate. Thus, using the chain of these transformation matrices and the joint variables, anything along the chain of the mechanism can be expressed in the World coordinates and be rendered on the screen. Thus, because the local coordinate of the endpoint of the articulated chain in Figure 11.10 is simply $^2(L3, 0, 0)$,

Endpoint of articulated chain in global coordinate (Frame 0)

$$
= {}^0 T_1 * {}^1 T_2 * {}^2 (L3, 0, 0)
$$

When there are multiple degrees of freedom in one joint, we can establish multiple coordinate systems for each degree of freedom at the location of the joint (there will be no link length between these coordinate systems).

The forward kinematics formulation and the 4×4 transformation matrices can easily be used with joint velocities or joint acceleration to compute displacements of limbs of the character in local or global coordinates. The same kinematic equations of motion seen in Chapter 10 apply here.

TABLE 11.2. D–H Parameter Table for the Articulated Chain Shown in Figure 11.10

Joint number	a_{i-1}	Θ_i	d_i	α_{i-1}
1	0	Θ_1	0	0
2	0	Θ_2	L1	−90
3	L2	Θ_3	0	0

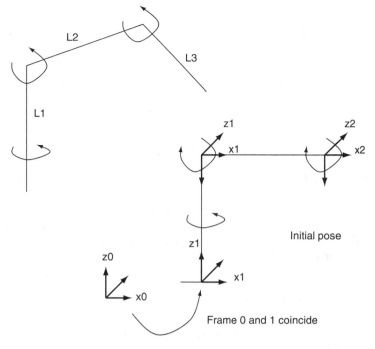

FIGURE 11.10. An example of an articulated chain and coordinate system assignment.

$$X = T(\theta)$$
$$dX' = T'(\theta)$$
$$X_{\text{New}} = X_{\text{Old}} + T'(\theta)^* \delta t$$

where θ represents the joint angles and the X represents the Cartesian coordinates of a point on the articulated chain.

Although the forward kinematic motion formulation can be used to control how a character moves by specifying the appropriate joint angle profiles in time, this method is not very intuitive (see Figure 11.11). For instance, to specify a walking motion of a human character with a thigh, knee, and an ankle, three joint angles must be specified with respect to time. It is not obvious what kinds of series of values will produce a natural humanlike walking motion. One method of producing natural motion is to use key framing. The user manually specifies a few intermediate poses of the leg segments, and the joint angles at these intermediate poses are extracted. Then the rest of the required series of joint angles is obtained by interpolating between these key frame joint angles. This method is more intuitive (although manual) because the user works with the leg segments visually in the 3D space, not in the numerical joint space.

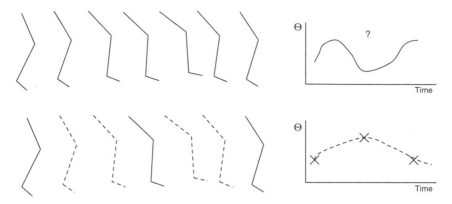

FIGURE 11.11. A human leg animation sequence. Figuring out the continuous joint angle profile in time is not intuitive (upper). The modeler can specify key postures and figure out the intermediate joint angles by interpolation. Still, this can be imprecise depending on the number of key postures (lower).

Inverse Kinematics

It would be nice, with the hierarchical chain of limbs, if the user could simply specify the motion profile of the endpoint of the articulated chain (such as the hand) in the 3D Cartesian space, and the appropriate joint angles be computed automatically. This is called the inverse kinematics problem: figuring out the joint angles from the end effector position (any point along the chain of limbs; see Figure 11.12). Thus forward and inverse kinematics equations can be written as

$$X = f(Q): \text{Forward kinematics}$$

$$Q = f^{-1}(X): \text{Inverse kinematics}$$

where Q represents the joint angles and X represents the 3D Cartesian coordinate values of the end effector.

The problem is that a closed form solution of f^1 is very difficult to obtain when the number of joints exceeds three or more. $f(Q)$ already consists of nonlinear terms including sine and cosine functions. Moreover, there may be many sets of joint angles that can produce a given location or orientation of the end effector. Thus, one way to overcome this problem is to solve the problem in the differential space, which linearizes the problem space. From the forward kinematics equations, we can obtain, by differentiating the equation with respect to time,

$$X' = J(Q)Q'$$

$J(Q)$, which relates the joint angle velocity to the end effector velocity, is called the Jacobian. The inverse of $J(Q)$ is computed to obtain the differ-

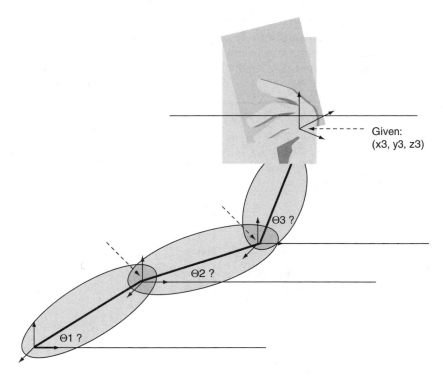

Given:
(x3, y3, z3)

$\Theta 3$?

$\Theta 2$?

$\Theta 1$?

FIGURE 11.12. The inverse kinematics problem.

ential form of the inverse kinematics equation. Because this technique linearizes a nonlinear problem, the equation is only an approximated solution, valid only at a given joint configuration and a given instant of time ($J(Q)$ changes in time).

$$Q' = J^{-1}(Q)X'$$

Thus, we can compute the joint angles using the above formulation in this way. Starting from a known initial configuration Q_{init} and given a goal position of the end effector X_{Goal},

$Q_{Current} = Q_{init}$ /* Initialization */

LOOP until ($X_{Goal} - X_{Current}$ < small threshold)   /* end loop when arrived at goal */

  1. $X_{Current} = f(Q_{Current})$ /* forward kinematics */

  2. Compute $\delta x = X_{Goal} - X_{Current}$

  3. Compute $J(Q_{Current})$ and $J^{-1}(Q_{Current})$

  4. Compute $Q' = J^{-1}(Q_{Current})X'$

  5. $Q_{Current} = Q(t + \delta t) = Q_{Current} + Q'^* \delta t$

That is, at every simulation tick, the new updated end effector position is computed from the old joint angles using the forward kinematics equation.

Then a new δx is computed from which J and J^{-1} are newly computed with the old Q'. Using the new J and J^{-1}, a new Q' is computed, and the joint angle is updated for that small time duration δt. The matrix J^{-1} is rank deficient (many solutions exist) and we can solve for the pseudo inverse J^+.

$$J^+ = J^T(JJ^T)^{-1}$$

The use of pseudo inverse produces a particular selection of Q' that happens to have a characteristic of minimizing the joint angle rates. Other techniques exist that looks for a different Q'. An example is presented for a simple kinematic shown in Figure 11.13. Suppose that we have the following forward kinematics equations

$$X = R\sin\theta_1$$
$$Y = -R\cos\theta_1$$
$$Z = d - T$$

where R and θ_1 are the joint angles and d and T are constants (link length and offset). Instead of trying to figure out the closed form solution for R and θ_1, we differentiate the equations with respect to time.

$$dX = dR\cos\theta_1 - R\sin\theta_1 d\theta_1$$
$$dY = -dR\sin\theta_1 - R\cos\theta_1 d\theta_1$$
$$dZ = dZ$$

In matrix form, the above equations become

$$\begin{pmatrix} dX \\ dY \\ dZ \end{pmatrix} = \begin{bmatrix} \cos\theta 1 & -R\sin\theta 1 & 0 \\ -\sin\theta 1 & -R\cos\theta 1 & 0 \\ 0 & 0 & 1 \end{bmatrix} \begin{pmatrix} dR \\ d\theta 1 \\ dZ \end{pmatrix}$$

$$J = \begin{bmatrix} \cos\theta 1 & -R\sin\theta 1 & 0 \\ -\sin\theta 1 & -R\cos\theta 1 & 0 \\ 0 & 0 & 1 \end{bmatrix}$$

There exist more elaborate inverse kinematics methods and we do not cover them here. Incorporating dynamics for an articulated chain is an even more

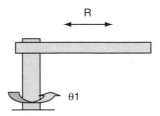

FIGURE 11.13. A simple kinematic chain with one rotary joint and one prismatic.

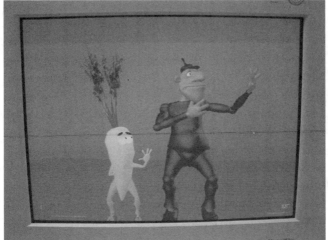

FIGURE 11.14. A motion capture system.

difficult problem. A direct motion capture (direct recording of joint angles using sensors worn by an actor; see Figure 11.14) is often used to overcome this problem.

Summary

Animating human characters is important because any realistic virtual environment will need living and moving entities in it. Accomplishing character animation starts with modeling of its form as a mesh or hierarchy of limb meshes and defining a skeleton structure for control. Appropriate parts of the character mesh are bound to the skeleton and can be moved by moving the underlying skeleton. The skeleton is simply a hierarchy of coordinate systems, and the hierarchy can be specified methodically by using the Denavit and Hartenberg parameters and conventions. The forward kinematics can be solved by formulating the relative orientation and location of neighboring coordinate systems (or bones) in terms of the changing joint angles. Using the forward kinematics formulation, a motion can be created by changing the joint angle values. The inverse kinematics lets users specify a convenient point (such as the end effector of the articulated chain) along the articulated chain and figures out the joint angles (the reverse problem of forward kinematics). It is usually more intuitive to specify motion with end effector positions and compute the joint angles instead. Generating realistic dynamic motions with forces and torques is very difficult and often a direct motion capture is used and adapted in real-time.

Pondering Points

- Model a ball-socket shoulder joint using the Denavit and Hartenberg convention.
- How can we use pre-captured (or modeled) motion data in a real-time interactive virtual environment?
- How can motion capture data captured for a certain actor be applied to a differently sized character?
- How can we connect two different motion profiles in a smooth manner?
- How would it be possible to model and simulate the bulging landscape of the skin due to muscle movements?
- Facial movement mostly occurs by muscle movements. However, the animation technique introduced in this chapter uses a bone-(skeleton)-based animation. What kind of underlying control structure might we need for facial animation?
- A face has a distinct landscape (e.g., high nose, cheekbones, round eyes). Modeling a face as a flat surface and pasting a picture may fall short of producing realistic effects. We can put more effort into modeling a face with more geometric details. How can we paste a picture more effectively on a facial model with more geometric details?
- What do you think is the minimum level of detail for representing humans or animals in virtual environments? Discuss it in terms of not only visual features, but others (aural, behavioral, haptic, etc.).
- For the Ship Simulator example, animate an arm (touching the Steering-Wheel and the Engine Lever) using a simple inverse kinematics model (e.g. three degrees of freedom).

Epilogue
Virtual Space, the Final Frontier

Other Important Subareas of Virtual Reality (VR)

In this book, I have covered some essential topics in building VR systems. It started with laying out the requirements and making rough specifications using storyboards and other constructs. The first phase of development focused on verifying the basic functionality and performance of the intended system. This led to the next phases of development where more VR-oriented elements would be added such as 3D multimodal interaction, collision handling, physical simulations, and character animations. By no means, are the topics or components of VR covered in this book exhaustive. For instance, one important aspect of VR in terms of promoting the sense of user-felt presence is the interaction with other "living" entities (rather than just manipulating static objects). This is possible mainly by: (1) building a networked and shared virtual environment and having multiple users interact with one another, and/or (2) employing autonomous entities controlled by artificial intelligence for believable interaction [Sin99;Rab02]. Another emerging area in VR is image-based rendering [Mcm95]. The goal of image-based rendering is to model virtual environments using a set of images. The image from a viewpoint where an image was not sampled is generated, for instance, by mixing or warping already sampled images from nearby viewpoints. However, image-based rendering requires high computational load and large storage capacity and is limited in providing interactivity.

A closely related area is computer vision. Computer vision is important for VR in at least the areas of (1) vision-based tracking [Reh94], and (2) model reconstruction (also known as image-based modeling). Vision-based tracking is attractive because the user is free of tether, and cameras are becoming more and more ubiquitous. The heavy computational load needed for vision-based algorithms is becoming less of an issue with the ever-increasing computational power of today's PCs. Using textures or environment maps is a simple form of image-based modeling. A more advanced form is to extract 3D models from images for quick constructions of photo-realistic 3D models [Deb96]. A more futuristic avenue for VR is happening with the advances in neurotechnology and brain science, to be more specific, in efforts to directly interface with the human nervous system. For instance, neurotechnology has already advanced to a level to restore (limited) vision to the blind [Wir02]. One obvious application of such technology is in creating display systems for VR by tapping directly into our sensory nervous system (input to the brain). However, interpreting neural signals (for control) would be a far more challenging problem (output from the brain).

Finally, in order for VR to take its place as one of the mainstream media for digital content, it is vital that research and industry produce more usable and effective authoring tools. It is easy to recognize the successes of the WYSIWYG (What You See Is What You Get) types of computer-based tools for creating documents, presentations, movies, 3D models, and even short animations. Likewise, the proliferation of VR technology and VR-based contents will also depend on the WYFIWYG (What You Feel Is What You Get) [LeeG04] type of authoring tools that can help developers compose, reuse, and integrate different components at the level of virtual objects and entities, and at the level of systemwide functionality (e.g., sensing, display, collision, performance management, etc.).

Is VR Really Any Good?

In this book, I have claimed that the two main pillars of VR (as distinguished from mere 3D interactive graphics) were 3D multimodality and the sense of user-felt presence. However, partly due to the different definitions of presence put forth by a number of different people, there has been much debate over whether other conventional media (such as books, movies, 3D games) can induce the sense of presence (or immersion) as well. Such an issue is important for identifying and establishing the uniqueness and value of virtual reality systems. For instance, if indeed it is possible to induce psychological immersion by manipulation of story, plots, and abstract interaction, then the digital content such as the interactive story or games can be conveyed sufficiently using conventional desktop interfaces rather than employing expensive and often difficult to use and engineer VR setups. This warrants a bit more explanation about the concept of presence as follows.

VR for Spatial Presence

One of the important and defining goals of virtual reality systems is to create presence and to fool the user into believing that one is, or is doing something "in" the synthetic environment. Many researchers have defined and explained presence in different ways [ISP04]. Historically, in the context of virtual reality, the concept of presence has been much associated with spatial perception as its informal definition of "feeling of being there" suggests [Hee92;ISP04]. Similarly, many studies have identified system elements that contribute to enhanced user-felt presence, and many of them are spatial or perceptual cues such as providing a wide field of view display, head-tracking, stereoscopy, 3D sound, proprioception, maps/landmarks, and spatial interaction [ISP04].

Other studies in presence have challenged this view and attempted to widen the concept to include psychological immersion, thus linking higher-level and "nontechnological" elements (processed in a top-down fashion in our brain) to presence such as story and plots, flow, attention and focus, identification/empathy with the characters, social interaction, emotion, pre-knowledge, and so on [ISP04;Riv03;Sas03]. One can argue that there is a (evolving) dichotomy within the concept of presence as illustrated in Table E.1 (the table should be taken as an illustration; that is, in reality, the separation is not as clear cut).

Thus, scholars now generally agree that there are different types of presence, such as spatial presence, social presence, and psychological (or conceptual) presence [ISP04]. Among them, the *spatial* presence (also known as physical presence) refers to the sense of physical and concrete space, often dubbed as the sense of being there (e.g., virtual environment). Spatial presence bears particular importance to virtual reality "technologists" interested in providing location-based experiences, because it is seemingly (although not proven) more dependent on the "form" (or system/hardware/technical) factors of the VR system. Spatial presence is formed as a product of a bottom-up perceptual process that gathers spatial cues to actively place and register the user in the surrounding environment. Thus, in general,

TABLE E.1. The dichotomy within the concept of presence [LeeS04]

	Nonspatial presence	Spatial presence
Nature	Conceptual/cognitive/psychological/ social (e.g., feeling of being in an abstract space or part of a story, "I felt like I was James Bond")	Perceptual/physiological (e.g., feeling of being in concrete space, "I felt like I was on the moon")
Individual Difference	More subjective	More objective
Space [Wat01]	Conceptual/abstract	Concrete/physical
Formation	Formed as byproduct of voluntary and conscious top-down processing (high level) Involves rational, abstract, and logical reasoning	Formed as byproduct of involuntary bottom-up processing of raw sensory cues (low level) Involves reflexive behavior responsive to stimuli
Factors	Nontechnological (content): story, plot, attention, focus, abstract interaction, role playing, emotion, social interaction (deliberate) nonrealism, etc.	Technological (form): display, bodily interaction, FOV, motion, shadow, graphic realism, texture resolution, simulation/motion realism, exposure time, etc.

employing expensive VR devices can be superfluous if the purpose of the system is nonspatial. On the other hand, VR as a technology will have a unique value in providing strong spatial context for those applications that require it, such as many training and educational systems. For instance, a virtual training system for finding the fire exit will require provision of strong spatial cues so that training effects can transfer to the real situation.

References

[Ber00] Berthoz, A. (Translated by Weiss, G.). *The Brain's Sense of Movement*, Harvard University Press, Cambridge, MA, 2000.

[Bern97] Bernstein, D., Clark-Stewart, A., Roy, E., and Wickens, C., *Psychology* (4th ed.) Houghton Mifflin, Boston, 1997.

[Boe88] Boehm, B. "A Spiral Model for Software Development and Enhancement," *Computer*, Vol. 21, No. 5, pp. 440–454, 1988.

[Bol80] Bolt, R.A. "Put-That-There, Voice and Gesture at the Graphics Interface," *ACM Computer Graphics*, Vol. 14, pp. 262–270, 1980.

[Bou01] Bourg, D., *Physics for Game Developers*, O'Reilly, Sebastopal, CA, USA, 2001.

[Bow05] Bowman, D., Kruijff, E., LaViola, J., and Poupyrev, I., *3D User Interface: Theory and Practice*, Addison-Wesley, Reading, MA, 2005.

[Bow99] Bowman, D., Davis, E., Badre, A., and Hodges, L., "Maintaining Spatial Orientation during Travel in an Immersive Virtual Environment," *Presence: Teleoperators and Virtual Environments*, Vol. 8, No. 6, pp. 618–631, 1999.

[Bro77] Brooks, F., "Computer Scientists as Toolsmith – Studies in Interactive Computer Graphics," in *Proceedings of IFIP*, pp. 759–763, 1977.

[Bys99] Bystrom, K., Barfield, W., and Hendrix, C., "A Conceptual Model of the Sense of Presence in Virtual Environments," *Presence: Teleoperators and Virtual Environments*, Vol. 8, No. 2, pp. 241–244, 1999.

[Can86] Canny, J., "Collision Detection for Moving Polyhedra," *IEEE Transactions on Pattern Analysis and Machine Intelligence*, Vol. PAMI-8, No. 2, 1986.

[Car00] Carroll, L., and Tenniel, J., *Alice's Adventures in Wonderland and Through the Looking Glass*, Reissue Edition, Signet Classics, New York, Dec. 2000.

[Car80] Card, S., Moran, T., and Newell, A., "The Keystroke Level Model for User Performance Time with Interactive Systems," *Communications of the ACM*, Vol. 23, No. 7, pp. 398–410, 1980.

[Car98] Carroll, J. M., *Making Use Cases: Scenario-based Design of Human-Computer Interactions*, MIT Press, Cambridge, MA, 1998.

[Che95] Chen, S., "QuickTime VR - An Image-based Approach to Virtual Environment Navigation," *ACM Computer Graphics*, pp. 29–38, 1995.

[Chu01] Chung, J., Kim, N., Kim, G.J., and Park, C.M., "Low Cost Real-Time Motion Tracking System for VR Application," in *Proceedings of International Conference on Virtual Systems and Multimedia*, pp. 383–392, 2001.

[Cim04] Cimitile, A., "Requirements," Unpublished presentation document available at: http://web.ing.unisannio.it/cimitile/ing-soft/dispense/Requirements-1.pdf, 2004.

[Cor02] Corradini, A., Wesson, R.M., and Cohen, P.R., "A Map-based System Using Speech and 3D Gestures for Pervasive Computing," in *Proceedings of the IEEE International Conference on Multimodal Interfaces*, pp. 191–196, 2002.

[Cra86] Craig, J., *Introduction to Robotics: Mechanics and Control*, Addison-Wesley, Reading, MA, 1986.

[Cri04] Cristiano, G., "Storyboard Home Study Course," On-line document available at: www.dicomics.com/storyboardschool/eng/index.htm, 2004.

[CRL04] CRLOpto Limited, UK, "HMD's and Microdisplay Basics," Company document available at: www.crlopto.com/products/pdfs, 2004.

[Cru93] Cruz-Neira, C., Sandin, D., and DeFanti, T., "Surround Screen Projector Based VR: The Design and Implementation of the CAVE," *ACM Computer Graphics*, Vol. 27, No. 2, pp. 135–142, 1993.

[Deb96] Debevec, P., Taylor C., and Malik J., "Modeling and Rendering Architecture from Photographs: A Hybrid Geometry- and Image-based Approach," *ACM Computer Graphics*, pp. 11–20, 1996.

[DeM79] DeMarco, T., *Structured Analysis and System Specification*, Prentice-Hall, Englewood Cliffs, NJ, 1979.

[Din99] Dinh, H.Q., Walker, N., Hodges, L.F., Song, C., and Kobayashi, A., "Evaluating the importance of multi-sensory input on memory and the sense of presence in virtual environments," in *Proceedings of the IEEE Virtual Reality*, pp. 222–228, 1999.

[Dud00] Duda, R., "3D Audio For HCI," On-line document available at: interface.-cipic.ucdavis.edu/3D_home.htm, 2000.

[Eva] Evans, F., Skiena, S., and Varshney, A., "Vtype: Entering Text in a Virtual World," submitted to *International Journal of Human-Computer Studies*.

[Fit54] Fitts, P., "The Information Capacity of the Human Motor System in Controlling the Amplitude of Movement," *Journal of Experimental Psychology*, Vol. 47, pp. 381–391, 1954.

[Fow97] Fowler, M. and Scott, K., *UML Distilled: Applying the Standard Object Modeling Language*, Addison-Wesley, New York, 1997.

[Fuk97] Fukumoto, M. and Tonomura, Y., "Body Coupled FingeRing: Wireless Wearable Keyboard," Proc. Of ACM Computer Human Interaction, p.147–154, 1997.

[Gol99] Goldstein, M. and Chincholle, D., "Finger-Joint Gesture Wearable Keypad," in *Second Workshop on Human Computer Interaction with Mobile Devices*, 1999.

[Got96] Gottschalk, S., Lin, M., and Manocha, D., "OBBTree: A Hierarchical Structure for Rapid Interference Detection," *ACM Computer Graphics*, pp. 171–180, 1996.

[Gra98] Grasso, M.A., Ebert, D.S., and Finin, T.W., "The Integrality of Speech in Multimodal Interfaces," *ACM Transactions on Computer–Human Interaction*, Vol. 5, No. 4, 1998.

[Gro98] Groen, J. and Werkhoven, P.J., "Visiomotor Adaptation to Virtual Hand Position in Interactive Virtual Environments," *Presence: Teleoperators and Virtual Environments*, Vol. 7, No. 5, pp. 429–446, 1998.

[Har90] Harel, D., "STATEMATE: A Working Environment for the Development of Complex Reactive Systems," *IEEE Transactions on Software Engineering*, Vol. 16, No. 4, pp. 403–414, 1990.

[Hee92] Heeter, C., "Being There: The Subjective Experience of Presence," *Presence: Teleoperators and Virtual Environments*, Vol. 1, pp. 262–271, 1992.

[Hen04] Henderson, T., "How Do We Know Light Behaves as a Wave?" On-line document available at: www.glenbrook.k12.il.us/gbssi/phys/Class/light/u2l1e.html, 2004.

[Hof97] Hoffman, W., "Database Design for Visual Simulation and Entertainment", *SIGGRAPH 97 Course Notes on Designing Real Time Graphics for Entertainment*, 1997.

[Hor97] Horry, T., Anjyo, I., and Arai, F., "Tour into the Picture," *Proc. of ACM Annual conf. on Computer Graphics and interactive Techniques (SIGGRAPH 97)*, pp. 225–232, 1997.

[How02] Howe, R., "Haptic Reseach: Tactile Display," On-line document available at: haptic.mech.northwestern.edu/TactileDisplay.html, 2004.

[IEE94] IEEE (The Institute of Electrical and Electronics Engineers, Inc.), IEEE 1220, 1994: IEEE-STD 1220–1994 - *Trial Use Standard for Application Management of the Systems Engineering Process*, February, 1995.

[ISP04] International Society of Presence Research (ISPR), "What is Presence?" On-line document available at: http://ispr.info, 2004.

[Jan02] Jang, Y., Yang, U., and Kim, G.J., "Designing a Vibro-Tactile Wear for Close Range Interaction for VR based Motion Training," in *International Conference on Artificial Reality and Telexistence*, 2002.

[Kam01] Kammermeier, P., Buss, M., and Schmidt, G., "A Systems Theoretical for Human Perception in Multimodal Presence Systems," *Transactions on IEEE/ASME Mechatronics*, Vol. 6, No. 3, pp. 234–244, 2001.

[Ken95] Kendall, A., "A 3D Sound Primer: Directional Hearing and Stereo Reproduction," *Computer Music Journal*, Vol. 19, No. 4, pp. 23–46, 1995.

[Kil00] Kilchenman, M. and Goldfarb, M., "Implications of Haptic Interface Force Saturation on the Haptic Display of Detail," in *ASME International Mechanical Engineering Congress and Exposition*, DSC, Vol. 69–2, pp. 1125–1131, 2000.

[KimN00] Kim N. and Kim, G.J., "Menu Presentation and Selection in Virtual Environments," in *Proceedings of IEEE International Conference on Virtual Reality* (Poster Session), p. 281, 2000.

[KimS] Kim, S. and Kim, G.J., "Using Keyboards with Head Mounted Displays," in *Proceedings of ACM SIGGRAPH International Conference on Virtual-Reality Continuum and Its Applications in Industry* (VRCAI 2004), June, 2004.

[Kra01] Kraemer, A., "Two Speakers Are Better than 5.1," *IEEE Spectrum Magazine*, Vol. 40, No. 7, pp. 70–74, May, 2001.

[Kwo01] Kwon, D., Yang, G., Lee, C., and Shin, J., "KAIST Interactive Bicycle Simulator," *Proceedings of IEEE International Conference on Robotics and Automation*, Vol. 3, p2325–2330, Seoul, Korea, 2001.

[LeeG02] Lee, G., Kim, G., and Park, C., "Modeling Virtual Object Behavior within Virtual Environment," in *International Conference on Virtual Reality Software and Technology*, p. 41–48, 2002.

[LeeG04] Lee, G., Billinghurst, M., and Kim, G.J., "Occlusion Based Interaction Methods for Tangible Augmented Reality Environment," in *ACM SIGGRAPH International Conference on Virtual-Reality Continuum and Its Applications in Industry*, p. 419–426, VRCAI2004, June 2004.

[LeeG04] Lee, G., Nelles, C., Billinghurst, M., and Kim, G.J., "Immersive Authoring of Tangible Augmented Reality Applications," in *Proceedings of IEEE and ACM*

International Symposium on Mixed and Augmented Reality (ISMAR), p.133–141, 2004.

[LeeS04] Lee, S. and Kim, G.J., "Formation of Spatial Presence: By Form or Content?" in *Proceedings of the International Presence Workshop*, pp. 20–27, 2004.

[LeeSY04] Lee, S., Chen, T., Kim, J., Han, S., Kim, G.J., and Pan Z., "Using Virtual Reality for Affective Properties of Product Design," in *Proceedings of IEEE International Conference on Virtual Reality*, p. 287–292, 2004.

[LeeSY05] Lee S., Sukahtme, G., and Kim, G.J., "Haptic Teleoperation of a Mobile Robot: A User Study," *Presence: Teleoperators and Virtual Environments*, Vol. 14, No. 3, 2005.

[Lia94] Liang, J., and Green, M., "JDCAD: A Highly Interactive 3D Modeling System," *Computer and Graphics*, Vol. 18, No. 4, pp. 499–506, 1994.

[Lin95] Lin, M. and Manocha, D., "Fast Interference Detection between Geometric Models," *Visual Computer*, Vol. 11, pp. 542–561, 1995.

[Lub99] Lubeke, D., "A Developer's Survey of Polygonal Simplification," in *IEEE Virtual Reality Conference Tutorial 7 Course Notes*, 1999.

[Mae99] Maestri, G., *Digital Character Animation*, New Riders, Indianapolis, Indiana, USA, 1999.

[Mat04] Half Keyboard Research, "Matias Half Keyboard Research," On-line document available at: www.halfkeyboard.com/halfkeyboard/index.html, 2004.

[McG76] McGurk, H. and MacDonald, J. W., "Hearing Lips and Seeing Voices," *Nature*, Vol. 264, pp. 746–748, 1976.

[McK92] McKenna, M. and Zelzer, D., "Three Dimensional Visual Display Systems for Virtual Environment," *Presence: Teleoperators and Virtual Environments*, Vol. 1, No. 4, p. 421–458, 1992.

[Mcm95] McMillan, L. and Bishop, G., "Plenoptic Modeling: An Image-based Rendering System," *Proc. of ACM Annual conf. on Computer Graphics and interactive Techniques (SIGGRAPH 95)*, pp. 39–46, 1995.

[Mil56] Miller, G., "The Magic Number 7 Plus or Minus Two: Some Limits on Our Capacity for Processing Information," *The Psychological Review*, Vol. 63, pp. 81–97, 1956.

[Mil94] Milgram, P., Takemura, H., Utsumi, A., and Kishino, F., "Augmented Reality: A Class of Displays on the Reality-Virtuality Continuum," *SPIE*, Vol. 2351, *Telemanipulator and Telepresence Technologies*, 1994.

[Min97] Mine, M.R., Brooks, F.P., Jr., and Sequin, C.H., "Moving Objects in Space: Exploiting Proprioception in Virtual-Environment Interaction," *Proc. of ACM Annual conf. on Computer Graphics and interactive Techniques (SIGGRAPH 95)*, 1997. p. 19–26

[Min98] Miner, N. and Caudel, T., "Computational Requirements and Synchronization Issues for Virtual Acoustic Displays," *Presence: Teleoperators and Virtual Environments*, Vol. 7, No. 4, pp. 396–409, 1998.

[Mit93] Mitsutake, N., Hoshiai, K., Igarashi, H., Sugioka, Y., Yamamoto, Y., Yamazaki, K., Yoshida, A., and Yamaguchi, T., "Open Sesame from Top of Your Head - an Event Related Potential based Interface for the Control of the Virtual Reality System," in *Proceedings of IEEE International Workshop on Robot and Human Communication*, pp. 292–295, 1993.

[Mol02] Moller, T.A. and Haines, E., *Real Time Rendering*, A.K. Peters, Wellesley, MA, 2002.

[Moo04] Moon, T. and Kim, G.J., "Design and Evaluation of a Wind Display for Virtual Reality," in *ACM International Conference on Virtual Reality Software and Technology*, p. 122–128, 2004.

[Moo88] Moore, M. and Wilhelms, J., "Collision Detection and Response for Computer Animation," *ACM Computer Graphics*, Vol. 22, pp. 289–298, 1988.

[Mor03] Morie, J. et al., "Sensory Design for Virtual Environments," *SIGGRAPH 2003 Sketch*, July 2003.

[Ope04] OSG Community, "OpenSceneGraph: Introduction," On-line document available at: http://openscenegraph.sourceforge.net/introduction/index.html, 2004.

[Ovi03] Oviatt, S.L., "*Multimodal Interfaces,*" The Human-Computer Interaction Handbook: Fundamentals, Evolving Technologies and Emerging Applications, Lawrence Erlbaum, Hillsdale, NJ, pp. 286–304, 2003.

[Ovi99] Oviatt, S.L., "Ten Myths of Multimodal Interaction," *Communications of the ACM*, Vol. 42, No. 11, pp. 74–81, 1999.

[Pal95] Palmer, I. and Grimsdale, R., "Collision Detection for Animation using Sphere Trees," *Computer Graphics Forum*, Vol. 14, No. 2, pp. 105–116, 1995.

[Par02] Parent, R., *Computer Animation: Algorithms and Techniques*, Morgan-Kaufmann, San Francisco, 2002.

[Pau95] Pausch, R., Burnette, T., Copeheart, A.C., Conway, M., Cosgrove, D., DeLine, R., Durbin, J., Gossweiler, R., Koga, S., and White, J., "Alice: Rapid Prototyping System for Virtual Reality," *IEEE Computer Graphics and Application*, Vol. 15, No. 3, pp. 8–11, 1995.

[Pou02] Poupyrev, I., personal communication, 2002.

[Pou96] Poupyrev, I., Weghorst, S., Billinghurst, M., and Ichikawa, T., "The GoGo Interaction Technique: Non Linear Mapping for Direct Manipulation in VR," in *Proceedings of 1996 ACM Symposium on User Interface and Technology* (UIST), pp. 79–80, 1996.

[Pou98] Poupyrev, I., Weghorst, S., Billinghurst, M., and Ichikawa, T., "Egocentric Object Manipulation in Virtual Environments: Empirical Evaluation of Interaction Techniques," *Computer Graphics Forum, Eurographics*, Issue 17, No. 3, pp. 41–52, 1998.

[Pre94] Preece, J., Rogers, Y., Sharp, H., Benyon, D., Holland, S., and Carey, T., *Human Computer Interaction*, Addison-Wesley, Reading, MA, 1994.

[Rab02] Rabin, S., *AI Game Programming Wisdom*, Charles River Media, Hingham, Massachusetts, USA, 2002.

[Ram98] Ramachandran, V.S. and Blakeslee, S., *Phantoms in the Brain*, Harper Collins, New York, 1998.

[Reh94] Rehg, J. and Kanade, T., "Visual Tracking of High DOF Articulated Structures: An Application to Human Hand Tracking," in *Proceedings of Third European Conference on Computer Vision* (ECCV'94), Springer-Verlag, pp. 35–46, New York, 1994.

[Rhe91] Rheingold, H., *Virtual Reality*, Summit Books, New York, New York, USA,1991.

[Ric04] Rickleephoto, "Using Fresnel lens to create a collimated display system," Company document available at: www.rickleephoto.com/rlcoll.htm, 2004.

[Ric94] Richard, P., Burdea, G., Gomez, D., and Coiffet, P., "A Comparison of Haptic, Visual and Auditive Force Feedback for Deformable Virtual Objects," in *Proceedings of ICAT Conference*, pp. 49–62, 1994.

[Ric96] Richard, P., Burdea, G., Birebent, G., Gomez, D., Langrana N., and Coiffet, P., "Effect of Frame Rate and Force Feedback on Virtual Object Manipulation," *Presence: Teleoperators and Virtual Environments*, Vol. 5, No. 1, pp. 95–108, 1996.

[Riv03] Riva, G., Davide, F., and Ijsselsteijn, W.A., Being There: Concepts, Effects and Measurement of User Presence in Synthetic Environments, Ios, Amsterdam, 2003.

[Roh94] Rohlf, J. and Helman, J., "IRIS Performer: A High Performance Multi-processing Toolkit for Real-time 3D Graphics," *ACM Computer Graphics*, pp. 381–394, 1994.

[Sal01] Sallnas, E.L., Kirsten, R.G., and Calle, S., "Supporting Presence in Collaborative Environments by Haptic Force Feedback," *ACM Trans. on Computer-Human Interaction*, Vol. 7, No. 4, pp. 461–476, 2001.

[Sas03] Sas, C. and O'Hare, G., "Presence Equation: An Investigation into Cognitive Factors Underlying Presence," *Presence: Teleoperators and Virtual Environments*, Vol. 12, No. 5, pp. 523–537, 2003.

[See04] SeeReal Technologies, "Autostereoscopic Display System," On-line document available at: www.seereal.com/EN/products_principle_js.en.htm, 2004.

[Sen61] Heilig, M., "Sensorama: A Totally Mechanical VR Device (One Person Theater)," *Invention*, 1961.

[Seo02] Seo, J. and Kim, G.J., "Design for Presence: A Structured Approach to Virtual Reality System Design," *Presence: Teleoperators and Virtual Environments*, Vol. 11, No. 4, pp. 120–126, 2002.

[SGI02] Silicon Graphics, Inc., "OpenGL Performer Getting Started Guide," Company Document (No. 007-3560-003), 2002.

[Shi01] Shimojo, S. and Shams, L., "Sensory modalities are not separate modalities: Plasticity and interactions," *Current Opinion in Neurobiology*, Vol. 11, pp. 505–509, 2001.

[Shi03] Shim, W. and Kim, G.J., "Design for Presence and Performance: A Case of the Virtual Fish Tank," *Presence: Teleoperators and Virtual Environments*, August, Vol. 12, No. 4, p. 374–386, 2003.

[Sho92] Shoemake, A., "A User Interface for Specifying 3D Orientation using a Mouse," in *Proceedings of Graphics Interface*, pp. 151–156, 1992.

[Sin99] Singhal, S. and Zyda M., *Networked Virtual Environments: Design and Implementation*, ACM, New York, 1999.

[Sla95] Slater, M., Usoh, M., and Steed, A., "Taking Steps: The Influence of a Walking Technique on Presence in Virtual Reality," *ACM Transactions on Computer-Human Interaction*, Vol. 2, No. 3, pp. 201–219, 1995.

[Sla97] Slater, M. and Wilbur, S., "A Framework for Immersive Virtual Environments (FIVE): Speculations on the Role of Presence in Virtual Environments," *Presence: Teleoperators and Virtual Environments*, Vol., No. 6, pp. 603–616, 1997.

[Smi04] Smith, C., "Human Factors in Haptics Interaces," On-line Document available at www.acm.org/crossroads/xrds-3-3.html#2, 2004.

[Sor00] Sowizral, H., Rushforth, K., and Deering, M., *The Java 3D API Specification*, 2nd ed., Addison-Wesley, Reading, MA, 2000.

[Sri92] Sriram, D., Logcher, R., Grouleau, N., and Cherneff, J. "DICE: An Object-Oriented Programming Environment for Cooperative Engineering Design," *AI in Engineering Design*, Vol. 3, pp. 303–366, 1992.

[Sto95] Stoakley, R., Conway M., and Pausch, R., "Virtual Reality on a WIM: Interactive Worlds in Minature," in *Proceedings of ACM Conference on Human Factors in Computing Systems*, pp. 265–272, 1995.

[Tat00] US Navy, "Tactile Situation Awareness System (TSAS), Information Through the Sense of Touch," On-line document available at: www.namrl.navy. mil/accel/TSAS, 2000.

[Vir04] VirTouch Inc., "Innovative Tactile Solutions for the Blind," On-line document available at: www.virtouch2.com, 2004.

[VKB04] VKB Ltd., "The Projection Keyboard," On-line document available at: http://vkb.co.il, 2004.

[VRM96] VRML Architecture Group, The Virtual Reality Modeling Language Specification: Version 2.0, Document available at: vrml.sgi.com/moving-worlds, 1996.

[Wal99] Waller, D., "Factors Affecting the Perception of Inter Object Distances in Virtual Environments," *Presence: Teleoperators and Virtual Environments*, Vol. 8, No. 6, pp. 657–670, 1999.

[Was04] Washburn, D. and Lauriann, J., "Could Olfactory Displays Improve Data Visualization?" *Computing in Science and Engineering*, Vol. 6, No. 6, pp. 80–83, November 2004.

[Wat01] Waterworth, J. and Waterworth, E., "Focus, Locus and Sensus: The 3 Dimensions of Virtual Experience," *Cyberpsychology and Behavior*, Vol. 4, No. 2, pp. 203–214, 2001.

[Wel96] Welch, R. B., Blackmon, T. T., Liu, A., Mellers, B. A., & Stark, L. W., "The effects of pictorial realism, delay of visual feedback, and observer interactivity on the subjective sense of presence," Presence: Teleoperators and Virtual Environments, 5, 263–273, 1996

[Wic83] Wickens, C.D., Sandry, D., and Vidulich, M., "Compatibility and Resource Competition Between Modalities of Input, Output and Central Processing," *Human Factors*, Vol. 25, pp. 227–248, 1983.

[Wir02] Kotler, S., "Vision Quest: A Half Century of Artificial Sight Research Has Succeeded, and Now This Blind Man Can See," *Wired Magazine*, September, 2002.

[Wol97] Wolfe R., "Teaching Texture Mapping Visually," *ACM Computer Graphics*, Vol. 31, No. 4, p. 66–70, 1997.

[Yan01] Yang, U., Ahn, E., Baek, S., and Kim, G.J., "Just Follow Me: VR Based Motion Training System," Emerging Technologies, *Proc. of ACM Annual conf. on Computer Graphics and interactive Techniques (SIGGRAPH 2001)*, pp. 126, 2001.

[Yan02-a] Yang, U. and Kim, G.J., "Implementation and Evaluation of "Just Follow Me: An Immersive VR-based Motion Training System," *Presence: Teleoperators and Virtual Environments*, Vol. 11, No. 3, pp. 304–323, 2002.

[Yan02-b] Yang, U., Jang, Y., and Kim, G.J., "POS.T.Wear: Vibro-tactile Interface Design for Near-body Space Interaction in VR-based Motion Training System," in *International Conference on Artificial Reality and Telexistence*, 12th ICAT, pp. 4–9, 2002.

[Yan03] Yang, U., "Multimodal Interaction in Personal Space for VR-based Motion Training System," Ph.D. dissertation, Pohang University of Science and Technology, 2003.

[Yan04] Yanagida Y. et al., "Personal Olfactory Display with Nose Tracking," in *Proceedings IEEE Virtual Reality Conference*, pp. 43–50, 2004.

[You00] Young, H., *University Physics* (10th ed.), Addison-Wesley, Reading, MA, 2000.

[Zac98] Zachmann, G., "Rapid Collision Detection by Dynamically Aligned DOP Trees," in *Proceedings of IEEE VRAIS Conference*, p. 90–97, 1998.

[Zha01] Zhang, Z., Wu, Y., Shan, Y., and Shafer, S., "Visual Panel: Virtual Mouse, Keyboard Mouse, Keyboard and 3D Controller with an Ordinary Piece of Paper," in *Proceedings of ACM Workshop on Perceptive User Interfaces*, p. 1–8, 2001.

Index